BETTER
BY
MISTAKE

BETTER BY MISTAKE

The Unexpected Benefits

of Being Wrong

ALINA TUGEND

RIVERHEAD BOOKS

a member of Penguin Group (USA) Inc.

New York

2011

RIVERHEAD BOOKS
Published by the Penguin Group
Penguin Group (USA) Inc., 375 Hudson Street, New York, New York 10014,
USA • Penguin Group (Canada), 90 Eglinton Avenue East, Suite 700, Toronto,
Ontario M4P 2Y3, Canada (a division of Pearson Penguin Canada Inc.) • Penguin Books Ltd,
80 Strand, London WC2R 0RL, England • Penguin Ireland, 25 St Stephen's Green,
Dublin 2, Ireland (a division of Penguin Books Ltd) • Penguin Group (Australia),
250 Camberwell Road, Camberwell, Victoria 3124, Australia (a division of Pearson Australia
Group Pty Ltd) • Penguin Books India Pvt Ltd, 11 Community Centre, Panchsheel Park,
New Delhi–110 017, India • Penguin Group (NZ), 67 Apollo Drive, Rosedale, North Shore 0632,
New Zealand (a division of Pearson New Zealand Ltd) • Penguin Books (South Africa)
(Pty) Ltd, 24 Sturdee Avenue, Rosebank, Johannesburg 2196, South Africa

Penguin Books Ltd, Registered Offices: 80 Strand, London WC2R 0RL, England

Excerpts from "The Wisdom of Deliberate Mistakes" by Paul J. H. Schoemaker and Robert E.
Gunther (*Harvard Business Review*, June 2006) are reprinted by permission of the *Harvard Business
Review*. Copyright © 2006 by the Harvard Business School Publishing Corporation. All rights
reserved.

Library of Congress Cataloging-in-Publication Data

Tugend, Alina.
Better by mistake : the unexpected benefits of being wrong / Alina Tugend.
p.   cm.
ISBN 978-1-59448-785-9
1. Failure (Psychology).   2. Errors.   3. Fallibility.   4. Success—Psychological aspects.
I. Title.   II. Title: Unexpected benefits of being wrong.
BF575.F14T84   2011   2010037057
155.2'4—dc22

Printed in the United States of America
1   3   5   7   9   10   8   6   4   2

Book design by Meighan Cavanaugh

In memory of my grandmother, Irene Tugendreich

In honor of my parents, Tom and Rachel Tugend

With great love to Mark, Ben, and Gabriel

CONTENTS

BETTER
BY
MISTAKE

Introduction

This book began when I made a mistake in a column for *The New York Times*. My first instinct, when the minor error was pointed out, was to disown it or cover it up. To rationalize that a correction was not really needed. Then I did what a good journalist should do and told my editor. She graciously acknowledged that she should have caught the error, and we submitted a correction, which ran a few days later. But it bothered me. Not so much the mistake, but the fact that in the world today—in our personal lives, our social interactions, and our workplaces—mistakes are viewed as "bad." Whatever happened to the platitudes that we hear throughout school—at least in the first few years—that reassure us that we need to make mistakes in order to learn?

A friend of mine loves to tell the anecdote of driving her son home from kindergarten and asking what he learned. "Nothing," he said. "Nothing?" she asked. "You didn't learn a single thing?" "No," he replied. "My teacher said you learn by making mistakes, and I didn't make any today." Imagine if that attitude survived throughout our lives. If, when we thought about how our day went, we didn't regret our mistakes, but proudly thought about those we had made and how we had learned from them.

So I wrote a column about the inherent tension between what we're told—that we must make mistakes in order to learn, how all great leaders and inventors have embraced them—and the reality that we often get punished for making mistakes and therefore try to avoid them—or cover them up—as much as possible. I discussed research, which I will expand on in this book, showing how parents and teachers often unwittingly encourage such an error-avoidance mindset and how such children grow into adults who fear and dread making mistakes.

At first glance, this doesn't seem so ominous—while perhaps we can lighten up a little, in general shouldn't we try to avoid blunders? It depends. Yes, we don't want to make the same error over and over. But that is different from thinking that we not only can but must do everything perfectly, and if we don't, we are failures. Such a mindset creates marriages and relationships where people exert enormous amounts of energy blaming each other when something goes wrong rather than finding a solution. Where defensiveness and accusations take the place of apologies and forgiveness. It creates workplaces where taking chances and being creative while risking failure is subsumed by an ethos of mistake-prevention at the cost of daring and innovation. Or conversely, workplaces where superstars are never challenged; rather, they are rewarded for making really bad decisions. And we end up with a culture where people feel shame at making mistakes—big or little—and pass this shame on to their children.

This topic seems particularly pertinent now. Over the time that I was working on this book, we all watched, astonished, as banking institutions that seemed—at least from the outside—as solid as stone imploded, taking the economy down with them. We wondered who was responsible for the wave of home foreclosures, for the job losses, for the uncertainty and anxiety that touched almost all of us. As I write this, a congressional commission is still holding hearings trying to figure out who screwed up, and how. The list of potential suspects is long. But besides the satisfaction of placing blame, will we learn anything from the mistakes that cost so many people so much?

Social psychologists Carol Tavris and Elliot Aronson write in their book *Mistakes Were Made (But Not by Me)*: "Most Americans know they are supposed to say, 'we learn from our mistakes,' but deep down, they don't believe it for a minute. They think that mistakes mean you are stupid. Combined with the culture's famous amnesia for anything that happened more than a month ago, this attitude means that people treat mistakes like hot potatoes, eager to get rid of them as fast as possible, even if they have to toss them in someone else's lap." And in this fast-paced world of increasingly complex choices, every decision can seem like a potential mistake. Which phone company, which health plan, which retirement fund? Even advances that in many respects have made lives better, such as medical procedures that prolong the lives of the elderly or fertility options that allow those who once would have been childless to have children, come with a cost. We have more choices, but we also have more opportunities to make the wrong choices, and we are plagued by doubts that we will make a crucial mistake that could prove catastrophic.

The column I wrote struck a chord; it was one of the *Times*'s "most e-mailed" articles after it was published (the paper does track such things), and I received many, many e-mails from readers not only relating their own anecdotes about learning from mistakes, but also, surprisingly to me, filled with gratitude. One reader told me that the column was being passed around her workplace to help transition it from a place of mistake avoidance to one of acceptance. A teacher wrote in to say he was going to read it to the elementary school children he teaches in rural Kansas. Typical was one from Vige Barrie, a director of media relations at Hamilton College: "Thank you for your article—I wish I had read it 50 years ago, but nevertheless, I still found it immensely reassuring!" Or from Elizabeth Leong in Springfield, Massachusetts: "As an attorney in constant fear of making mistakes and who is not open enough to 'the process' . . . and as a mother of two young children who wants them to not follow in her footsteps in this regard, I thank you."

These responses made me realize that the fear of making mistakes is a cudgel that hangs over so many of us, preventing us from not only taking risks in our personal and professional lives, but even more important, really accepting—not just giving lip service to—the truth that we all are human and imperfect. Of course, there are big mistakes and small ones and varying levels of consequence. A pilot error that crashes a plane full of people is not in the same league as a minor mistake in a law brief or forgetting to pick up your child from dance lessons. And this book does look at how those in professions that hold lives in their hands develop responses to mistakes. But for most of us, a mistake does not cost a life. I think almost everyone can relate to an anecdote told in a 1999 research paper by a British academic, Patricia Bryans, on what men and women learn from making mistakes at work.

A student of hers, "David," was a night-shift supervisor at a food-production factory, responsible for mixing the recipes. One night, just when he was about to start production, he realized that he had mixed ten times too much of one ingredient. Like me, David was tempted to ignore and cover up his mistake and go ahead, knowing that the product would taste awful but look fine. Instead, he confessed, held up production while everything was cleaned out, remixed the batch, and left work. The next day, his manager summoned him to his office and issued a formal written notice saying that if David made one more mistake, he could be fired. David, naturally, was very upset about this and his attitude toward his job changed completely. "He now took every opportunity to sneer at what they 'preached' about quality. He started to look for another job. His eagerness to learn and improve was severely diminished. His major learning from that experience seemed to be that he should never have owned up to his mistake," Bryans wrote.

All too often, we come away with David's lesson about making a mistake: Ignore it, blame someone else, rationalize it—do anything to avoid admitting it because you just might put yourself in a position of weakness.

Now if David constantly messed up the baking process, putting in ten cups of flour when one is required, then his manager would be right in issuing a warning—and then firing him if need be. But if this was David's first mistake—or even second, within a certain period of time—then his manager could have discussed how the mistake happened to see if there was a systemic problem, and he could have acknowledged that, indeed, we're all human and mistakes *do* happen.

This book looks at why such a seemingly obvious and helpful solution is, in reality, so difficult. While the answers aren't easy, I hope the reader will gain some insight into why we react the way we do when we blunder—or when others do—and how we can change that. By delving deeply into why and how we react to errors, we can learn how to acknowledge mistakes without foisting the blame onto others or beating ourselves up. That allows us to be more open to the valuable lessons that mistakes can offer—and will ultimately improve our work and our relationships with our bosses, spouses, and children.

One last point about my mistakes column. At the end, I jokingly told readers that "old habits die hard," and that if they see any mistakes, don't bother to tell me. Guess what? As much as people hate to make mistakes, they love pointing out ones others have made. A number of readers couldn't resist gleefully noting an editing typo. To those folks, I simply say: Please read this book.

1.

(Mis)Understanding and (Re)Defining Mistakes

Every time I would be at, say, a dinner party and the topic of this book would come up (I don't know how *that* would happen), someone inevitably would say, "Well, how do you define mistakes?" I would respond with an elaborate spiel, which usually left the listener bewildered and me hoping for another glass of wine. Because defining a mistake, it seems, is almost as difficult as, well, defining happiness. First of all we turn to the dictionary, which offers us "an incorrect, unwise or unfortunate act or decision caused by bad judgment or lack of information or care." That seems to cover it all, more or less. We've got chance (unfortunate, lack of information), we've got deliberate action (unwise, bad judgment, lack of care), and we've got the physical or mental component (act or decision). While seemingly useful, the definition is so broad that when parsed carefully, it becomes useless. A mistake is a typo, a mistake is prescribing the wrong medicine, a mistake is forgetting your car keys, a mistake is misreading signs resulting in a fatal crash.

The dictionary separates out error, which is "something in a piece of work that is incorrect, such as a misspelling or a misprint." When British academic Patricia Bryans asked participants in a study to provide a definition of mistakes, they "largely agreed that the key issues were misjudgment and adverse consequences which were unplanned. For them, it was the scale of the consequences which differentiated mistakes from errors or slips."

Even then, a real mistake can vary widely. It can be an accounting error that costs thousands or millions of dollars, it can be a newspaper article that cites incorrect information, it can be a teacher scolding the wrong pupil for misbehaving. But it can also be leaving a sponge in a patient during surgery, causing a fatal infection, or wrongly diagnosing an illness. It can be misreading information from air-traffic controllers and crashing a plane full of people. All these are considered mistakes as well. As we can see, our society does not offer many subtle gradations of mistakes, nor does it easily distinguish between bad and good mistakes. In writing about how mistakes can foster innovation, Charles Prather, a company president and senior fellow at the University of Maryland, notes that unfortunately we don't have a word in English that means "a well-reasoned attempt that didn't meet expectations."

James Reason, a professor of psychology at the University of Manchester in England, has written extensively on human performance and the prevention of errors in hazardous fields. While most of us aren't astronauts or nuclear power plant operators, the intensive study of errors in high-risk fields offers great insights into what causes people to make mistakes and what works best to prevent them. Some of the findings may not be applicable to us, whose greatest challenge may be driving to the office; however, much of it—with a little adaptation—is. Although the expertise may be different, human reaction and behavior, for the most part, translate across professions. That is why, as we'll see later, the medical profession is looking so closely at work done on pilots and error to see how it can help reduce mistakes in the medical field.

Reason defines an error as the failure of a planned sequence of mental or physical activities to achieve its intended outcome when these failures cannot be attributed to chance. A slip or lapse is when an action does not go according to plan—when we push a door instead of pull it to open it or more frighteningly, step on the gas instead of the brake. We meant to pull, we meant to step on the brake, but for some reason we didn't. A mistake, however, is when the plan itself is inadequate to achieve its objectives. To explain the difference, Reason looks at two different nuclear power plant emergencies: In 1979 at Oyster Creek, an operator intended to close pump discharge valves A and E, and inadvertently closed B and C also. All natural circulation to the reactor core area was shut off. That was a slip of action—the worker had the right intention, but failed to execute it properly. In Chernobyl in 1986, a previous operator error had reduced the reactor power to well below 10 percent of maximum—despite strict safety procedures prohibiting any operation below 20 percent of maximum. Nonetheless, a team of operators and electrical engineers continued with a planned test program. This and subsequent violations of safety procedures resulted in a double explosion at the reactor core, ultimately releasing a large amount of radiation into the air. Chernobyl's workers didn't accidentally push the wrong button—they went ahead as planned but the plans were not enough for safe operating conditions. Of course, we can't be too rigid about this terminology—slips and mistakes can overlap, or both can contribute to an accident. And while it's helpful to tease out these differences in defining mistakes, throughout this book—in order to avoid being overly repetitive and because in everyday language we don't adhere to such fine distinctions—I use the terms "mistakes," "errors," "slips," "lapses" as well as "blunders," "goofs," and "screw-ups" interchangably.

We usually judge the severity of a mistake by the outcome, or, as Bryans says, the scale of the consequences. A mistake that causes death is usually the most drastic, and that is why the procedures of doctors and pilots have been studied so intensively. A mistake can occur with the best information and the best intentions or through carelessness or lack of knowledge. Although the definition of mistake can be fluid, I believe it stops being a mistake when deliberate wrongdoing or malfeasance is involved. Granted, the line between the two can be slim or virtually nonexistent at times—those who voted in favor of funding the second Iraq war, for example, such as Hillary Clinton, later called it a mistake based on bad information. Others no doubt would argue that it was not a mistake but willful ignorance or political expediency. There is enough to write about, however, without dipping into criminal activity, and as much as possible I will leave that one aside in this book.

Reason's book *Human Error*, which was published in 1990, was part of an expanding body of literature looking at errors, and has become a classic in the field. The timing of publication was not accidental; the past decade or so had seen some horrendous calamities attributed to human error: In 1977, the Three Mile Island nuclear accident scared the hell out of those of us who remember the great (and ultimately unfounded) terror that this would be the nuclear meltdown that we all feared. It was followed in the 1980s by the Bhopal tragedy in India, the *Challenger* space shuttle explosion, Chernobyl, and the King's Cross subway fire in London—separate catastrophes over ten years that cost countless lives and, particularly in the case of Bhopal and Chernobyl, generations of human and environmental disaster. As Reason noted: "There is nothing new about tragic accidents caused by human error, but in the past, the injurious consequences were usually confined to the immediate vicinity of the disaster. Now, the nature and scale of potentially hazardous technologies . . . means that human errors can have adverse effects upon whole continents over several generations."

On the face of it, Reason notes, the odds against an error-free performance of any kind seem overwhelmingly high. He points to the apparently simple task of boiling an egg. You can crack the egg when taking it out of the carton. You can spill the water. You can forget to turn on the stove. You can forget to turn off the stove and boil the water dry. If this seems so difficult, think about driving a car. If one really dwells on it, it seems, well, impossible. It's amazing we ever get up in the morning, let alone have breakfast. But, Reason reassures us, our errors are not as abundant as we may think, nor are they as varied as it would appear, given the vast potential for making them. Human error is actually more predictable than we would think—not that we necessarily know when a particular mistake will be made by whom, but given this task to be performed under these circumstances, we will probably make errors around this point and they will probably take this reliable form. For instance, in January, most banks will receive checks with the previous year written on them. No one can say exactly how many checks will be misdated, or who in particular will forget to write the correct year, but we know every year those errors are going to happen. This type of error is called "strong habit intrusion" and is the most common of all error types.

A concept that is key to how we think about errors is that of differentiating between active and latent errors, a distinction that has become important in trying to understand and prevent mistakes, particularly in high-risk fields, but is applicable just about anywhere. An active error, for example, is the pilot crashing the plane. The latent error is a design malfunction causing the plane to roll unexpectedly, which the pilot couldn't control. I will delve into this more in later chapters, but Reason notes that it is often the latent errors that pose the greatest threat to safety in a complex system, because they can be unrecognized and subsequently cause multiple types of active errors. To use Reason's analogy, "active failures are like mosquitoes. They can be swatted one by one, but they still keep coming. The best remedies are to create more effective defenses and to drain the swamps in which they breed. The swamps . . . are the ever present latent conditions."

An example of how latent failures can lead to a tragedy is apparent in examining the explosion of the space shuttle *Challenger* in 1986. I happened to be working for an education newspaper in Washington, D.C., when the *Challenger* was set to launch. For the first time, a schoolteacher, Christa McAuliffe of New Hampshire, would be going up in space. So for us in the education world, that was a pretty big deal. One of our reporters went to cover the launch out of Cape Canaveral, but I, like most Americans, didn't worry about the potential danger involved, since space shuttle flights seemed almost as safe as scheduled airline flights. I was in a taxi returning from an interview when the driver turned to me and said, "It blew up." I didn't know what he was talking about. "It blew up," he repeated. "The spaceship." I remembered suddenly that the *Challenger* was launching that day and immediately understood. When I arrived at the office, grim reporters were crowded into the editor's office. Plans were being made for how to cover this once-happy story. I was dispatched to New Hampshire to talk to those who had known McAuliffe and, if possible, her students. They had worn party hats and gathered in the school cafeteria to watch the liftoff, and instead saw her die in a fiery explosion. "I was confused when I saw everyone's head go down," Alex Scott, a sophomore at the time, told me. "I thought we'd go back to class and she'd be up in space."

As REASON POINTS OUT, described in purely physical terms, the explosion of the space shuttle "was brutally simple. A rubbery seal, called an O-ring, on one of the solid rocket boosters split shortly after lift-off, releasing a jet of ignited fuel that caused the entire rocket complex to explode." But how that came to be, he continues, is a nine-year "complicated tale of incompetence, selective blindness, conflicting goals and reversed logic." As far back as 1977, engineers discovered in test firings of the solid rocket booster that casing joints expanded instead of tightening, as they were designed to do. It was also discovered that one of the two O-ring joint seals frequently became unsealed, failing to provide the backup it was supposed to. Tests over the next nine years sought different methods to fix the problems, but at the same time some engineers downplayed the concerns, saying they were unlikely to occur in flight and constituted an "acceptable risk." Communications errors also led to the disaster, as one set of engineers did not talk with another set; in addition there was a conflict between engineering data and management judgments. Finally, the temperatures at launch time were much colder than anticipated, causing the O-rings to become less resilient. So the latent problems of incomplete and sometimes misleading information, poor communication, and an overriding desire to look at best-case rather than worst-case scenarios spanning nearly a decade led to the active failure of the blowout of one of the primary booster O-rings. And seven astronauts died.

In writing this book, I often emphasize the "good" part of mistakes. That doesn't necessarily mean that the mistakes themselves are good, but their aftermath—tracing back why we made them and what we learned from them—can be very helpful in avoiding mistakes in the future. If we make them not because we are careless or lazy but because we are willing to experiment, venture off the accepted path and try something hard, then that's a "good" reason to make mistakes. And if, in the aftermath of a mistake, we are willing to look back and figure out what went wrong (and if it was because we were careless or lazy, then try to correct that for next time), then that's a "good" outcome. For example, as a journalist, I will, as I've mentioned, every once in a while have a blunder of mine appear in print. I hate it. But (after cursing and trying to figure out if there's someone else I can blame) I usually sit down and try to understand how it happened and see if I can prevent it from happening again. And I usually do—for a while. And then I make a different type of mistake.

We prize quotes from geniuses like Thomas Edison, who said, "I am not discouraged, because every wrong attempt discarded is another step forward," and Albert Einstein, who opined that "anyone who has never made a mistake has never tried anything new." Those mistakes handily fit into the definition of "to wander or stray," because, as we well know in hindsight, Edison and Einstein often strayed down many wrong—or at least less-trod—paths in order to make great discoveries. And this fits into the definition offered by Bryans's subjects that mistakes are "misjudgment and adverse consequences that were unplanned." Surely Edison and Einstein and other brilliant thinkers have misjudged and experienced adverse consequences and failure, but in the end, the results are what count. But no doubt there are many failed inventors or scientists or mathematicians who worked as hard as Edison and Einstein, but because they were not as smart or lived in the wrong time or had more bad luck—or any confluence of reasons—will not be hailed as geniuses. Or maybe they will be, but only in retrospect. How do we judge their mistakes? Did they drag their families down into poverty in vain pursuit of their dreams? Did they work hard and fail, but feel that the process itself was an accomplishment, to pass on to future generations?

Once we put mistakes under the microscope, attempting to define and categorize them becomes a dizzying morass of overlapping circles. Bill Gore, founder of the company that produces the breathable waterproof fabric Gore-Tex, distinguished between "above the line" mistakes and "below the line" mistakes. The latter threaten to sink the ship, while the former do not. Above-the-line mistakes show that managers are willing to experiment, think, and challenge, while below-the-line ones are so enormous that they bring on disaster. But Gore also told each associate that it was his or her responsibility to know where the water line was. It doesn't mean that large risks shouldn't be taken, but that they should be considered very carefully and taken only after everyone who might be affected is consulted. The trouble is, as two British psychologists referring to the Gore quote said, "Too many employers confuse the two types and punish them equally." But it is not just employers who confuse them. All too often I, and many people I know, fear and react to small slips as if they are huge blunders. To use Gore's terminology, we give equal weight to a minor above-the-line error—breaking a deck chair, say—and a major below-the-line one, like running into an iceberg. The result of this is that we fear making any mistakes, because we view them all as catastrophic.

But defining a mistake or error or slip or lapse or whatever we want to call it only goes so far. "If you want to understand human error," writes Sidney Dekker, author of *The Field Guide to Understanding Human Error*, "you have to assume that people were doing reasonable things given the complexities, dilemmas, trade-offs and uncertainty that surround them. Just finding and highlighting people's mistakes explain nothing. Saying what people did not do, or what they should have done does not explain why they did what they did."

We've always been told to put ourselves in someone else's shoes, and simplistically speaking, that's what we need to do. We often look at how people made mistakes from the outside rather than understanding how they (and we) made certain decisions based on the information available at the time. Dekker talks about the tendency to examine the mistake from outside the tunnel, where we can clearly see every twist and turn, every possible problem, and observe where every road leads. How different that is from being in the tunnel, where we have to make split-second decisions, perhaps based on faulty data and unclear directions, often while we are stressed or scared. There's a name for this: hindsight bias. That bias makes us assume that a bad outcome could only be preceded by a bad process. It causes us to oversimplify history relative to how people understood it at the time it was happening.

I grew up acutely aware of hindsight bias. My father, a Jew, left Germany in 1939, a bit late, historically speaking. As I grew older and more aware of history, I would question him—as did many others—about how his parents could possibly have stayed in Berlin so long, when they had a chance to get out earlier. Well, of course, we see the 1930s in Germany as an inexorable march to the gas chambers. But if you were living there at the time, as my father was, things were not so obvious. His family was forced to relocate to another part of town, but it certainly was not clear that things were going from worse to worst. My father still played soccer with his friends, he still had a child's worries. The perspective of his family was that Germany was a civilized country that they had lived in and loved for generations, and that it was momentarily going through a dreadful period. How could they even imagine a Holocaust? It took my grandfather moving to England for a job in 1937 and seeing the full horror to insist that his wife and children leave. He was outside the tunnel, while they were still in it. As historian Barbara Tuchman said, "Every scripture is entitled to be read in the light of the circumstances that brought it forth. To understand the choices open to people of another time, one must limit oneself to what they knew; see the past in its own clothes, as it were, not ours."

With hindsight bias we tend to think that a sequence of events is linear, inevitably leading to one outcome. It causes us to be hard on ourselves and others. For example, I once wrote a column quoting a woman from Berkshire, England, which she, as the English do, pronounced BARK-sher. Having lived in London for seven years, I knew of this pronunciation quirk. But when I was writing the story, I Googled "Barkshire," with an *a*, and results came up indicating it was a place in England. I spelled it that way and it was printed. An alert (if annoying) reader quickly e-mailed to tell me it was spelled "Berkshire," with an *e*. Trying to justify my error, I pointed out to my husband that "Barkshire" had come up when Googled. He, in turn, pointed out that only about four thousand examples of "Barkshire" appeared on the screen, compared with more than 1 million for "Berkshire," and that in the future I should be aware of the number of results that appear when Googling, because Google lists things spelled incorrectly as well as correctly. I was angry at myself—how could I have done something so stupid? In hindsight, it looked oh-so-obvious. But it was simply something I had never thought about. I learned from that experience. My error, though maddening to me, obviously wasn't all that serious. Yet hindsight bias permeates all accidents. As the chairman of the investigation of the 1988 Clapham Junction railway accident in Britain—in which thirty-five people were killed and five hundred injured—wrote: "There is almost no human action or decision that cannot be made to look flawed and less sensible in the misleading light of hindsight. It is essential that the critic should keep himself constantly aware of that fact." Even if that critic is oneself.

And we can't learn from every error. Or rather, we can't always learn the lesson we assume we're supposed to learn. While writing this chapter on a laptop while on vacation in California, I saved it and saved it and saved it and then attached it to an e-mail as a safety precaution. Guess what? When I called it up to work on it, an earlier version—missing about one thousand precious words—came up. No matter how much I searched, I could not find the later version. To this day, I don't know what happened. So there was no technical lesson to be learned here. But what I did know—learned from incidents in the past, when computers had gobbled up my writing—was that stomping around and crying and slamming things just wastes time. I was fuming, but the only way to feel better was to sit down and reconstruct it as best I could. That was the lesson I had learned, and it served me well this time.

We've talked about how we try to differentiate mistakes and how our culture, our environment, our personality, and our biases shape how we respond and learn from them. But what can we understand by looking directly at how the brain itself reacts to mistakes? As the ability to research and "read" the brain becomes ever more sophisticated, scientists are formulating new theories that may help us comprehend some of the genetic underpinnings in how we react to mistakes. It was back in the early 1990s that scientists at the University of Dortmund in Germany first began discovering how the neural system processes errors. Researchers were monitoring some subjects' brains using an electroencephalograph (EEG) during a psychological experiment and noticed that, whenever the subject pressed the wrong button, the electrical potential in the frontal lobe suddenly dropped about 10 microvolts. Scientists at the University of Illinois confirmed the effect, which they referred to as error-related negativity or ERN—the combined electrical activity of millions of neurons in the brain. This ERN occurs about 50 to 100 milliseconds after making an error, such as, say, hitting the wrong keystroke. The ERN occurs in the part of the brain called the medial frontal cortex, which is the region of the brain that monitors negative feedback, action errors, and decision uncertainty—and is "an overall supervisor of human performance."

Researchers found that if more weight is added to that error—such as winning money if you get the activity right or losing money if you get it wrong—then electrical charges of the ERN drop even more, anticipating the incentive or the punishment. And a slightly more delayed ERN, known as a feedback ERN, crests 250 to 300 milliseconds after an outcome and occurs in reaction to an unfavorable response. The feedback ERN also may appear in situations in which a person faces difficult choices—known as decision uncertainty—and remains conflicted even after making the choice. It doesn't have to be a major dilemma—a feedback ERN may occur after picking a checkout line in a supermarket and then realizing that it's moving slower than the one you were going to pick (doesn't that always happen?). I can only imagine what was going on in my brain the time I wrote an e-mail complaining about my boss and then clicked send—milliseconds before I realized that I had sent it *to* my boss. I did some fast tap dancing to explain to him that it was all a joke. I doubt he bought it.

But in addition to recognizing errors, the brain must have a way of adapting and responding to them. Scientists have also discovered, through this research, that people often react to errors by slowing down after a mistake, presumably to more carefully analyze a problem and to switch to a different strategy for tackling a task, says Markus Ullsperger, a professor of biological psychology at Radboud University Nijmegen in the Netherlands, who has written a great deal on this subject. "Such behavioral changes represent ways in which we learn from our mistakes in hopes of avoiding similar slipups in the future." For instance, after my missent e-mail, I learned to type in the e-mail address *after* I've finished writing the entire message—and to double-check the address.

In 1998, two Japanese neuroscientists trained three monkeys to either push or turn a handle in response to a visual signal. The monkeys, naturally, would push the handle if they received a reward. But when the researchers successively reduced the reward for pushing, the monkeys would, after a few times, switch to turning the handle instead. While this was happening, the scientists looked at what was happening inside the monkeys' brains and found that four neurons were activated, but only if the monkeys learned from the incident and changed their behavior. That is, the neurons didn't activate if the monkeys kept pushing the handle, despite receiving a lesser reward. Ullsperger notes that these findings give us information about what and how rewards can be used for the purpose of altering behavior and how negative feedback can be used as a guide for improvement.

Scientists around the world have built on these findings to tease out how and why the brain seems to respond to mistakes. For example, experiments show that the neurotransmitter dopamine plays a role in how we process errors. Dopamine neurons generate patterns based on experience—if this happens, then that will follow. Something called the Iowa Gambling Task, which was developed by neuroscientists and is well known in psychological circles, helps prove this point. It works this way: A player is given four decks of cards and $2,000 of play money. Each card tells the player whether he won or lost money, and the object is to win as much money as possible. But the cards are rigged, with two decks paying out small amounts of money, like $50, but rarely causing a player to lose money. The other two decks have high payouts, but also high losses. So if a player pulls from the first deck—the one that gives low but steady payouts—she will come out far richer in the end. It takes an average of fifty cards before people begin to pull regularly from the more profitable first deck and about eighty cards before they can explain why they do that.

But according to Jonah Lehrer's book *How We Decide*, the neuroscientists Antonio Damasio and Antoine Bechara found that by hooking the players up to a machine that measured the electrical conductance of their skin, the players became more nervous after taking only ten cards from the less-profitable decks—although they weren't even aware of it. "The emotions knew which decks were dangerous," Lehrer writes. "The subject's feelings figured out the game first." How does this work? Dopamine. Scientists at the University of Iowa and the California Institute of Technology watched a patient undergoing brain surgery for epilepsy while playing the Iowa Gambling Task—the patient was given local anesthesia but remained conscious during the procedure. If the player chose the bad deck, the dopamine neurons immediately stopped firing. The player experienced negative emotion and learned not to draw from the deck again. If his choice was accurate, then he felt the pleasure of being correct and wanted to do the same thing again.

What's interesting is that people who produce too little dopamine in their bodies, such as those who suffer from Parkinson's disease, a degenerative disorder of the central nervous system, tend to learn more from negative feedback than from positive feedback. In one study, researchers asked nineteen healthy people and thirty Parkinson's patients to choose one symbol from a pair of symbols. The symbols were arbitrarily labeled "incorrect" or "correct." The healthy people learned from the positive feedback, choosing the correct symbols and avoiding the incorrect ones equally. But those with Parkinson's were more likely to reject the symbols labeled "incorrect" than to select the ones labeled "correct." That is, they learned more from their errors than from their hits. But once they took medication that boosted brain levels of dopamine, they reacted more strongly to positive feedback than to negative feedback.

Lehrer points out that the best way to become an expert in your field is to focus on your mistakes, "to consciously consider the errors being internalized by your dopamine neurons." He looked at what led to the success of Bill Robertie, who is a grand master in chess, a world-class poker player, and a world champion backgammon player. "After Robertie plays a chess match or a poker hand or a backgammon game, he painstakingly reviews what happened. Every decision is critiqued and analyzed. Even when Robertie wins—and he almost always wins—he insists on searching for his errors, dissecting those decisions that could have been a little better." We need to learn from mistakes not just because it might be an emotionally healthier way to live, but also because, as Lehrer says, "expertise is simply the wisdom that emerges from cellular error. Mistakes aren't to be discouraged. On the contrary, they should be cultivated and carefully investigated."

One of the very important aspects of much of the research being done in this field is that it begins to help us understand mental flexibility—why some people have the adaptive ability to avoid making the same mistakes over and over. As Ullsperger says: "Errors are a condition calling for behavioral adjustments." In other words, an error is a signal that we've done something wrong and we need to change our behavior to avoid doing it again. And scientists also discovered, interestingly enough, that the neuron activity that occurs just after an error begins in childhood—around eight to ten years old—and increases in early adulthood. This shows that the ability to monitor our errors grows as we do.

My somewhat absentminded husband is a great example of this. He used to drop his keys just about anywhere in the house, which meant a frantic search for them every morning. Eventually, he figured out that if he put the keys in the bowl near the front door in the evening when he walked in, he would find them in the same place every morning. And it also works when he puts his billfold, train pass, and cell phone in the same place on his dresser. But if he is distracted, or terribly tired, he sometimes forgets to leave them in their usual place, and the search in the morning begins anew. My sons, however, have yet to learn this lesson. Despite the fact that I constantly tell them to find one place for their precious items, like their cell phones, they have a tendency to leave them lying around any old place. The constant cry in our house is, "Have you seen my . . . ?" They blame each other, they blame the cleaner, they blame me. Eventually they find the missing cell phone or keys (and rarely apologize to any of us). But they still haven't learned that much of this brouhaha could be avoided if they found a consistent storage place for these items.

Ullsperger noted that if we understand how the brain adjusts to changeable conditions, we also learn about changes in brain activity that lead to errors. As a long-term perspective, this may help us understand the conditions under which errors are made. Possibly we will be able to predict certain errors, "a first step in the direction of avoiding them before they occur."

These experiments focusing on ERN have also provided insight into psychiatric illnesses, such as obsessive-compulsive disorders. Those with OCD can pathologically inflate small mistakes and worry that they are always on the verge of goofing up, leading to checking rituals, such as returning to the house a dozen times to ensure that the gas is turned off. Experiments such as these indicate that "hyperactive error signals" in the brain—or blowing up small mistakes—can be found in people with OCD, as well as, to some extent, those with Tourette's syndrome and even depression. It may seem as if we've wandered far afield, but Stephan Taylor, an associate professor of psychiatry at the University of Michigan who has conducted research in this area, says OCD reflects normal, everyday concerns that get hijacked by extreme doubts, and that it's "sometimes a blurry line between pathology and normal." Almost all of us have experienced that sinking feeling when we forget to take care of something important, such as turning off the stove. We may go back and check, and then move on. People with OCD can't be satisfied; they go back to check again and again. "It's as if they have a permanent error signal for some acts," Taylor says.

OCD is a clinical anxiety disorder, and I am certainly not saying that most of us who fear mistakes suffer from it. But if you put OCD at one end of the continuum of those who compulsively dread doing something wrong—and this dread impairs their level of functioning—it's not that far down the scale to perfectionists. Perfectionists often get caught in the endless cycle of regret and blame that makes it difficult, if not impossible, to move on from their mistakes. "Perfectionism," says Jeff Szymanski, executive director of the Obsessive Compulsive Foundation in Boston, is "a phobia of mistake-making. It's the feeling that if I make a mistake, it will be catastrophic." What's so interesting about perfectionism is that it is not some new phenomenon growing out of our multitasking, hard-driving twenty-first-century life. Rabbi Irving Greenberg, a Jewish scholar, notes that to practice Judaism is to strive for perfection. But he also says the conundrum is that "those who have internalized Judaism's drive for perfection find it difficult to admit their own imperfections, so how can they obtain forgiveness?" Maimonides (back in the twelfth century!) said that the "indispensable but most difficult first step in repentance is to admit the flaw or sin." The trouble, Greenberg says, is that in the fantasy of perfection, many people believe that admitting a flaw or failure—and even asking for forgiveness—permanently destroys the original "perfect" wholeness, which can never be restored.

Most of us know the story of how Moses became angry at his followers for creating the Golden Calf to worship while he was busy getting the Ten Commandments on Mount Sinai—and in his fury at his people's lack of faith, he smashed the tablets. The original tablets symbolized unattainable purity, Greenberg says, and once Moses destroyed them, he and his followers had to work through heartbreak, reconciliation catharsis, and ultimately the creation of new tablets. This new set of tablets was "the product of hard-won repentances built on realism, forgiveness, and acceptance of others' limitations," Greenberg writes. "Out of our brokenness we become stronger than when we claimed to be whole." The idea that life should not and cannot be perfect is also exemplified by a tradition among some old-time quilters to deliberately make an occasional flaw in their work to spoil the perfection. Otherwise, the fear was that the devil would like it too much and grab the needleworkers up in their sleep.

Wait a minute here. Aren't we always complaining that things are going to hell in a handbasket—that no one really cares about doing a good job? Why not strive to be the very best you can be? Up to a point, being a perfectionist isn't a bad thing; in fact, it may mean you have very high standards and you often meet those standards. Those who have perfectionist tendencies without having those tendencies rule—or ruin—their lives are what psychiatrists call "adaptive" perfectionists. They find it very important to do certain things in the right way, but this need doesn't hinder their lives and can actually help them achieve great success. For instance, Szymanski told me, he likes all the glasses in his kitchen cupboard lined up a certain way. That doesn't mean he freaks out if someone changes them (as friends sometimes do for fun), or that everything else in his house is equally ordered. He also strives to be the best executive director and psychiatrist that he can be. But he knows he's not a great tennis player, and that's okay with him—it doesn't mean he'll give it up because he's not world-class, or line up a pro to work with him seven days a week. He's okay being okay at some things.

On the other hand, what psychiatrists call maladaptive perfectionists need to be the best at everything, and if they make a mistake, it's a crisis. It's also not just about how they perceive themselves, but about how others perceive them: they believe they will lose the respect of friends and colleagues if they fail. They have to hit all their marks all the time. Their need for perfection can also sabotage their own success. They don't turn in projects on time because they're not yet perfect. They can't prioritize between what needs to be done quickly and what can be put on the back burner. They want to rigidly follow rules in order to get things "right," and this often means they're terribly uncreative, since creativity involves making mistakes, Szymanski says. Even worse, they don't learn from their mistakes, because if, God forbid, one occurs, it should be concealed like a nasty secret. So they can't get crucial feedback—feedback that would both stop them from making similar mistakes in the future and make them realize that it's not a disaster—because they won't risk punishment or alienation for a blunder. And such a drive for perfection takes a heavy psychological toll, because every flaw, no matter how small, is cause for agony.

"A lot of people are proud perfectionists," Szymanski says. "If you take away their perfectionism, they see themselves as chaotic and slovenly. They don't see an in between." They also feel that they simply have high standards and that it's the rest of the world that falls short. The problem with maladaptive perfectionists, Szymanski says, is not that they shouldn't have goals, but that those goals are often unrealistic and inevitably lead to a sense of failure. A quote I once read seems to sum up perfectly the difference between striving for excellence and striving for perfection: "Excellence involves enjoying what you're doing, feeling good about what you've learned, and developing confidence. Perfection involves feeling bad about a 98 [out of 100] and always finding mistakes no matter how well you're doing."

There is some controversy in the field among those who study perfectionism about whether, in fact, the term "adaptive perfectionism" is valid, as, by their very nature, perfectionists have trouble adapting. Randy O. Frost, a psychology professor at Smith College in Northampton, Massachusetts, who has studied perfectionism for years, says he would prefer the term "positive achievement striving," but he acknowledges that that phrase is going to be a tough one to sell. It's also important to remember that very few fit neatly into one category or another—we all tend to be on a continuum of perfectionism.

One of Frost's studies shows how fearing criticism prevents maladaptive perfectionists from improving. He asked fifty-one women undergraduates—some considered high in perfectionist traits (more maladaptive) based on a scale developed by Frost and his colleagues (see below) and some considered low (adaptive and nonpefectionists)— to reword a passage from an introductory writing composition text as succinctly as possible without changing its meaning or deleting any important themes or ideas. The assignment was then graded by two college professors who were blind to the differences in the participants. The findings? Those high in perfectionism wrote passages that "were judged significantly poorer in quality than subjects low in perfectionism." Perhaps, Frost theorized, that is because maladaptive perfectionists avoid writing tasks, procrastinate about them, and avoid having others review and comment on their work to a greater extent than nonperfectionists. "The result may be that those perfectionists don't practice writing in any consistent way and don't benefit from feedback on their work," he wrote. "Consequently, they may not develop the same quality of writing skills as nonperfectionists. . . . Perfectionists seem to be motivated by a fear of failure and . . . new tasks are viewed as opportunities for failure rather than accomplishments."

Here is the scale Frost uses to measure perfectionism:

MULTIDIMENSIONAL PERFECTIONISM SCALE

Please circle the number that best corresponds to your agreement with each statement below. Use this rating system.[1]

	STRONGLY DISAGREE . . . . STRONGLY AGREE				

1. My parents set very high standards for me.　　1　2　3　4　5

2. Organization is very important to me.　　1　2　3　4　5

3. As a child, I was punished for doing things less than perfectly.　　1　2　3　4　5

4. If I do not set the highest standards for myself, I am likely to end up a second-rate person.　　1　2　3　4　5

---

[1]The test is not evaluated as a whole, but in subsets. The Concern over Mistakes (CM) subscale (items 9, 10, 13, 14, 18, 21, 23, 25, 34) reflects negative reactions to mistakes, a tendency to interpret mistakes as equivalent to failure, and a tendency to believe that one will lose the respect of others following failure. The average is 20, a high score is 27.

Personal Standards (PS) (items 4, 6, 12, 16, 19, 24, 30) reflects the setting of very high standards and the excessive importance placed on these high standards for self-evaluation. The average is 26, a high score is 31.

The tendency to believe that one's parents set very high goals constitutes the Parent Expectations (PE) scale (items 1, 11, 15, 20, 26). The average is 15, a high score is 19.

The perception that one's parents are (or were) overly critical constitutes the Parental Criticism (PC) scale (items 3, 5, 22, 35). The average is 7, a high score is 10.

Doubting of Actions (D) (items 17, 28, 32, 33) reflects the extent to which people doubt their ability to accomplish tasks. The average is 9, a high score is 12.

The Organization (O) (items: 2, 7, 8, 27, 29, 31) average is 23, while the high is above 29. A high score in this area might not be a problem, Frost notes, as it may indicate an adaptive rather than a maladaptive perfectionist.

	STRONGLY DISAGREE . . . . STRONGLY AGREE				
5. My parents never tried to understand my mistakes.	1	2	3	4	5
6. It is important to me that I be thoroughly competent in everything I do.	1	2	3	4	5
7. I am a neat person.	1	2	3	4	5
8. I try to be an organized person.	1	2	3	4	5
9. If I fail at work/school, I am a failure as a person.	1	2	3	4	5
10. I should be upset if I make a mistake.	1	2	3	4	5
11. My parents wanted me to be the best at everything.	1	2	3	4	5
12. I set higher goals for myself than most people.	1	2	3	4	5
13. If someone does a task at work/school better than me, I feel like I failed the whole task.	1	2	3	4	5
14. If I fail partly, it is as bad as being a complete failure.	1	2	3	4	5
15. Only outstanding performance is good enough in my family.	1	2	3	4	5

	STRONGLY DISAGREE . . . . STRONGLY AGREE				

16. I am very good at focusing my efforts on attaining a goal.　　1　2　3　4　5

17. Even when I do something very carefully, I often feel that it is not quite done right.　　1　2　3　4　5

18. I hate being less than the best at things.　　1　2　3　4　5

19. I have extremely high goals.　　1　2　3　4　5

20. My parents have expected excellence from me.　　1　2　3　4　5

21. People will probably think less of me if I make a mistake.　　1　2　3　4　5

22. I never felt like I could meet my parents' expectations.　　1　2　3　4　5

23. If I do not do as well as other people, it means I am an inferior human being.　　1　2　3　4　5

24. Other people seem to accept lower standards from themselves than I do.　　1　2　3　4　5

25. If I do not do well all the time, people will not respect me.　　1　2　3　4　5

26. My parents have always had higher expectations for my future than I have.　　1　2　3　4　5

	STRONGLY DISAGREE . . . . STRONGLY AGREE				
27. I try to be a neat person.	1	2	3	4	5
28. I usually have doubts about the simple, everyday things I do.	1	2	3	4	5
29. Neatness is very important to me.	1	2	3	4	5
30. I expect higher performance in my daily tasks than most people.	1	2	3	4	5
31. I am an organized person.	1	2	3	4	5
32. I tend to get behind in my work because I repeat things over and over.	1	2	3	4	5
33. It takes me a long time to do something "right."	1	2	3	4	5
34. The fewer mistakes I make, the more people will like me.	1	2	3	4	5
35. I never felt like I could meet my parents' standards.	1	2	3	4	5

Highly perfectionist people fear making mistakes before and during a task, and they beat themselves up after they're finished. In a study of athletes, those more concerned about making mistakes than their teammates tended to have more difficulty forgetting about flubs that they made on the playing field, had more social concern (such as "I let down the team"), and felt more pressure to overcome the mistakes. They also were more likely to report that the images of the blunder influenced them for the remainder of the game and that they had a lower level of confidence following the game.

Frost asked university students—some who ranked high and some low on the perfectionism scale—to complete the Stroop Color Naming Task, in which they are asked to name a color, but the word "red," for example, appears in blue letters. It's a difficult test and most people make a lot of errors. Then they did a much easier color-naming exercise. When asked questions afterward, those higher in perfectionism reacted more negatively to their mistakes than did their counterparts, showed lower confidence in their ability to do the task, believed others judged them more harshly, and reported being more likely to conceal the details of their performance from others. Frost and his colleagues also found that those who leaned more toward perfectionism believed that "they should have done better," although—and here's the kicker—they did not believe they made more mistakes than the less-perfectionist participants. They simply reacted more negatively to the ones they made. (The experiment did not report which group actually made a greater number of errors.)

There are ways that those with super-perfectionist traits can try to take things down a notch. They can try to break tasks down into more manageable bites, so they don't feel overwhelming. They can work on getting more feedback at an early point in a project to get a reality check. They can learn to prioritize and set deadlines, so they don't get subsumed in every project to the detriment of other needs. This is where self-help books can be helpful, Szymanski said, by providing such strategies. However, a problem arises when a perfectionist knows the strategies and won't use them. That's when therapy might be necessary.

It's good to remember that while we often think of saints as the ultimate perfectionists ("I'm no saint, you know!"), in the Catholic tradition the saints were not always, well, saintly. As Thomas Craughwell, author of the pithily named book *Saints Behaving Badly*, put it: "The Catholic calendar is full of notorious men and women who turned their lives around and became saints. St. Camillus de Lellis was an Italian mercenary soldier, a card sharp and con man. For six years St. Margaret of Cortona lived as a Tuscan nobleman's mistress. St. Moses the Ethiopian led a gang of cutthroats in the Egyptian desert. And St. Pelagia was the porn queen of fifth-century Antioch." Of course, they went through great suffering to become saints—but the point is, they made their fair share of mistakes. And most of us aren't aiming for canonization.

Perfectionism is fear not just that a particular gaffe will be discovered or elicit punishment, but that it will lead to another—and another. And in particular, in this age of YouTube, twenty-four-hour news stations, and the Internet's perpetual motion, what once would have been a blooper that lived for a few days and died can now resonate far beyond its natural life. Ironically, while I argue that people need to be more open about mistakes, television—first through *Jerry Springer*–like programs and more recently reality shows, which follow people's lives with microscopic intensity and blow all missteps out of proportion—has created a bizarre ethos where people share their mistakes with millions of viewers. Those mistakes can range from addiction to choosing the wrong lover to a failed home renovation. But they project a paradoxical message about how we should think about mistakes.

There is the makeover genre of reality television, in which an expert shows you where you went wrong and how to do better in decorating your home, dressing yourself, disciplining your children (or all three if you're lucky). I confess, I like watching these types of shows, although their rigid formulas soon become dull: the expert points out everything you've done wrong, maybe with a small dose of humiliation thrown in, shows you what to do right, and reveals the new look (which, of course, means much more than just a new look—it's a whole new outlook! A whole new life!), as the participants gush gratitude for this chance to learn and change.

In some ways, do these shows teach us that we all make mistakes and can all learn from them? Maybe, but within a severely limited context. What they tell us, says Mark Andrejevic, author of *Reality TV: The Work of Being Watched*, is that we have complete control over the ability to fix our mistakes—which can be empowering in a certain way: I'm told that I am solely responsible for whether I'm overweight or not—it has nothing to do with forces beyond my control. But then the contradiction is that it takes an expert to show me how to do everything right. The popular reality show *The Biggest Loser* is an example of this, where severely overweight people work out strenuously for six to ten hours a day with a personal trainer and learn healthy eating habits. No one can argue that teaching people about exercise and eating right is good, but the message is that anyone can do this if they just have enough willpower—and apparently no job, because you're exercising throughout most of the day. It also doesn't show the dangerous practices some contestants engage in off-camera, such as self-induced dehydration.

As Andrejevic points out, these shows also don't talk about other social issues contributing to weight gain, such as the food industry, economics, and advertising, and they strongly downplay the role of genetics. Of course, who would want to watch a program like that? But the message is, then, not surprisingly, a simplistic and conflicting one—only you have the power to fix your mistakes, and by extension, you have no excuse for not perfecting yourself. But you can only do it in this certain way that our experts say is right. And rarely do the shows (*The Biggest Loser* and a few others have on occasion) go back to see if the results have stuck. So it appears that once you resolve a problem, it stays resolved—no typical ups and downs of real life. "The confessional is always, 'I learned so much by going through the process. I learned how to do things right by being forced to confront them,'" Andrejevic told me. "But the message is, if I made these mistakes on my own, I wouldn't change. I needed the apparatus of publicity and the initial humiliation. None of this says you can do this at home."

The other types of reality shows, the docudramas that show us the hilarious goings-on of celebrities or regular folks (who just happen, say, to have sextuplets) do in some ways offer the message that we're all human and we all make mistakes. But because these blunders are presented for "entertainment" purposes only, understanding and resolving the problems has no place on the shows' agendas. They're used so people can shout and cry and blame one another, as well as, of course, keep us riveted to our screens. And once again, mistakes get a bad rap.

So what have *we* learned, going through our own process—perhaps in a less entertaining but hopefully more enlightening way—of trying to define mistakes? Well, there are many different kinds, and often the apparent cause really hides the many underlying mistakes that contributed to error. That to really understand why someone made an error, we have to understand the process they went through through their own eyes. That we're learning more every day about how the brain reacts to mistakes. That we all—from Moses to us—must acknowledge that we can never be perfect, nor should we try to be. We should remember what Reason said: "Errors are . . . the inevitable and usually acceptable price human beings have to pay for their remarkable ability to cope with very difficult informational tasks quickly and, more often than not, effectively." But defining mistakes and acknowledging that we all make them is only the beginning. It doesn't do us much good unless we also try to change our approach—when we and others make mistakes—in ways that will benefit us and those around us.

2.

IT STARTS EARLY

I FIRST HEARD ABOUT CAROL DWECK IN AN ARTICLE that ran in *New York* magazine back in 2007. The story, "How Not to Talk to Your Kids: The Inverse Power of Praise," introduced me and my many friends who e-mailed the article around—I think I received it at least five times—to her research on how praise can encourage children to fear mistakes.

Dweck is a professor of psychology at Stanford University whose highly influential research has closely examined children's reactions to mistakes. She found that children commended for being smart are often less willing to take chances than those praised for making a greater effort. When we applaud children for their intelligence, she said, "we tell them that this is the name of the game: Look smart, don't risk making mistakes." I read her research and my mind started reeling. How often do I tell my children that they are smart? I don't think it is an inordinate number of times, but I certainly use that as one way to describe them. In fact, I probably use it more as a punishment than praise. When they have dawdled over their homework, when they have seemed deliberately dense about doing something I've requested, I've snapped at them, "You're smart, you can do this."

My God! Here I am, unwittingly depriving them of the willingness to take on challenges, creating children who would rather play it safe than risk doing something new and different. Then I calmed down. If this was true, it was simply one of the many, many parental mistakes I will make over my lifetime.

However, I didn't forget Dweck's advice. I tried to talk more about effort with my sons, to emphasize how proud we are of them if they try hard even if they don't succeed. We happened to take the boys—then eleven and eight years old—skiing for the first time right after I read the article, and I remember, somewhat awkwardly, trying to praise them for the good effort they made skiing down the slopes rather than simply telling them they skied well. I sounded a bit like someone practicing a foreign language—and my husband looked at me rather strangely—but Dweck's research had made an impact. A few years later, when I wrote the *New York Times* column that initiated this book, I returned to Dweck, this time interviewing her over the phone. She explained her research a little more in-depth—and it struck me anew how interesting it was.

A petite, sharply dressed woman, Dweck is low-key but passionate about her work. As a child she was always focused on being—and appearing—smart, and her sixth-grade teacher, Mrs. Wilson, helped etch the importance of this on her young brain. Mrs. Wilson seated the students in her class in IQ order, and only the highest IQ students were awarded the honors of carrying the flag, clapping the erasers, and taking a note to the principal. Where did Dweck fall in this ranking? Row 1, seat 1. "I was one of the perfect little girls," she told me. "I hated mistakes." As a graduate student at Yale, Dweck started off studying animal motivation and learned helplessness: the animals sometimes didn't do what they were capable of doing because they had given up after numerous failures. Dweck wondered how this translated to humans—why do some children quit in the face of failure while others are motivated? At the time, it was believed that learned helplessness could be overcome with enough successes. Dweck theorized that the difference between the helpless response and its opposite, the determination to master new things and surmount challenges, lay in people's beliefs about why they had failed. People who attributed their failures to lack of ability, Dweck thought, would become discouraged even in areas where they were capable. Those who thought they simply hadn't tried hard enough, on the other hand, would be fueled by setbacks. This became the topic of her Ph.D. dissertation. So when trying to untangle why and how all of us respond to mistakes and where it all begins, her research seemed crucial.

That is why I found myself one chilly winter day in Palo Alto, California, sitting at a picnic table in the playground at Ohlone Elementary School watching Russell, a thoughtful ten-year-old with glasses, dark hair, and red Crocs on his feet, intently doing a puzzle.

Allison, a graduate student at Stanford University, sat across from Russell, as he easily finished the questions about which pattern would likely complete the picture.

Russell eagerly looked up as Allison graded it.

"You got nine out of nine—you must have worked hard," she told him.

Then Russell was asked, if he had a choice, would he choose to do:

1. "Problems that aren't too hard, so I don't make too many errors."

2. "Problems that are pretty easy so I'll do well."

3. "Problems that I'm pretty good at so I can show that I'm smart."

4. "Problems that I'll learn a lot from even if I won't look so smart."

Russell chose number 4.

Then Allison pulled a fast one on him. She gave him a second quiz that clearly had Russell stumped. No longer whizzing through, he went slower and slower as he labored over the questions.

He got only three right. "That's a lot worse," Allison bluntly told him.

Russell was then given a choice between taking home the first puzzle or the second one. He chose the second, the one he didn't do as well on. Finally, Russell was given a paper wheel with a green part that stated, "I didn't work hard enough," and a red part that stated, "I'm not smart enough."

He could adjust the wheel so it was all red, all green, or a combination of the two. Using the wheel, Allison asked Russell to explain why he thought he didn't do well on the second quiz.

He moved it around until it was largely green: "I didn't work hard enough."

"The problems were also harder," he added.

Allison had a final surprise for Russell: the second test he had been given was really for much older students, so he did very well for a ten-year-old. Russell smiled and loped off.

Clara, another ten-year-old, came out next, sporting a Berkeley sweatshirt and a headband, her hair swept back in a ponytail. Allison began the whole procedure over again, but this time when Clara did well on the easy puzzle, she told her, "You must be really smart." Clara beamed. Next, when Clara was asked to choose what kind of problem she would like next, unlike Russell, she chose number 3—"Problems that I'm pretty good at so I can show that I'm smart."

After getting only three right on the second quiz, Clara looked embarrassed. When asked which puzzle she would take home, she volunteered that she would rather take home the easier one that she had done well on. When given the wheel, Clara said she didn't do well primarily because she just wasn't smart enough. So, praised for being smart, Clara wanted easy puzzles so she could continue looking smart and thought her failure on the difficult puzzle was because she wasn't smart enough. Praised for effort, Russell and another girl, Sonya, were willing to try the more difficult puzzles and believed it was hard work, rather than smarts, that would help them do better.

This is a microcosm of the research Dweck and her graduate students did with four hundred fifth-graders in New York City schools. Of those praised for effort, 90 percent chose the harder set, just like Russell. Of those praised for being smart, the majority chose the easy test, so they could continue looking smart, like Clara. "One thing I've learned is that kids are exquisitely attuned to the real message, and the real message is, 'Be smart,'" Dweck told me. "It's not, 'We love it when you struggle, or when you learn and make mistakes.'"

Allison didn't ask the kids to complete the other section of the experiment when I was visiting, but I have to say that once I learned about it, it became my favorite part. In the original experiments, after scoring poorly on the test that was too hard—but without being told it was above their grade level—the children were told to write anonymously to students in another school explaining the test and telling their score. Of those who were told they were smart, 37 percent lied about their scores, while only 13 percent of those who were praised for their effort did.

What Dweck's research showed is that whether or not we think we have the innate talent or skills to do something—as opposed to believing that in general we can work and improve ourselves in most areas—has a significant effect on how we view mistakes. Those who see their abilities as fixed, as innate and inflexible, are "entity" believers in psychological parlance, or as Dweck terms it, they have "fixed mindsets." They fear mistakes because they think they are simply not smart or talented enough to do the task required and they learn to be defensive and foist blame on anything or anyone but themselves. Those who hold "incremental" beliefs, or in Dweck's language, "growth mindsets," see ability as a malleable quality and therefore believe that with enough effort they can over-come obstacles. They may not embrace mistakes, but they tend to see them more as part of the process of learning than as a reflection of their intelligence or abilities.

Children as young as three or four years old showed similar tendencies: preschoolers who were praised for being "good draw-ers" were subsequently more afraid of making a mistake than those praised for "doing a good job drawing." But even more important, to my mind, is that Dweck tested her ideas on children of differ-ent backgrounds: lower-income groups and minorities, who are too often left out of such psychological studies. In a study published in 2007, Dweck and two colleagues looked at four successive groups of entering junior high school students at a New York public school to see how well they did in math. The group of 373 moderately high-achieving students was 55 percent African-American, 27 per-cent South Asian, 15 percent Latino, and 3 percent East Asian and European American. Of those, 53 percent were eligible for free lunches, meaning they were from low-income homes.

The students were given a questionnaire at the beginning of their junior high experience asking them how much they agreed or disagreed with statements like "You have a certain amount of intelligence and you really can't do much to change it" and "You can always greatly change how intelligent you are." It also assessed their views of effort, such as "The harder you work at something, the better you will be at it" and "To tell the truth, when I work hard at my schoolwork, it makes me feel like I'm not very smart." Nearly two years after completing the questionnaire, Dweck found out that those students whose answers put them more in the fixed mindset camp generally did worse in math than those in the growth mindset.

Then, for one semester, Dweck and her researchers worked in another secondary school in New York, this time including lower-achieving students. The population was approximately half African-American and half Latino. The students were told they would have eight twenty-five-minute sessions, one per week, "about the brain." All the students learned similar information about the physiology of the brain and study skills, but those in the experimental group were also taught that intelligence is malleable and can be developed. Those in the control group were not given such lessons. At the end of the sessions, teachers were asked to write about individual students who had shown changes in their motivational behavior after the workshop and to describe the changes. The teachers did not know which group the students were in—in fact, the teachers didn't even know there were two distinct groups. Twenty-seven percent of students in the experimental group were mentioned by their teacher as showing positive change, compared with only 9 percent of the control group.

It is important to note that Dweck is not arguing that everyone has exactly the same potential in every area or will learn everything with equal ease. Rather, she believes that the intellectual ability of any given individual can always be developed further, and that we limit ourselves when we proclaim, "I'm just not a math person," or "I don't have the writing gene."

Now I want to tell you something about the little experiment I witnessed in Palo Alto. Three out of the four children I observed reacted just as expected to Dweck's experiment. But Ryan, a small boy with a froggy voice who was praised for being smart, still wanted to take home the harder test "so I can get better," and emphatically said that the reason he didn't do well was "all because I didn't work hard enough." He added, "If we put our mind to something, we can do anything." Ryan didn't fit into the pattern. This doesn't discount the findings, by any means, but it does tell us that many different facets go into behavior and beliefs—and how we react and learn to react to mistakes.

First of all, there's simply how we're hardwired. My two sisters and I, raised by the same two parents, have radically dissimilar temperaments and interests. My sons, besides their intense love of sports, have such opposite personalities that they could have been raised on different planets. As researchers increasingly use MRIs to see how parts of the brain react to different tasks, they're developing fascinating new ideas regarding the genetic components of personality traits that we previously had attributed much more to nurture than to nature. For instance, who would think there might be a genetic component to learning from mistakes? But a team of neuroscientists from Germany reported in 2007 that people with a particular gene variation have greater difficulty learning from negative reinforcement than those without the gene variation. That means those with the gene variation are slow to learn from bad experiences and mistakes.

Of course, environment is also crucial—socioeconomic class, culture, and ethnicity all come into play when delving into how we respond to mistakes and our willingness to learn from them. It starts with not only the overt messages but also the covert messages our parents and other authority figures gave us. Do we tell our children that "it's okay to make mistakes" and then yell at them for spilling milk? (Step right next to me if that's the case.) Do we say that learning is a process, yet seem more interested in results? And in the classroom, does the teacher seem more involved with those who excel than with those who struggle? On the soccer field, are children told "anyone can succeed" but receive an underlying message that some kids have what it takes and some kids don't?

So we throw all these ingredients into a pot—genetic makeup, parenting, class, and culture—and try to sift through them. While we may not be able to parse exactly what comes from where, there are some critical findings about how we regard our ability to learn and our reactions to mistakes. Before getting to that, it's important to focus on what the terms "ability" and "effort" mean, and how we perceive them at different stages in life. John Nicholls, a pioneer in looking at children's concepts of ability and effort, concluded that younger children tend to conflate effort and ability, and how they relate to outcome. For example, some studies have shown that preschoolers and kindergartners often think that smart people do well because they work hard and not-so-smart children do poorly because they don't work hard enough. As they grow, children begin to distinguish between ability and effort, but will be inconsistent in attributing outcome to one or the other. Older children, on the other hand, often believe that smart students don't have to work hard and, conversely, those who do work hard must be dumber. Researchers in the field differ on how porous these age differences are, and some, like Dweck, have conducted experiments that demonstrate that even very young children can be influenced to have a fixed mindset or a growth mindset. But age clearly plays a role.

Second, one person can have both incremental and entity beliefs, depending on the situation and the subject. A student can have a fixed mindset about her competence in sports, but an incremental belief about her ability in mathematics or writing. Take this study done of teenagers of Mexican descent in Southern California. Researchers used questionnaires to assess their beliefs about entity and incremental beliefs in the areas of general intelligence, mathematics, science, and English. On the basis of their answers, four students were determined to have a complete fixed-mindset outlook, thirty-seven were labeled as growth mindset, and sixteen as mixed. Then six girls and seven boys—four from the first group, three from the second, and six from the last—were pulled out for one-hour follow-up interviews.

The ones with the growth mindsets only expressed views that fit perfectly with the theory of growth mindset. For instance, Pablo said, "I think everyone can learn if he wants, except that there are some things that take longer to learn, and that's all. It's like everything. One can learn anything, just wanting to."

INTERVIEWER: "Okay. What about those that take longer to learn? Why is that so?"

PABLO: "I couldn't say. I think that . . . I guess they understand things slower."

INTERVIEWER: "So do you think that that person is less intelligent or the same, just slower?"

PABLO: "They are equally intelligent, it's just that they take longer to think about things."

Julian, on the other hand, had mixed views: "I feel that I know something and that I have a certain amount of intelligence, but that I can't change it—can't make it better or use it."

Then he goes on to say that in fact, "in some subjects you can and others you can't. In math, sometimes yes, but biology is not the same. I don't think I could change."

INTERVIEWER: "What's the difference between math and biology? Why can you change it in math and not in biology?"

JULIAN: "Biology has strange words and they all seem similar at times, and not so in math."

INTERVIEWER: "Why do you think that you can't change your intelligence in any subject?"

JULIAN: "Due to the subject: it depends on the subject."

Of course, Julian is right, even if he can't articulate it that well. Both innate intelligence and effort do matter. Everyone is not starting with the same genetic material. Look, I know I'm a terrible singer. I enjoy singing, but the surprised looks from strangers when I'm caught doing it—say, at a concert—tipped me off long ago that I'm somewhat, shall we say, lacking in the musical arena. I also know that if I had pursued singing lessons and really worked at it, I could have become passable—just. I would never, however, have become a professional vocalist.

The key question is how much we believe we can do with what we were born with. If we believe our smarts or skills are pretty much set in concrete, we are going to avoid and dread mistakes, because what do they show us except that we've screwed up? If we believe that with more effort we can keep getting better and better (even if we'll never win that Grammy), then we can view mistakes less harshly and as part of an overall process of growing and learning.

The idea that ability trumps effort is a very American notion, which is odd because it runs counter to another quintessentially American narrative: the Horatio Alger tale, that with hard work and perseverance, anyone can climb to the top in this country. When Barack Obama was elected president, his rise was lauded as an "only in America" story. So how do the two ideas mesh? I believe that we give lip service to one—we're a nation of unlimited potential—and yet increasingly internalize that without some great talent or luck, we might as well throw in the towel. And speaking of towels (or laundry), my ten-year-old son, Gabriel, has taken this all to its logical conclusion. When I ask him to put away his clothes, he tells me, "I'm not a good folder." I realize it's his way of getting out of an unwanted chore (I wasn't born yesterday!), but he also believes that there *are* good folders and bad ones. Which there are. But not because we were born that way—because we've been forced to practice. So if children believe that working hard doesn't matter, that either you've got it or you don't, then mistakes are simply signs of failure. Learning from them doesn't really matter, because we all know that either you're smart or you're not (or a good folder or not). The only purpose mistakes serve is to show you up. And sadly, that's what too many of us—children and adults alike—think.

It's interesting to note that far more than many other cultures,

Americans enthusiastically embraced the intelligence test, first created by French psychologist Alfred Binet. The idea that intelligence
could both be measured (as a "quotient," thus coining the idea of
an "intelligence quotient," or IQ) and that it was relatively fixed
was one that a lot of American psychologists liked and was widely
lauded by educators. Most other countries were far less keen on IQ
tests and used them, if at all, in a much more limited manner than in
this country. And, as we have seen in more recent times, culture and
environment, not just innate smarts, do indeed affect how children
perform on IQ tests.

In his best-selling book *Outliers*, Malcolm Gladwell tries to
puncture the illusion that has become so prominent in our society:
that certain people are just born great and others aren't. "We are so
caught up in the myths of the best and the brightest and the self-
made that we think outliers spring naturally from the earth," he
writes. Rather, he comes to what shouldn't be a particularly radical view, but seems to be, these days: that "achievement is talent
plus preparation." K. Anders Ericsson, a professor of psychology
at Florida State University, has spent years studying what makes
world-class successes—whether they play sports, chess, or the violin. The concept that the best naturally rise to the top like cream
belies the fact that very hard work is often behind the accomplishments. In his research on expertise, Ericsson determined that it
usually takes a top achiever ten years of what he calls deliberate
practice to become great. And deliberate practice means working
with 100 percent concentration in a structured environment, focusing on improving and overcoming weaknesses in one small area at
a time. In fact, Ericsson says he has not found any genetic evidence

that accomplishments are linked to individual differences in genes except height—it's hard to become an NBA basketball player if you're short or an Olympic gymnast if you're tall.

Now here's another contradiction I found myself wrestling with: On the one hand, the competitive nature of the American classroom and the individualistic nature of American culture are being blamed for the difficulty many of us have grappling with mistakes and failure. On the other hand, many bemoan what they see as the coddling of our children—the constant praise and rewards, the trophies for every participant, the fear of saying anything that might remotely be taken as criticism. All children must be special. All children must be gifted. While Garrison Keillor's Lake Wobegone, where all children are above average, is a mythical place, too many parents seem to believe it can be true.

Huh? So how does that all fit together? Well, one way to get a handle on it is to look at a child-rearing philosophy that emerged more than a hundred years ago, lay dormant, and then took off with a vengeance in the 1960s: that of the importance of children's self-esteem. According to Martin E. P. Seligman, who has spent a lifetime studying the development of happiness in children, the concept was first introduced by William James, the father of modern psychology. It then lay dormant throughout two world wars and the Depression, when American psychology was dominated by theories that human beings are at the mercy of forces beyond their control. Then the 1960s came along, as "America moved into an era of unprecedented wealth and power, with individual consumption driving the economy. Self-direction rather than outside forces became the primary explanation of why people do what they do.

The time was now ripe for the resuscitation of self-esteem." That occurred in 1967, when a young California psychology professor proposed that self-esteem was crucial for child-rearing, and he devised a test to measure it using such statements as "I often wish I were someone else," "It's pretty tough to be me," and "I'm pretty happy." (For me, this would all change depending on what day—or hour—you asked me.) Good self-esteem was defined as feeling positive about yourself, and it became generally accepted that the job of parents and teachers is to make sure their children and students possessed it. Thus sprang up the "Everybody is a star" philosophy, according to which everybody is special and everybody gets an award for everything.

The trouble is that low self-esteem was seen as the cause of poor grades, depression, unpopularity, and a whole host of other modern-day plagues. If you could just raise self-esteem, the thinking went, then all those other problems would disappear. But as Seligman says, "Does failure cause low self-esteem or does low self-esteem cause failure?" Modern research, he argues, finds that there is no evidence that "self-esteem causes anything at all." Rather, and this is crucial, "self-esteem is caused by a whole panoply of success or failures in the world." Children (and everyone) feel better when they feel competent, when they are able to master a subject, and, in regards to our subject of mistakes, when they are allowed to goof up and make errors and learn that they can recover. That is why the concept of resiliency—how well a child can recover from the inevitable ups and downs—has replaced self-esteem as a goal in creating happy and successful children and adults. The truth is, children (and, indeed, all of us) need to succeed at some things but not at everything. And that is why, while they shouldn't fail all the time, they must fail sometimes.

"While we do not want our children to face ongoing failure, to attempt to overprotect them and rush in whenever we fear they might fail at a task robs them of an important lesson, namely, that mistakes are experiences from which to learn," write Robert Brooks and Sam Goldstein, two prominent child-development experts. "It also communicates another subtle or perhaps not-so-subtle message to a child: We don't think you are strong enough to deal with obstacles and mistakes. The ways in which children understand and respond to mistakes and setbacks are a key component of a resilient mindset." Resilient children, Brooks and Goldstein argue, attribute mistakes, particularly if a task is achievable, to things they can change. They also look for parents and other adults who can help them. Resilient children have "the insight and courage" to recognize when a task may just be beyond their abilities. While they may be temporarily cast down, they don't see themselves as failures, and they eventually direct their energies toward other tasks. "These children possess one of the most important features of a resilient mindset: the belief that adversity can lead to growth. They view difficult situations as challenges rather than as stresses to avoid." Children who are not resilient, on the other hand, usually see mistakes and failures as beyond their control. They see themselves as overall losers and failures rather than as having difficulty in one particular area of their life.

Does this sound familiar? "When children possess this kind of mindset and believe that they do not have the ability to learn from mistakes, they often try to mask this feeling by relying on self-defeating ways of coping, such as quitting at tasks, blaming others, denying responsibility." I've seen that in myself and in my sons. If mistakes are seen as a basis for learning, their self-esteem and resilience will thrive, Brooks and Goldstein say. If not, if they "feel trapped by their mistakes, their self-worth and confidence will diminish, making it even more difficult for them to perceive the possible positive aspects of mistakes and failure."

As parents, we can try to back off, let our children fall down and get up and fall down again. Even if that means they make mistakes that make them (and us) unhappy.

Wendy Mogel, a psychologist, wrote a book a number of years ago about just this, *The Blessing of a Skinned Knee.* "When we treat our children's lives like we're cruise ship directors who must get them to their destination—adulthood—smoothly, without their feeling even the slightest bump or wave, we're depriving them," she writes. Mogel, who uses the Torah, the key text in Judaism, as a framework for best-practice child-rearing, talks about the three different types of sin in Judaism. The first and most benign is *cheit,* or inadvertent sin (mistake!). It is also used in archery to refer to missing the mark or aiming off course. For *cheit*—the lost jackets, spilled milk, forgotten lunches—the consequence of the poor judgment is the teacher itself, and, Mogel says, the lesson learned is as precious as money and more important than whatever was lost or spilled. But we deprive our kids of the reward if we, as the parent, insist on being the teacher and the fixer, rather than letting the lesson learned be the teacher.

This can seem obvious and easy, but somehow in our culture it often just feels like poor parenting. Not only do I feel bad about my children paying a price for their blunders, but I suspect that other parents are judging both me and my children, and finding us wanting. I feel that their children miraculously remember every item every time and that those perfect parents will be critical of me for not rescuing my children by rushing to fix the problem. Intellectually I know it's ridiculous, but deep down, where I scold myself over every mistake, where a persistent belief that I should be perfect clings tenaciously, I believe it. The reality, of course, is that berating a child for making a mistake and then grudgingly fixing it is far worse. Even kindly jumping in to protect my child from real or potential mistakes does not help. If they forget their baseball gloves, my sons may have to come up with another solution besides speed-dialing my cell phone. Perhaps asking the coach if he has an extra glove? Asking a friend to share? And if that doesn't work, they will have to face the consequences of an annoyed coach or the indignity of sitting on the bench while others practice fielding. They might learn not just to remember their gloves, but also that making a mistake is not the end of the world.

For parents, it's often hard to know when to rescue their children and when the children need to resolve their own problems. Of course, as children age, the balance shifts. But the key is not to be too rigid about it. Author Barbara Coloroso divides parents into the brick-wall parent, the jellyfish parent, and the backbone parent. The brick-wall parent adheres to rigid views of when to help. Never deliver the forgotten band instrument or science report. Their motto is: "Let 'em learn." The jellyfish parent scurries over to the school, French horn in hand, as soon as the call comes. The backbone parent takes the situation into consideration. For example,

Coloroso said, her daughter called to ask if she would bring her backpack to school. Coloroso was busy and asked what was so important in the backpack that couldn't wait another day. It turned out that her daughter's cards for her second-grade Valentine's Day party were in the backpack. Sure, Coloroso could have said just give them out tomorrow, but the embarrassment and distress her daughter would have suffered would have outweighed any lesson she might have learned. I, for instance, will usually bring a forgotten lunch to school if I'm called and I'm available, because my children rarely forget them—and none of us is perfect. If it became a habit, however, they would have to go a little hungry as incentive to remember next time.

A friend of mine, whom I'll call Joelle, had that very tough choice to make when her son Dan entered his freshman year in high school. He didn't do his homework and didn't take school seriously. Joelle knew something was wrong, and it was confirmed when he received his midterm report card, which showed he was in danger of failing most of his classes. "My husband and I sat down with him and told him he had to step it up and he got mad at us," she said. "So we said, 'If you want us to step out, we will, and you will suffer the repercussions.'" That meant that if he failed his classes, he would have to go to summer school and miss attending his beloved summer sleepaway camp. So Joelle didn't talk with his teachers, didn't get on his case about homework. And Dan failed.

"It was the worst summer we've ever had," Joelle said. Dan stuck to the agreement and took summer school and a separate program on study skills. Because he buckled down and held up his end of the bargain without too much whining, they agreed he could spend the last two weeks of summer, after school ended, at his camp (sounds like backbone parents to me). He never failed a class again—and is now in college. "He managed to figure out what he needed to do to pass the classes," Joelle said. "I could have been a helicopter parent, but at some point he had to learn by failing. If I saved him, what kind of adult would he be? What kind of employee would he be?" As Coloroso says, "How we respond to their many mistakes, occasional mischief, and rare mayhem can help provide the wherewithal for our children to become responsible, resourceful, resilient, compassionate humans who feel empowered to act with integrity and a strong sense of self or to become masters of excuses, blaming, and denial who feel powerless, manipulated, and out of control."

One of the difficulties, of course, is finding the right way to scold or criticize so your child doesn't feel crushed. Seligman offers two examples of a parent who has had it up to here with her ten-year-old daughter bugging her little brother:

"Elena, this teasing has got to stop. What has gotten into you today? You are such a wonderful big sister. You teach Daniel games. You share your toys. But today you haven't been nice to him at all. You know I don't like this kind of behavior, Elena. I want you to apologize to Daniel, and if you tease him again today, you will not be allowed to play outside after dinner. Is this clear?"

Here's the other option:

"Elena! I am sick of this! Why are you always such a brat! Here I plan a nice day for the three of us and you go and ruin it. I don't know why I even bother trying to do fun family things when, without fail, you pull some stunt that spoils everything."

Okay, no prizes for guessing that Option 1 is the right one. But sadly, Option 2 sounds all too familiar—perhaps because it could have come out of my mouth. Now, I dislike those books that tell you how patient and kind and understanding you should be with your children when you're this close to sending them off to boarding school, but I do find this reminder helpful. In the first scolding, the mother points out that it's a specific and temporary problem, that usually she's a good big sister but this time she's getting out of control—and there's an explicit punishment if it doesn't improve. The second one characterizes Elena's behavior as permanent and unchangeable—you're always a brat, always causing the family misery. I try—*try*—to keep the words "always" and "never" out of my vocabulary when reprimanding my children.

A good parent can have a huge impact on a child's ability to accept or reject mistakes and criticism. The same, of course, is true with teachers. Wendy Bray, a graduate student at the University of North Carolina, Chapel Hill, wrote her Ph.D. dissertation on learning from mistakes during classroom discussions of mathematics. She looked at "Lincoln Heights" (a pseudonym), a large urban elementary school in the southeastern United States where the majority of students live in poverty and don't speak English as their first language. Bray observed four third-grade teachers giving math lessons in their classrooms for one school year. She offers the stark contrast of a teacher, "Ms. Rosena," who used errors as a way of getting the kids to learn, and another teacher, "Ms. Larsano," who didn't.

After a lengthy discussion, Ms. Rosena told her class—which was made up of third-graders who had failed and were repeating the year—to take game pieces to represent the twenty-four children in the classroom and arrange the pieces in equal rows. She then had the children partner up and exchange solutions and asked them to give a thumbs-up if they understood their partner's solution. Some children did understand their classmates' answers, some didn't. Then several solutions were discussed by the whole class, including Jeremy's. Jeremy had put fourteen pieces in one crooked row and ten in another.

> Ms. ROSENA: "Jeremy, can you explain to the class how you came up with this arrangement?"
>
> JEREMY: "Well, I put one row, I mean one column of fourteen dots and another column of ten."
>
> Ms. ROSENA: "Okay, so this is fourteen [indicates the first column; Jeremy nods] and this is ten [indicates the second column; Jeremy nods]? And that is twenty-four. But my question was to show the twenty-four children in equal rows. What does this mean to you—equal rows? What does this mean?"
>
> JEREMY: "Like if you have two, you need to put two blacks on the other side."
>
> Ms. ROSENA: "If you have two on this row, you must have two on the second row. Did you do that?"
>
> JEREMY: "No . . . but if I have fourteen and fourteen . . . that would be twenty-eight."
>
> Ms. ROSENA: "If you have fourteen and fourteen, that would be twenty-eight. Okay. Is there a way that you can arrange this to make twenty-four? To have equal rows making twenty-four in total?"

At this point, Ms. Rosena opens it up to the class, and one student tentatively suggests twelve rows of two. They try that.

Bray points out that Ms. Rosena didn't just correct the work—she had one student try to make sense of it, then gave the class the opportunity to study it as well, then they all tried to figure out a solution. The mistakes were used to teach the mathematical idea of equal groups, which is central to understanding multiplication and division. "By mid-year," Bray writes, "Ms. Rosena's students appeared to view mistakes as part of the learning process. They did not seem uncomfortable or unhappy when their flawed solutions were shared. Quite the opposite, students appeared motivated to understand correct and flawed solutions." By spring, students were commenting on other students' solutions without being prompted by the teacher.

Ms. Rosena's teaching stemmed partially from her own school experience. She told Bray: "When I was in school, I was not good in math. So the teachers were always showing off the people who . . . were right. But they never took my way of solving the problem and explained to me why it was wrong. So I never really quite got how to do it right. I think that we are focusing on what students are doing right and sometimes not enough on what they are doing wrong."

Ms. Larsano had a very different approach. She asked the class—composed of children who were just learning English—to answer the question "Twenty-three candles are arranged with three in each row. How many rows are there?" Five students put their solution on the board, and Ms. Larsano pointed to Andre's, which had three rows of eight.

MS. LARSANO: "What's the total?"

SOME STUDENTS: "Twenty-four."

MS. LARSANO: "Twenty-four. But I started out with how many?"

SOME STUDENTS: "Twenty-three."

MS. LARSANO: "Twenty-three. So I have how many extra?"

SOME STUDENTS: "One."

MS. LARSANO: "One extra. So I have to take one from here. [She erases the extra candle, then points out that the rows are no longer equal. Then she tells Andre:] I'm not telling you that you are wrong, I am just explaining to you what you did. So he put that twenty-four divided by eight equals three. So he did have three groups. The only problem was that he put one more. But it's okay, it's a model."

Unlike Ms. Rosena, Ms. Larsano controlled most of the exchange, didn't let the children figure out why Andre's solution was incorrect and work through how to fix it, and reassured Andre that he wasn't really wrong, even though he was. Ms. Larsano told Bray that it was a priority of hers to be encouraging and supportive of students when they shared ideas publicly. "She intentionally avoided actions that she perceived might hurt students' feelings or discourage them from participating in the future," Bray writes. And unlike Ms. Rosena, who believed that examining mistakes would help her children develop an understanding of the underlying concept, and a flexibility that would allow them to try different approaches to solving problems, Ms. Larsano believed that students didn't really have the ability to understand math problems before they had been taught procedures, and that her role as a teacher was to provide necessary explanations and direction on how to solve those problems. And like all the other teachers except Ms. Rosena, Ms. Larsano believed that exposing flawed solutions might confuse children, who had fragile mathematical understanding.

There is another lesson that the children in Ms. Rosena's class came away with and that is to be part of what is called "a community of learners." That meant the students all had a stake in and felt engaged in *each other's* learning as well as their own. That is in contrast to Ms. Larsano, who saw herself as largely the sole source of knowledge.

Although many factors go into children's success on tests, it's interesting to note that Ms. Rosena's class achieved a 78 percent pass rate on the math standardized achievement test, compared with 43 percent in Ms. Larsano's. Even more startling is that another classroom of similar students—who were repeating a year—achieved only a 30 percent pass rate. "That Ms. Rosena's students scored so well is really amazing considering how far behind they started and how children who have a history of failure tend to continue to fail," Bray told me. Ms. Rosena viewed students' flawed answers—and this is crucial—*not* as errors, but as partially correct solutions with underlying logic. This approach contrasts with the way many of us think: that faulty solutions are the result of careless mistakes or unfounded guesses. So Ms. Rosena didn't just correct incorrect answers; she dug deep to understand where the students went wrong and to see whether their answers were grounded in a misunderstanding of a fundamental mathematics concept. If such an approach is extrapolated beyond mathematics and the classroom, think of what we can learn. To be okay with mistakes and build on them. To understand that there's often more than one way to attack and solve a problem. To be confident enough to question the answers of our peers, our teacher, or our boss. And to learn for the sake of learning, not simply to get the right answer.

I have to say, it took me a while to untangle what I saw as another inconsistency rearing its ugly head. The psychologist John Nicholls argues that in classrooms that rely on competitive situations, children tend to focus on how much innate ability they and others have, while in noncompetitive situations they tend to focus on effort and learning for learning's sake. But some of the methods that I had learned were used in Asian classrooms—such as making grades, on both tests and report cards, public for all to view—seem as if they would foster rivalries among students rather than collaboration. And, indeed, having a student work out a problem in front of a class and allowing others to point out its flaws, rather than addressing the mistake in private, also seems to be an approach that would pit students against one another rather than create a supportive working environment. I'll discuss this more in a subsequent chapter, but this seems important to point out here. Ultimately, though, an interesting cross-cultural experiment made me realize that it's not the behavior itself but how we interpret the behavior that can make a situation competitive or cooperative. Gail Heyman, a professor of psychology at the University of California, San Diego, and some colleagues in China looked at how children viewed a child talking about doing well in academics and athletics—such as scoring very well on academic tests or booting in several goals in a soccer game—to a group of peers who did worse. In one study, of ten- and eleven-year-olds, 76 percent of the Chinese participants but only 50 percent of those from the United States predicted that such a disclosure would motivate the poorer performers to study harder. Even more striking, 86 percent of the American students thought that the successful child was showing off, while 68 percent of the Chinese students inferred that the speaker was trying to help those who performed less successfully.

Right here we can tie together two different strands—fixed and growth mindsets and how we react to mistakes or doing poorly and how it affects our self-esteem. I would wager that the Chinese students who believed that the better-performing speaker was trying to help them—rather than flaunt his superiority—viewed learning with a growth mindset rather than a fixed mindset. This growth mindset helped the Chinese students view their more successful peer as offering help rather than attacking their self-esteem. With fixed mindsets, we would rather look down on people who do better than learn from them. Carol Dweck and her colleagues have studied just this issue—what attributes affect how we try to repair self-esteem after doing poorly. When I was at Stanford, a graduate student administered the experiment to me. In the initial experiment, the participants, who were told it was a speed-reading study, were divided into two camps—those who read an essay about how intelligence is largely genetically determined and cannot change, and those who read an essay about how intelligence can grow and develop if you work at it. I read the one about how scientists discovered that intelligence was innate and you can't do much about it—an essay that was mighty persuasive, even though I knew it was largely false. I then read a dense and virtually incomprehensible excerpt from Freud's *The Interpretation of Dreams*, and answered eight multiple-choice questions, most of which I guessed at. I ranked in the 37th percentile, not knowing that was the score handed out to all participants no matter how well or poorly they really did. Even though I *knew* the point of the experiment, I was bummed. I started feeling tired and irritated, and even a little flustered. Then I was given a table of eight past participants who had ranked from the 97th to the 14th percentile and told they had each written three strategies about how they had worked on the experiment. I knew the point of this part of the experiment, so I opted out, but here is what Dweck discovered: Far more of those who had read about intelligence being fixed chose to look at the strategies of students who had performed worse than they did, while those who read about growth mindsets more often looked at the strategies of those who had done better. In other words, those in the fixed-mindset group wanted to feel superior to those who had done poorly, while those in the growth-mindset group wanted to learn from those who had done better.

Such insight may help explain why Chinese, Japanese, and people of other cultures are more comfortable with their grades' being made public and their mistakes' being spotlighted than many in the United States. We believe we can all help one another learn when we believe we're all capable of learning. Hazel Markus, a professor of psychology at Stanford University who has written extensively on Japanese and American culture, says part of this attitude can be traced back to the process of self-criticism, which is deeply ingrained in Japanese and Chinese culture. "It's cultivated from the earliest days at school," Markus told me. "At the end of the day they sit in a group and ask, 'How did our day go today? What did we like? What went wrong? What mistakes did we make?' The children might say, 'We didn't have time to finish our pictures,' or, 'Kenji fell down on the playground and everyone was upset.' Often they talk as a group first, but then get down to individuals, and talk about their own work—'I didn't finish my painting,' 'I forgot my lunchbox.' The next part is 'What am I going to do tomorrow?'— 'How will I remember to bring my lunchbox?' It is constantly done in a developmentally appropriate way." She went on: The Japanese "have the idea of time as cyclical, and with that comes the idea that there are good times and bad times, there are successes and failures— they're all part of life, the yin and the yang. In America, we tend to believe that life should be one success after another. In Japan you cannot succeed unless you fail. It's hollow."

I truly believe that it is possible—although certainly not easy— to create a world where children understand that learning, whether at home, in school, or later, on the job, is an ongoing process and not solely tied to rewards, whether in the form of grades or money. Encouraging children to accept blunders more readily is not simply a matter of assuring them that "Mommy makes mistakes, too," or that "we all goof up," but shifting some unspoken but very real paradigms that exist, especially in the more affluent parts of our society. One is that every child will be successful in everything. Another is that every child will be above average (statistically impossible, but somehow socially desirable). A third is that if they are not successful it's because something is "wrong" with them that can be "fixed."

In Nicholls's concept of a successful learning environment, he is not saying that everyone must be seen as equal or as above average. Rather, he is saying that it is possible—although certainly not simple—to create an atmosphere in which almost everyone is working up to his or her potential, and therefore has feelings of competence and accomplishment.

It can seem overwhelming to think in terms of societal change—after all, we're just individuals trying to do the best we can. But change really can begin at home—that doesn't mean it should end there, but it sure is a good starting place. As a parent, I know how easy it is to get caught up in the frenzy to raise children who are good at academics and sports and socializing and maybe with a musical or art talent thrown in as well. I know how easy it is to lose sight of *why* we want them to accomplish those goals and simply focus on the results—it's the end of the world if he doesn't make the tennis team; maybe she should play violin and flute; and oh God, what if they don't get into a good college? Daniel Pink, author of *Drive: The Surprising Truth About What Motivates Us*, talks about how parents focus so hard on cognitive skills, such as reading and writing, but we're not very good at teaching "noncognitive skills," like sticking with it when the work gets tough, and understanding that failure and disappointment are part of success. "Are we establishing a generation literate in perseverance?" he asks.

When I feel myself getting carried away, I call one of my friends, part of an informal support group, who will talk me down. These are friends with the same values and outlook as me, and who remind me of what's important and what's not. We are parents who hope that our children will find a number of interests they are passionate about and good at, but acknowledge that they may be—gasp—middling or even worse in other areas. And that even effort, although very important, does not always guarantee success. We try not to lose sight of stressing the importance of attributes that sometimes get buried in the rush to the top—kindness and generosity and making the world a better place. We try to remind each other that our children won't always be the best or even the second or third best, and that they and we will inevitably make lots of mistakes. And that that really is okay.

3.

"Fail Often, Fast, and Cheap"

I first wrote a draft of this chapter in early 2008. Do you remember that time? The stock market was bullish, and houses seemed to be as solid an investment as gold—so much so that real estate brokers joked that all you needed to get a mortgage was to prove you were breathing. Bernie Madoff was still enjoying a reputation as a Wall Street genius. And my husband had a job as a business editor at a magazine, earning the highest salary he had ever received. While as journalists we were still earning a pittance compared with our investment banker friends, life seemed pretty good. But by the end of the year, all had changed. Not since 9/11 had the world felt so upside down. It seemed like every day—in fact in some cases, it was every day—that my husband's BlackBerry buzzed with some unbelievable news. Within a few days in mid-September 2008, word came that Lehman Brothers was collapsing, the government was bailing out AIG with an $85 billion loan, Asian and European markets were panicking, and Merrill Lynch hastily agreed to sell itself to Bank of America in a desperate effort to avoid Lehman's fate. It never seemed to end. By early 2009, the term "underwater" no longer referred to snorkeling in the Caribbean, but to owing more on your house than it was worth. And my family couldn't escape the economic firestorm. The company my husband worked for, owner of a once very profitable chain, folded his magazine in spring 2009.

So, my draft—and our lives—needed a hefty revision. But although I'm certainly going to look at some of the mistakes some very smart men and women on Wall Street made—which helped guide us into the worst recession since the Depression—that's not going to be my focus. Plenty of books have already come out and no doubt will continue to pour forth, written by people much more expert than I, that concentrate in exhaustive detail on every meeting, every player, every decision. But I would be doing a disservice to the vast majority of us who continue (hopefully) to work as teachers or lawyers or office managers or health care providers in examining solely what happened on Wall Street. The point of this chapter is to look not at things that are largely out of our control, but at those that we can change.

Remember poor David from our introduction, who made a mistake in baking, rectified it, but was still chastised by his boss and threatened with losing his job? When I started looking at mistakes in the workplace, I took David as the archetypal problem: a worker blunders, has to decide whether to cover it up or make good, does the right thing, and unluckily has a boss who handles it in all the wrong ways. The result is an angry and demoralized worker. I think we've all been there. But where does another worker—a much more lavishly compensated one, I assume—fit into this model? Someone like Lou Pai, who launched Enron's power-trading business. Pai was celebrated in a book about Enron, yet Pai's group lost tens of millions of dollars trying to sell electricity to residential consumers in newly deregulated markets. The problem was that states that were opening their markets to competition were still setting rules that gave traditional utilities big advantages. "It doesn't seem to have occurred to anyone that Pai ought to have looked into those rules more carefully before risking millions of dollars," Malcolm Gladwell wrote in a *New Yorker* article. Pai then moved on to build the commercial outsourcing business, where he ran up several more years of heavy losses before cashing in his stock in the company and walking away with $270 million. Of course, we don't have to go back as far as Enron to find people who made a fortune who in retrospect apparently were in way over their heads and steering straight into a crisis.

At first glance, David and Lou don't seem to have a whole lot in common. David had a job that was probably repetitive and didn't call for much creativity. His boss just wanted the process to run efficiently and the food to taste decent. Lou, on the other hand, had a job that required innovation and risk-taking, and he gave his bosses both of those things, big-time. So where is the similarity? Both learned the wrong lessons from their mistakes. David learned that he better lie or foist the blame on someone else the next time he screws up; Lou seems to have learned that even when idea after idea failed to pan out, he could keep on making high-priced mistakes because no one above him was going to call him on it—in fact, he was encouraged to keep trying. They are examples of how mistakes can be handled in vastly different ways, yet still have tremendously negative—and in some cases, far-reaching—consequences.

As we know, there are many different types of mistakes, different ways to respond, and different lessons to be learned. Chris Argyris, a professor emeritus at Harvard Business School, has spent decades writing about how employees and organizations learn from errors, and is considered one of the great theorists in organizational learning. Argyris argues that most responses to errors fall into the category of single-loop learning—when a mistake is detected and corrected without questioning the underlying values of the system. The phrase is borrowed from electrical engineering: a thermostat is defined as a single-loop learner. The thermostat is programmed to detect states of "too cold" or "too hot," and to correct the situation by turning the heat on or off. Double-loop learning, on the other hand, means to question the underlying factors themselves and subject them to critical scrutiny—in effect, it turns the question back on the questioner and asks not only about objective facts, but also about the reasons and motives behind those facts. "If the thermostat asked itself such questions as why it was set at 68 degrees, or why it was programmed as it was, then it would be a double-loop learner," Argyris writes in his seminal book *On Organizational Learning*. In other words, double-loop learning is a lot harder.

For example, a newspaper I worked for in the 1990s established a rule—no stories could "jump," or continue, off the front page.

While this is now far more common, it was quite radical in those days and created much dismay among reporters. It meant radically shorter stories. The reason given was that in focus groups, readers said they wanted shorter stories. The solution: banning stories from jumping. That was single-loop learning. But an in-depth look at the success of this solution by the *American Journalism Review* showed that newspaper editors might have pleased their readers if they had engaged in double-loop learning instead—finding out the reasons why readers said they wanted shorter stories, rather than simply taking the information at face value and fashioning a solution to address it. The shorter stories didn't attract more readers; in fact, in a later survey, almost half of the readers said they wanted more in-depth stories. It turns out that there are a lot of different kinds of newspaper readers and they want a lot of different things. Single-loop learning isn't able to address those complexities.

This doesn't mean all single-loop learning is bad—after all, it is necessary for routine, repetitive issues. Not all mistakes are alike, and not all require examining and challenging the surrounding criteria. Imagine an office where workers constantly debated every error—making the wrong change, mistyping a law brief—rather than simply correcting the problem. It might make for some interesting conversations, but no work would ever get done.

Sometimes, however, it may seem like single-loop learning is all that is necessary, but that just short-circuits the real learning process. Argyris gives the example of a CEO who found out that his company inhibited innovation in employees by subjecting every new idea to more than 275 checks and sign-offs. He promptly eliminated two hundred of them, and the result was a higher innovation rate. It sounds like a successful case of identifying a problem and resolving it, but it is only a case of successful *single-loop learning*, by ignoring a more fundamental problem—why the checks and sign-offs had been around for so long. A double-loop approach would require the CEO to ask employees who told him about the problem some tough questions, such as "How long have you known about the 275 required sign-offs?" and "What goes on in this company that prevents you from questioning these practices and getting them eliminated?"

Years of empirical research have shown that while most people will say that double-loop learning is desirable, it has proven difficult to implement and all but impossible in situations in which much is at stake. Part of the reason is that while people believe they are open and willing to learn, that is often not true. That's because—guess what?—most of us say one thing and do another. In fancier parlance, it is what Argyris calls the contradiction between a theory in use and an espoused theory. Espoused theory is what people tell you about the rules and beliefs that govern their actions. They usually tell you that open communication is best, that they strive to improve their performance, and that they are willing and happy to cooperate with their colleagues. But, Argyris says, observe these same people's behavior and "this espoused theory has very little to do with how they actually behave." For example, the professionals in one of his case studies said that they believe in continuous improvement, and yet they consistently acted in ways that made improvement impossible. Or, as my father used to tell me, "Do as I say, not as I do."

This is not surprising to Elliot Aronson and Carol Tavris, the social scientists who wrote *Mistakes Were Made (But Not by Me)*. They have spent decades looking at how people justify their behavior. I didn't find it shocking that we all invest energy justifying bad decisions or blunders, but I was surprised at just how much. If we spent half that much energy owning up to our responsibilities rather than hiding from them, we might actually get things done much more effectively and with a great deal less angst. In *Mistakes Were Made*, Aronson and Tavris write that all of us share the impulse to excuse what we do, to convince ourselves that we didn't act in a bad or irrational way and avoid taking responsibility for harming someone. "Most of us find it difficult, if not impossible, to say, 'I was wrong; I made a terrible mistake,'" the authors write. "The higher the stakes—emotional, financial, moral—the greater the difficulty." Self-justification is not the same as lying or making excuses; when we justify our actions we persuade ourselves that we did a good thing or at least not a bad thing. And self-justification is not necessarily wrong, as I've said before—it can stop us from endlessly agonizing about choices already made. Should I have painted the bathroom a different color? Should I have taken the other job? Should I have married Harry instead of Fred? But "mindless self-justification, like quicksand, can draw us deeper into disaster. It blocks our ability to even see our errors, let alone correct them."

Most companies—like most people—don't see themselves as promoting a work environment where mistakes are feared and avoided. They say they encourage risk taking and innovation, but in reality, they don't. Paul J. H. Schoemaker, chairman and chief executive officer of Decision Strategies International, discussed this in a *Harvard Business Review* article called "The Wisdom of

Deliberate Mistakes." He wrote, with Robert E. Gunther, that "although organizations need to make mistakes in order to improve, they go to great lengths to avoid anything resembling an error. That's because most companies are designed for optimum performance rather than learning and mistakes are seen as defects that need to be minimized." All too often, mistakes are treated as something shameful that should be flung aside as quickly as possible, rather than as something to be examined and learned from. And because of this, companies—and employees—fail to uncover systemic problems that may be leading to the errors. Take the time that management consultant Bob Kardon led a seminar at a conference for the National Council of Nonprofit Associations. The seminar was called "Mistakes" and attracted twenty leaders of statewide associations. The ground rules were that each participant had to tell about a mistake he or she had made as a leader and not tell how they corrected it or justified it. The leaders found it incredibly difficult. "Participants would often get uncomfortable hanging out there with a mistake and try to tell a redeeming anecdote about a success or recovery from the mistake. I enforced the ground rules and cut off the face-saving attempt." Kardon's exercise illuminates "just how difficult it is to say, 'Boy, did I mess up,' without the protective postscript of self-justification."

Schoemaker and Gunther broke down into four categories the reasons that they think most human beings are resistant to making mistakes and therefore play it safe:

- We are overconfident. We are often blind to the limits of our expertise. Inexperienced managers make many mistakes and learn from them. "Experienced managers may become so good at the game they're used to playing that they no longer see ways to improve significantly. They may need to make deliberate mistakes to test the limits of their knowledge."

- We are risk-averse because "our personal and professional pride is tied up in being right. Even if we exhibit humility in private about our knowledge or insight, we are very reluctant to submit our fragile egos to explicit tests that might show we have been wrong all along. Employees are rewarded for good decisions and penalized for failures, so they spend a great deal of time and energy trying not to make mistakes."

- We tend to favor data that confirm our beliefs, so we don't often see the alternatives. Consider NASA's effort to settle the debates among competing theorists about the moon's origin by distributing moon rocks to various laboratories for analysis. After studying the rocks, each research group was more convinced than ever that its own theory was correct. The scientists' self-serving, selective perceptions were largely unconscious, as such perceptions generally are.

- We assume feedback is reliable, although in reality it is often lacking or misleading, and we don't often look outside tested channels.

"Unfortunately, the people who most need to make mistakes are the ones least likely to admit it, and the same is true of companies,"

Schoemaker says. For example, he said, if *The New York Times* never published an article that it later regretted, "it's probably playing it too safe."

Speaking of the *Times*: The notorious Jayson Blair episode—which entailed a reporter's fabricating and plagiarizing stories for at least a year until he was finally discovered and forced to resign—was emblematic not just of a rogue reporter, but of a culture that ignored numerous warning signs. It was a workplace, manifested by managing editor Howell Raines, some said, that played favorites and had top editors who hated hearing unwanted truths. Linda Greenhouse—the Pulitzer Prize–winning Supreme Court reporter for the *Times* until she left in 2008—said in an interview that "there is an endemic culture at the *Times* that is not a Howell creation, although it plays to his vulnerabilities as a manager, which is a top-down hierarchical structure. And it's a culture where speaking truth to power has never been particularly welcome."

But how do you change a deeply embedded culture? That is the $64,000—or in these days of megabank meltdowns, $64 billion—question. Transforming a company's or profession's mores to ensure that mistakes are something we learn from—rather than something we hide—is a multipronged effort. After decades of studying and working with organizations' efforts to change themselves, to create an environment where double-loop learning exists, Chris Argyris has concluded that, not surprisingly, it is very complex, and requires fundamental change. That is largely because most workers tend to have very little control over their work environment or the tasks they do—even with the best-intentioned bosses and work cultures. The reasons are many; workers often say they want empowerment, but avoid it because it's scary and hard. Managers often espouse empowerment and may truly believe they are offering it to their employees, but they often undermine it by their words and actions.

Too often such leaders practice defensive routines to hide the truth when it's potentially embarrassing or threatening. We learn those routines early in life, and as adults we help create workplaces that support and reinforce these routines. The cycle becomes self-reinforcing, says Argyris. What this means is that a CEO might say he wants honest and open feedback on his leadership style from senior executives, but when it happens, that CEO lashes out. So the executives respond by creating rules among themselves about when it's okay to talk to the CEO and when it's not. They censor themselves.

A recurring theme, in work as in marriage, is that trust and openness determine to a large extent how mistakes will be handled from beginning to end. If they are not there, or perceived not to be there, then workers will attempt to cover up blunders, and organizational learning is cut off at the root. Some people will always have a harder time than others owning up to mistakes, but if a boss or colleague responds with blame, punishment, or humiliation, it sure helps employees learn a lesson, but it's the wrong one—keep your mouth shut and your head low next time you make a misstep. "It only takes one or two events like this before everyone gets the message that the consequences of mistakes are too high around here, and they begin to conceal mistakes," says Charles Prather, a company president who has written about mistakes and innovation.

Researchers from Stanford University and the University of

Southern California found that blame spreads like a virus once it starts. Nathanael Fast and Larissa Tiedens showed, using four experiments, that blaming behavior can be socially contagious. They didn't look at whether someone who is blamed for a wrongdoing turns around and places the fault on others. Rather, they examined how a blame culture can insidiously and even subconsciously spread. In one experiment, participants read a news clip about a failure by Arnold Schwarzenegger, the governor of California. Some participants read about how Schwarzenegger took full responsibility for the failure. Other participants read, instead, about how Schwarzenegger blamed others. All participants were then asked to recall and write about an unrelated failure of their own and then asked to explain what caused that failure. Those who read about Schwarzenegger blaming himself tended to take greater responsibility for their own self-described failures; those who read about the governor blaming others tended to hold others responsible for their own failures.

Fast and Tiedens took the question one step further; they discussed the likelihood that blaming is contagious because we're trying to protect our self-image when we think it's under assault. "When we see others protecting their egos, we become defensive, too," says Fast, the study's lead author. "We then try to protect our own self-image by blaming others for our mistakes, which may feel good in the moment." The question then is, are there ways to change that? In a final experiment, they repeated the same routine of having participants read about a failure. Some read about a director of a foundation, in this case, taking responsibility, while others read about the director assigning blame to others. One group of participants was then asked to select one "core value" from a list (music/art/theater; business/economics; social life/relationships; science/pursuit of knowledge) and explain why this value was important. The other group of participants was asked to choose a value from the same list, but the one that was least important to them and write about why it might be valuable to someone else. Then both groups were asked to once again write down a personal failure and explain why it occurred. The tendency for blame to spread was completely eliminated in the group that wrote about what was important to them and why that was so. That is because they had a chance to bolster their self-worth by reaffirming their values and therefore removed "their need to self-protect" by blaming others for failure, the researchers found.

Such experiments underline how important it is that business managers and leaders be very careful about how they criticize—they might want to consider doing it privately, Fast and Tiedens suggest, or publicly take ownership of failures rather than blaming others. In their book *Leaders: Strategies for Taking Charge*, Warren Bennis and Burt Nanus advise that institutions reward admissions of mistakes as part of the organizational culture. This is a change that must come from the top, and Bennis and Nanus offer a story about Tom Watson, Sr., IBM's founder. "A promising junior executive of IBM was involved in a risky venture for the company and managed to lose over $10 million in the gamble," they write. "It was a disaster. When Watson called the nervous executive into his office, the young man blurted out, 'I guess you want my resignation?' Watson said. 'You can't be serious. We've just spent $10 million educating you!'" Some companies have gone even further than simply learning from mistakes by, in a tongue-in-cheek way, actually rewarding them. For example, a group of presidents of Ann Arbor businesses handed out a "Golden Egg Award" to a member who got egg on his face trying something new. The winning president took the Golden Egg—an empty egg-shaped L'eggs pantyhose container, sprayed gold—back to his company for the month to proudly display it.

But wacky awards won't go far if the anti-mistake culture is deeply embedded in a management's style. One way to address this is to go back to Carol Dweck's "fixed" mindset versus "growth" mindset. We know how this can affect children's performance; what about managers in a workplace? Professor Peter Heslin of Southern Methodist University and his colleagues did some interesting experiments looking at one aspect of managers' mindset—how open they would be to acknowledging that a subordinate has improved or declined in work performance. They chose nuclear power plant managers, deliberately selecting a type of work that hinges very much on close observation of any performance problems—we certainly do not want people working at nuclear power plants to be laxly supervised. First the managers were assessed to determine, as well as possible, their type of mindset through an established survey called, impressively, "Beliefs About Human Nature." If you have a fixed mindset, for example, you would probably more strongly agree with "Everyone is a certain kind of person and there is not much they can really change about that." With a growth mindset, you would more likely agree with "People can substantially change the kind of person they are."

Each participant was asked to rank the comments from 1 (strongly disagree) to 6 (strongly agree). The researchers then assessed the managers as they were observing and evaluating a video of an employee's "poor" negotiation performance. The managers then observed and evaluated the same employee's video-recorded "good" negotiation performance in a similar situation. Managers deemed to have a fixed mindset initially gave the employee a ranking of 2.12, then raised it to 3.68. The managers with the growth mindset gave a ranking of 2.07 for the poor performance, then raised it to 4.12 after viewing the good performance. Heslin and his colleagues performed several more studies, all of which confirmed that those managers who believe that people don't really change were "disinclined to adequately alter either a positive or negative initial impression of an employee's performance." A fixed mindset, they found, led managers to "anchor" to an initial impression, good or bad. Those who believed that a worker was good, no matter what, wouldn't notice increasing mistakes. The managers who believed that a worker was a poor performer wouldn't notice when mistakes lessened. And either way, it creates a lousy work environment: if improvements aren't noticed, then employees usually become resentful and demoralized; if declines in performance aren't noticed, then mistakes made by "airline pilots, nuclear power plant operators, paramedics, surgeons or security guards could seriously compromise organizational effectiveness and human safety," Heslin writes.

A belief that abilities are innate and unalterable also makes it less likely that a supervisor will invest in coaching an employee to improve. As Heslin says, why bother if the person cannot really change? In addition, managers with fixed mindsets aren't willing to hear feedback that contradicts their own views, because they see it as a personal attack (see Stanley O'Neal, later in this chapter). Supervisors with a growth mindset are more likely to be able to take the criticism because they don't see it as a judgment of their competence, but as potentially useful insight. Bill Gates, founder of Microsoft, is often quoted as saying, "How a company deals with mistakes suggests how well it will bring out the best ideas and talents of its people."

In order for companies to accelerate their own learning and increase their competitiveness, Schoemaker says, they must make what he calls deliberate mistakes—that is, try something that common wisdom says won't work. He points to advertising pioneer David Ogilvy, who, when he tested his ideas, deliberately included ads that he thought would not work in order to test and improve his rules on evaluating advertising. "Most were, as expected, dismal failures, but the few that succeeded pointed to innovative approaches in the fickle world of advertising," he wrote. Deliberate mistakes, to me, sound very much like experiments, but the difference is that people usually design experiments to test their initial assumptions—for example, an advertising company may try many different approaches to see what works to sell its client's product, but it won't run an ad that it assumes will fail. "True deliberate mistakes," Schoemaker says, "are expected, on the basis of current assumptions, to fail and not be worth the cost of the experiment."

He used as an example the attempts by the Pentagon's Defense Advanced Research Projects Agency (DARPA) to meet a congressional mandate that one-third of U.S. military ground vehicles be autonomous—that is, unmanned and not remote-controlled—by 2015. Instead of turning to the most experienced people, DARPA did what many would consider a foolish mistake—it sought the help of amateurs, by sponsoring an unmanned-vehicle race across the California desert, offering $1 million to the winner. In 2004, Schoemaker says, it looked like a complete failure, as the competitors barely made it off the starting line. "But the experience revealed the flaws in 13 different approaches, helping builders quickly zero in on a design that would succeed." In 2005, DARPA doubled the prize money and five vehicles finished the 132-mile course, and "DARPA had set the stage for rapid success by deliberately encouraging a high failure rate." Not all companies can use this strategy—it depends on the costs and benefits. For example, drilling for oil where it is likely dry might be a deliberate mistake, but it would be so costly that it would be insane to try it. And companies need to not just make the mistakes, but analyze them to understand what went wrong and what went right. Procter & Gamble, for example, makes lots of deliberate mistakes. A saying at the company? "Fail often, fast, and cheap." And as we all know, in science "mistakes" have led to amazing discoveries—think Ben Franklin and his kite.

While success may be a bad teacher, failure isn't a very good one either if we don't recognize the lessons being taught. If a worker is discouraged from ever making mistakes, then she can't learn, and if a worker is encouraged to make tons of mistakes but never self-correct, then she can't learn. But finding ways to use both success and failure to create a satisfying work environment and help a company flourish is not easy, and people have to accept some real inconsistencies—such as that most companies can have both top-down controls and programs that empower people. Managers can minimize such inconsistencies by:

- realizing which tasks are routine and which aren't.
- understanding that you can't espouse empowerment and then put into place policies that undermine it—it just creates cynicism.
- encouraging employees to examine their own behavior. "One of the most helpful things we can do in organizations—indeed in life—is to require that human beings not knowingly kid themselves about their effectiveness," Argyris says.

Creating an environment where people learn the right lessons from mistakes doesn't mean everyone is nice to each other all the time. Remember our CEO who resolved the excess number of checks for new innovations by eliminating them but not by questioning why they existed in the first place? Well, questioning people might be seen as putting them on the spot: "Unavoidably digging deeper would have uncovered the employees' collusion with the inefficient process," Chris Argyris writes. "The motives were probably quite decent—they didn't want to open Pandora's Box, didn't want to be negative." But their behavior and that of the CEO "blocked the kind of learning that is crucial to organizational effectiveness. In the name of positive thinking, in other words, managers often censor what everyone needs to say and hear, a benevolent strategy that is actually anti-learning."

There are ways to resolve the conflict between fostering a

culture of learning from mistakes and still creating as positive a workplace as possible. In fact, the former chief ethics officer at Northrop Grumman, a global security company, established a program allowing managers to practice having unpleasant conversations constructively without being hurtful; such exercises appear to be increasingly common in large corporations. Researchers have determined that certain building blocks make a company of any size a "learning organization." One of those building blocks entails that employees feel "psychologically safe"—that is, are not scared to disagree with others, ask naive questions, or own up to mistakes. One way to make employees feel psychologically safe is for bosses to "fix the learning, not the blame," Charles Prather says. When people at all levels of a company learn to do this, it creates an environment where learning can take place and, ideally, a company's performance can improve. Changing a work culture where the focus is on fixing the blame is not easy, but studies have shown that it can be done. For example, Peter Heslin, in his research, found a way to shake loose some of the preconceived notions his nuclear power plant operators held. It involved, among other things, holding workshops over a period of time in which supervisors were given scientific testimony about how the brain can grow and evolve throughout life; participants talk about when and how they have seen people they know change and develop their abilities over time; and participants write an e-mail to a hypothetical protégé, "Pat," outlining evidence that abilities can be developed and giving anecdotes about how they have personally overcome professional development challenges. Six weeks later, those managers with "fixed mindsets" were more flexible and open in their judgments.

While most people will do anything to avoid making a mistake, research has shown that some people actually respond better to certain types of training when they are encouraged to make gaffes rather than to avoid them. Rutgers professor Stanley Gully and his colleagues conducted an experiment to perform computer simulations like actual navy radar tracking. The experiment was designed to emulate the workload and chaos of real-world decision-making situations, and required the participants to make four primary decisions about moving contacts on a screen as they approached their "ship." On the basis of information provided on the radar screens, they had to correctly identify the type (land, sea, or air), the class (military, civilian, or unknown), and its intent (peaceful, hostile, or unknown). The research subjects then had to decide whether to clear, monitor, warn, lock-on, or shoot the contact before it reached a specific area on the screen.

When trying to help people master complex techniques, organizations usually focus on minimizing mistakes, maximizing correct responses, and giving positive feedback; few actually encourage making errors. The trouble, as Gully states, is that "failing to fail can restrict individuals from exploring alternatives, inhibit risk-taking and perhaps lead to complacency." So he decided to see what would happen if some people were told mistakes were a good way to learn, some were told to try not to make any mistakes when learning, and a third, control group was given neutral advice about the learning process. Those encouraged to make mistakes were told things like, "It is likely that you [will] find yourself making mistakes. This is common; making errors is simply part of the learning process," and "Do not worry if you get confused while learning how the cue values relate to decisions. Making errors can help you learn the cue values and decision rules more effectively."

Those trained to avoid errors, however, were told that "while familiarizing yourself with the task, it is important to make as few mistakes as possible. Making errors will make it difficult to learn . . . and will prevent you from learning how to perform the task effectively."

Gully and his colleagues found that not everyone learned better by making mistakes, but those with certain types of personality traits—who are good at processing information, open to learning, and not overly conscientious—were more effectively trained by being encouraged to make mistakes rather than avoid them. In other research, Gully and colleagues found that telling people to perform well during training resulted in higher immediate performance; but it also resulted in shallower processing of information, more superficial learning, and less confidence. In contrast, those people who were told to learn—and not worry about mistakes—during training did more poorly initially but ended up with deeper processing of information, more complex learning, and more confidence about performance. Those in the latter group also showed higher performance when faced with a really challenging version of the task they were trained to perform. Fiona Lee, a professor of psychology and business administration at the University of Michigan at Ann Arbor, found the same results when surveying 688 employees throughout a large midwestern health care organization. They were learning a new website system that would provide administrators and caregivers with a single access point for retrieving up-to-date clinical information. There was no formal training course, so employees—who were divided into five status levels from doctors and administrators down to clerks and dieticians—had to learn by trial and error.

Lee and the other two researchers who studied the employees found that people were more willing to experiment with the new system—try out different software applications and test new features—when their department managers consistently did two things: explicitly stated that making mistakes would be okay, and didn't punish them for errors. Managers who gave mixed signals, such as encouraging experimentation but maintaining a reward system that punished failure, "created confusion and mistrust" among employees. As a result, Lee said, "experimentation was much rarer in those departments." The employees on the bottom status rung were also the most likely to have the greatest fear of failure, and used the system only when they were completely sure through their supervisor's words *and* actions that mistakes were to be expected. "Contrary to conventional wisdom, allowing employees room to fail didn't diminish their performance," Lee says. "Indeed, the employees who experimented the most ended up being the most proficient and satisfied with the new technology and the quickest to integrate it into their everyday work."

So what about the example of Lou Pai of Enron, whom I mentioned at the beginning of the chapter? If the recession of 2009 taught us anything, it's that those bankers and CEOs considered brilliant—and paid very well for that brilliance—knew a lot less than we thought they did. Again, there are many reasons for the economic collapse, but for the purpose of this book, I'll look at one: Why did so many highly educated, successful, and creative people make so many mistakes, and why weren't they stopped?

First let me go back to our single-loop/double-loop concept. Highly skilled professionals are frequently very good at single-loop learning, because they have spent much of their life doing well in academics, mastering one or a number of intellectual disciplines and applying those disciplines to the real world. But ironically, Chris

Argyris says, it is this very skill at specific problem-solving that helps explain why professionals are often so bad at double-loop learning. "Put simply, because many professionals are almost always success-ful at what they do, they rarely experience failure," he writes. "And because they have rarely failed, they have never learned how to learn from failure. So whenever their single-loop learning strategies go wrong, they become defensive, screen out criticism and put the 'blame' on anyone and everyone but themselves. In short, their ability to learn shuts down precisely at the moment they need it the most."

Very successful professionals tend toward perfectionism—not just doing a good job, but being the best. The flip side of the drive for success, however, is the fear of failure and the tendency to feel shame and guilt when they do fail to meet their high standards. Mistakes equal failure. These kind of driven people make up much of the workforce of high-flying companies, many of which revere talent—and degrees from prestigious universities—over almost everything else. So what's wrong with that? Don't we want talented workers to be valued and compensated? Don't we want to encour-age them to take risks? Indeed. Maybe. Not always. The star sys-tem, where individual brilliance is regarded above all else, may, in fact, be a bad way to run a company, Malcolm Gladwell writes in the *New Yorker* article "The Talent Myth." There are many reasons for the successes and failures of any corporation, but he compares the excessive focus of Enron on MBAs from good schools and hefty compensation and promotion of individuals who were perceived to be geniuses with the attitude at Southwest Airlines, which hires very few MBAs, pays its managers modestly, and promotes accord-ing to seniority. Southwest is vastly more successful and effective than its low-cost competitors and is still around, while Enron is gone. Carol Dweck argues that this adulation of talent proved fatal for Enron. "It created a culture that worshiped talent, thereby forcing its employees to look and act extraordinarily talented. Basically, it forced them into the fixed mindset. We know from our studies that people with the fixed mindset do not admit and correct their deficiencies." Executives confidently went on making multimillion-dollar mistakes and the culture was all about, as Peter Heslin says, "proving rather than improving" their ability.

If one looks back over the first decade of the twenty-first century, it is probably not coincidental that it began, more or less, with Enron's bankruptcy in 2001 and ended in 2010 with Wall Street just starting to pick itself up from near ruin. During that decade, over and over we saw chief executive officers walk away from beleaguered companies with golden—no, even platinum—compensation packages.

Merrill Lynch, Countrywide Financial, and Citigroup lost $20 billion as a result of investments in subprime and other risky mortgages. Yet their chief executive officers, E. Stanley O'Neal, Angelo Mozilo, and Charles O. Prince III, respectively, each left with fantastic compensation packages. O'Neal will make do with a $161 million retirement package; Mozilo with about $120 million in compensation and proceeds from the sale of his company; and Prince will be able to enjoy some mighty plush retirement years with a $68 million exit package (including a car and driver) upon his departure from Citigroup. And who can forget the stunning collapse of Bear Stearns, which, as a *New York Times* editorial put it, "gorged on the dubious subprime securities to boost its profits and share prices, helping to set up one of the biggest financial collapses since the savings-and-loan crisis in the 1980s." Yet its chairman and former chief executive James Cayne walked away with $40 million in cash between 2004 and 2006, as well as shares he sold worth millions more.

O'Neal is an example of an apparently brilliant man who was allowed—and took full advantage of—great latitude after he became president and chief operating officer of Merrill Lynch in 2001, and then CEO in 2003. For a while, his was a Wall Street success story; between 2002 and 2004, Merrill's after-tax profits nearly doubled, and in 2004 *Fortune* described O'Neal as a "turnaround genius." But as the economy took a downturn, so did Merrill's—and O'Neal's—fortunes. In October 2007 Merrill announced the company would be writing off almost $5 billion, by far the largest trading loss in history. O'Neal resigned in 2007 as Merrill became deeply entangled in the subprime mortgage mess. According to John Cassidy, writing in *The New Yorker*, O'Neal seemed to fall into the classic mistake—he relied on a small inner circle who did not challenge his assumptions: "There was no one who could stand up to Stan and tell him what was really happening." Some critics thought O'Neal should be fired rather than allowed to resign; others thought that his tenure overall, despite the losses, had been so successful that he did not deserve to be sacked. It didn't matter in the end: like many CEOs, under the terms of his employment he could be fired only for breaking Merrill's rules, for unethical conduct, or for breaching government laws or regulations. Actual performance doesn't seem to have played into it. And we seem to have learned nothing as the decade advanced: Richard Fuld, also known as the Gorilla of Wall Street, headed Lehman Brothers as it got deeper and deeper into the business of subprime mortgages. In what is now seen as a disastrous move, Lehman bankrolled lenders across the country that were making loans so complex that even those granting them often didn't understand them to borrowers who shouldn't have been given loans in the first place. The firm took all those loans, turned them into bonds, and passed on to investors billions of dollars of what is now toxic debt. For all this, Fuld was paid nearly $500 million until the end of his—and Lehman's—tenure.

Michael Jenson, a professor emeritus at Harvard's Graduate School of Business, reviewed contracts for top chief executives and found that in 44 percent of the cases, chief executives—even those convicted of fraud or embezzlement—could not be fired without a severance payment. In 94 percent of the contracts, those executives could not be fired for unsatisfactory work without a big severance package. There are many reasons that the alignment between pay and performance has grown so out of whack, but one of them is the growth of the star system within companies, which includes the belief that there is a small constellation of exceptionally brilliant leaders with some sort of innate talent out there who must be paid more than most ever dream of seeing in a lifetime. The fact that their performance often fails to live up to their billing seems to matter little, although, as Gladwell asks, "If talent is defined as separate from an employee's actual performance, what use is it exactly?" Or, as the caption of a 2009 *New Yorker* cartoon put it: "True, a salary cap on Wall Street may limit the talent pool, but on the other hand, if they get any more talented we'll all be broke." Warren Bennis, who is a pioneer in studying what makes good leaders—as well as an advisor to four presidents—says that one of the most dangerous myths out there is that great leaders are born, not made, and that there is some genetic factor to leadership. "This myth asserts that people simply either have certain charismatic qualities or not. That's nonsense; in fact the opposite is true." Of the ninety leaders studied by Bennis, a common theme was that they demonstrated persistence, commitment, and risk taking, but above all, learning. "The learning person looks forward to failure or mistakes," Bennis says. "The worst problem in leadership is basically early success. There's no opportunity to learn from adversity and problems." Or to quote the oracle Bill Gates again: "Success is a lousy teacher. It seduces smart people into thinking they can't lose."

What is also astonishing, as we learned when we were digging ourselves out of the rubble of subprime mortgages and credit-default swaps, is how little many of these superstars seemed to understand about what their companies were actually doing. Here is John Thain, the former Merrill Lynch chief executive, admitting as much in a speech: "There is no chance that pretty much anybody understood what they were doing with these securities. Creating things that you don't understand is really not a good idea no matter who owns it." That seems pretty safe to say. Yet at the end of 2009, when the unemployment rate was 10 percent (double what it was at the end of 2007), Wall Street bankers prepared to award themselves billions of dollars in bonuses in the new year—the largest compensation windfall in Wall Street history.

I asked Joe Nocera, an award-winning business columnist for *The New York Times* and editor of *The Smartest Guys in the Room*, a book about the Enron scandal, what the similarities and differences were in the mistakes that those at Enron and those at the Wall Street firms like Lehman, Bear Stearns, and others made. "The big difference was that the Enron guys were doing things blatantly crooked, and it's very hard to make the argument that Wall Street did things that were blatantly crooked. But the primary similarity was a kind of delusion." All the main players believed they were smarter than everyone and had figured out a system that couldn't fail. Until it did. There were, of course, some Cassandras out there warning that critical mistakes were being made, but they weren't listened to. This is largely because those doing the nay-saying worked out of risk management departments, which are generally viewed as the uninspired grunts compared with the creative stars. In fact, that is one lesson that may have been learned from this—the risk managers are now being given more credence, and are more likely to have the ear of the CEOs.

But as for other lessons? Don't hold your breath. "My view is that this is part of the human condition," Nocera said. "Every generation has to learn lessons. Crashes used to happen quite frequently—every five to ten years. It was a function of greed overcoming fear." But the combined impact of the Great Depression and World War II—more than fifteen years of deprivation—led to passage of numerous laws regulating banks and providing safety nets to investors: the Securities and Exchange Commission, or SEC, and the Federal Deposit Insurance Corporation, or FDIC, to name just two. The years of war and deprivation were so life-shaping that it took decades for the children of Depression-era parents to forget the mistakes of the past and decide that government doesn't really need to regulate business, that the market is always right, and that savings are a quaint anachronism. They discarded caution and embraced hubris. Those children—who are the ones who run government and business now—threw all those hard-earned lessons "out the window," Nocera said.

Carmen Reinhart, a professor of economics at the University of Maryland, says it all in the title of a book she coauthored, *This Time Is Different: Eight Centuries of Financial Folly.* "The same patterns emerge, but people don't think the old rules apply to them," she told me. "When the Mexican crisis occurred, the Asians said, 'That will happen in Mexico, it won't happen here.' Then when the Asian meltdown happened, the perception here was, 'That's happening in emerging countries.'" Each time, she said, people believe that because of new technology or policy, "the old rules of valuation don't apply." Around the world, she added, "People will tell you why this time it's different—why the bubble isn't a bubble." Although so much has changed over eight centuries, the "ability of governments and investors to delude themselves, giving rise to periodic bouts of euphoria that usually [end] in tears, seems to have remained constant."

But why don't we see what has consistently failed in the financial world and respond to it? For example, back in the 1950s, a British aircraft company called DeHavilland launched the first commercial jetliner, the Comet. After a few years of successful travel, the planes started having accidents—some fatal—that no one could figure out. Following extensive testing, it turned out that the design of square-cornered windows—rather than the rounded ones we're now used to—created metal fatigue and caused the planes to crack up midair. So, of course, that design was changed, and we've never gone back to square corners. In finance, on the other hand, we don't seem to build on past experiences. It would be as if airline manufacturers decided to go back to square windows because there hadn't been an accident in a number of years. "Finance is like sex," Nocera said.

"Every generation has to discover it for itself." But lest we get too gloomy, we may not learn to avoid financial crashes, but we have learned to better cope with the consequences. That includes pouring money into the economy—such as the $787 billion stimulus package passed by Congress in 2009—rather than aggravating the crisis with fiscal restraints. "We don't have a preventative vaccine, but we do have better treatment," Reinhart said.

Although it is easy and feels sort of good—okay, *really* good—to blame bankers for our current problems, they are not the only actors. Some people were certainly misled into believing they could afford homes they really couldn't, but there were many who knew they were getting in way over their heads and just ignored the red flags. Edmund Andrews, an economics writer for *The New York Times*, is a great example. If anyone should have avoided the mortgage catastrophe, he should have. He had written several articles during the 2000s warning about the growth of unsustainable mortgages—and before that had covered the Asian financial crisis of 1997, the Russian meltdown of 1998, and the dot-com collapse of 2000. He certainly knew how economies can soar and then crash just as fast. "But in 2004, I joined millions of otherwise-sane Americans in what we now know was a catastrophic binge on overpriced real estate and reckless mortgages. Nobody duped or hypnotized me. Like so many others—borrowers, lenders and the Wall Street dealmakers behind them—I just thought I could beat the odds," he writes first in a *Times* article and then in a book confessing his sins. He tells the story of a mortgage lender, Bob, who was more than willing to offer him a mortgage that was far too expensive for someone with Andrews's income and expenses—and Andrews took it. "As I walked out of the settlement office with my loan papers, I couldn't shake the sense of having just done something bad . . . but also kind of cool. I had just come up with almost a half-million dollars and I had barely lifted a finger. It had been so easy and fast. Almost fun." He acknowledges that he and his new wife "succumbed to magical thinking about ourselves, as well as about money." But inevitably, his debt spiraled out of control, and, Andrews says, he and his wife "hung ourselves with the rope they gave us." Andrews later said that emotions—the quest for happiness—trumped rational thinking. When we want something bad enough, it turns out, we can justify just about anything.

Even those of us who didn't engage in the housing frenzy may have been too willing to buy into the ideology that bigger and more are always better. We made the mistake of being too willing to forget history and to ride the wave of excess. For some, born in the 1970s and 1980s, good times were all they knew. One friend told me of sitting around his office at one point at the beginning of the economic downturn, talking about how he hoped his retirement accounts wouldn't go down. A younger colleague looked at him askance and said, "They can go down?" That was a lesson quickly learned.

So far I've looked largely at how others react to mistakes. But what about when you're the one who has blundered? It is nice if your coworkers are sympathetic, your boss understanding, and your customers willing to overlook it. But owning up honestly and straightforwardly to your own mistakes is a key part of the whole process. As we know, not every mistake is equal, and an appropriate response depends on the seriousness of the gaffe. Some missteps seem to be insurmountable, experts say, such as serious ethical lapses (Do the names Eliot Spitzer, former governor of New York, and Larry Craig, former senator from Idaho, ring any bells?) and/or criminal action. But what about relatively trivial failures of judgment or, say, just doing your job badly for whatever reason? I examine the role of apologies later, but let's touch on it here.

Holly Weeks, a consultant who has been working for the past twenty years with corporations on dealing with stressful conversations, writes in the *Harvard Business Review*: "Done right, an apology can enhance both reputations and relations. Done wrong, an apology can compound the original mistake, sometimes to disastrous consequences." The trouble is, as we know, most people—and companies—find it embarrassing to be wrong, and they often apologize poorly, too late, or not at all, which simply compounds the problem.

Take the Intel Pentium chip tale, a perfect example of the wrong way to apologize. In 1994, Intel testers discovered an error in the chip. Intel managers decided that the error wouldn't affect many people and didn't tell anyone outside the company. That might have worked in pre-Internet days, but not when word of a problem can travel as fast as disgruntled consumers can type. And while the company was right that the problem probably would not affect many users, by not announcing it, it looked like the executives were trying to hide something. Various Internet newsgroups picked it up, and in the first article to appear in in *Electronic Engineering Times*, Steve Smith of Intel dismissed the flaw, saying, "This doesn't even qualify as an errata [*sic*]." *The New York Times* ran an article two weeks later, as did the Associated Press. Inevitably, jokes about Pentium chips began to bounce around cyberspace, not something that enhances public trust in a company. While the controversy escalated, Intel remained silent. Its stock dipped. Finally, about six weeks after the error was made public, Intel apologized and offered to replace all flawed Pentium chips upon request, and set aside $420 million to cover costs. It hired hundreds of customer service employees to deal with customer requests and dedicated four full-time employees to read Internet newsgroups and respond immediately if necessary. A clear, upfront act of contrition and offer to replace all chips immediately probably would have forestalled a lot of Sturm und Drang. If Intel managers had thought about the psychology of failing to inform consumers and then dismissing the problem when customers were clearly upset, they might have realized that a full and immediate apology was the only way to defuse the situation.

The types of mistakes we make in the workplace may be of a different sort and have a different impact than those we make in other parts of our lives, but the tools we need to react to and learn from them in a positive manner are the same. While the reality is that we can only do so much without changing the culture of a workplace, individuals can start the process. As a manager, you can work to create a culture where blame is not the most common response to mistakes. Consciously aiming to reduce finger-pointing, to use mistakes as a way to teach rather than to punish, is a good first step. Being aware of contradictory messages—it's okay to blunder, but not really—is also crucial. So is not rushing in to repair an obvious error, but taking time to figure out why it happened and how it can be prevented in the future. As workers, we need to learn to recognize overconfidence and be willing to question common wisdom—and then question it again. We need to be able—and this is a really tough one—to think more in the long term and less in the short term, to not always see failure as a waste of time, but sometimes as a risk that can lead to success. We must really look at our own and others' efforts and accomplishments and not let reputations—good or bad—rest solely on past deeds. And finally, we need to man up and take real responsibility when things go wrong, rather than mouthing insincere platitudes or ignoring the problem altogether. None of this is going to be quick or easy, but it's important to remember the words of Nike's founder, Phil Knight, who changed the sports shoe industry: "The problem in America is not that we are making too many mistakes, but that we are making too few."

4.

IT'S NOT BRAIN SURGERY . . .
BUT WHAT IF IT IS?

WHEN STARTING THIS CHAPTER ON MEDICAL ERRORS, I decided to talk to my friend Rebecca, a pediatrician who specializes in children with diabetes, to see if I could glean some insight from someone who is in the trenches every day. I've read countless articles from medical journals, advocacy groups, and mainstream publications. I've absorbed the breadth and complexity of confronting and dealing with medical mistakes. But I wanted to get a more intimate sense of how someone like Rebecca, who has been a doctor for almost two decades, feels when an error occurs on her watch. Although luckily she has never been involved in a fatal mistake, she recounted a recent mistake by a resident on the team she oversees. It was a calculation error—the resident administering the insulin was supposed to base the amount of insulin on how many carbohydrates the child was consuming, but she accidentally calculated it using the number of calories. So the young girl received four times as much insulin as she should have. While that sounds highly dangerous, in reality, once the mother pointed out that the girl looked weak, she was immediately given something to eat and perked up. "We explained to the mother that there was a calculation error, we checked, and there were no long-term consequences," Rebecca said. Nonetheless, "the mother was hysterical. The resident was very upset and shaken."

It was clear that Rebecca took the error very seriously. And since Rebecca practices in one of the top hospitals in the country, there are rules and protocols in place every time a medical mistake occurs—even when there is no real effect on the patient. That one incident she told me about set into motion a whole procedure: the doctors, the support team, and a social worker discussed the blunder with the mother, acknowledging the accident and the cause, and an incident report was filed with the state.

The mistake in Rebecca's hospital was just one of many that no doubt occurred that week in hospitals around the country, and it happened a decade after the landmark study on medical mistakes, *To Err Is Human*. Published by the Institute of Medicine (IOM), which was established in 1970 under the charter of the National Academy of Sciences to provide objective advice to policymakers and health care professionals, the study immediately attracted enormous attention, among both health professionals and the public. Although a small cadre of experts had sounded the alarm about patient safety concerns in the 1990s—and then pushed for the IOM to examine the issue—most of us laypeople were blithely unaware of the extent of the problem. But the report changed that. A poll by the Kaiser Family Foundation taken a few weeks after the report's release found that 51 percent of the public was aware of its conclusions—which is pretty amazing if you consider that means that more than half of Americans knew about a medical report. But no wonder—the study cited a staggering statistic: at least 44,000 people and as many as 98,000 people die each year in hospitals in the United States as a result of preventable medical errors. One of the report's authors compared that figure to three fully loaded jumbo jets crashing every other day. Of course, as soon as those numbers were released, some in the medical field argued that they were exaggerated; others contended that they were an underestimate. But few disputed that too many medical errors happen and that the health care establishment has been far less forthcoming than those in other high-risk fields— such as aviation or nuclear power plant operations—in looking for ways to address and minimize such mistakes.

Let's return to definitions. The report defined medical error as "the failure of a planned action to be completed as intended or the use of a wrong plan to achieve an aim." The authors divided types of errors into four groups:

- Diagnostic, such as error or delay in diagnosis, failure to require the indicated tests, use of outmoded tests or therapy, and failure to act as a result of the monitoring or testing.
- Treatment, including error in performing an operation, test, or procedure, in administering treatment, in dose or

method of using drug, or avoidable delay in treatment and inappropriate care.

- Preventative, such as failure to provide preventative treatment or inadequate monitoring or follow-up of treatment.
- Other, including failure of communication, equipment failure, or other system failure.

The initial step, of course, was to examine why such errors occur. The report cited a number of reasons, including the decentralized and fragmented nature of the health care delivery system. Unlike in other fields, there is no one overarching organization that collects and has access to complete medical information. Health care, the report stated, is a decade or more behind most other high-risk industries, like aviation, in paying attention to basic safety, and this is due partially to the lack of one designated government agency devoted to improving and monitoring safety. Also, when patients see multiple providers in different settings, none of whom has access to complete information, it becomes easier for things to go wrong. The licensing procedures of health care professionals focus limited attention on the prevention of medical error. The severe costs and consequences of medical malpractice also play a very important role. And as noted, there is another reason why health care might lag behind other fields—because "the pilot has a certain enlightened self-interest—he is always the first to the crash site." That is not to minimize the very real pain doctors and nurses feel when a patient may have suffered due to an error on their part, but the primary incentive to save one's own life (as opposed to livelihood)—which is there for pilots, nuclear power plant operators, and the like—is not there for doctors.

But a key point made in the report is—and this is significant—that "the majority of medical errors do not result from individual recklessness or the actions of a particular group." In other words, this is not a "bad apple" problem. More commonly errors are caused by faulty systems, processes, and conditions that lead people to make mistakes or fail to prevent them. This is crucial, because while it is always grimly fascinating to read about a rogue doctor, the fact is, mistakes rarely can be attributed to the actions of a single person. Our British psychology professor James Reason, who writes on human error, addresses exactly this point when he refers to the "person approach" and the "systems approach." The person approach, which he calls "the dominant tradition in medicine, as elsewhere," blames people on the front lines—doctors, nurses, surgeons, pharmacists, and so on. With this approach, medical errors result from carelessness, negligence, forgetfulness, inattention, or poor motivation. From some perspectives, it has much to commend it, Reason writes. "Blaming individuals is emotionally more satisfying than targeting institutions. People are viewed as free agents capable of choosing between safe and unsafe modes of behavior. If something goes wrong, it seems obvious that an individual (or group of individuals) must have been responsible." But there are many problems with this approach, because if one person is blamed for a mistake, then all too often no further action will be taken—that is, there will be no detailed analysis of mishaps or near misses and therefore no way of uncovering systemic failures. Reason points out that "the complete absences of such a reporting culture within the Soviet Union contributed crucially to the Chernobyl disaster."

The systems approach, on the other hand, views humans as fallible, and errors as expected in even the best circumstances. "When an adverse event occurs, the important issue is not who blundered, but how and why the defenses failed," Reason states. In life-or-death situations, it is important to set up a system in which, to whatever degree possible, one person's error cannot sink the ship. Remember his definition of active and latent errors in an earlier chapter? Well, as the *To Err Is Human* report states, focusing on active errors lets the latent errors remain in the system, and "their accumulation actually makes the system more prone to future failure." While the current thinking about patient safety leans toward a systems rather than an individual approach, there is also a need to realize that blaming a system can in some cases allow people who really are at fault to escape responsibility. The trick is to balance finger-pointing with accountability.

Let me put a human face on what can too often sound like empty jargon. *To Err Is Human* was published at the end of a decade that saw some horrific medical mistakes. I'll focus on one: the case of Betsy Lehman, a thirty-nine-year-old health reporter for *The Boston Globe*, who was being treated for breast cancer with an experimental chemotherapy program. She died in 1994 of complications from an overdose of a medication that she was receiving for chemotherapy. The story, which made headlines across the country, was full of tragedy and irony. Lehman, as a reporter, took great interest in patient care issues. Her husband was a scientist at Dana-Farber Cancer Institute, where she was being treated. Lehman's autopsy showed that she was cancer-free, and it was not until two months after her death that a data entry employee noticed irregularities in the dosage: Lehman had received a quadruple overdose. Even worse, although Lehman and her husband knew something was terribly wrong with her reaction to the treatment, her medical team did not take it seriously. It became clear, a report on the situation by the Department of Veterans Affairs patient safety arm stated, that "three pharmacists, seven nurses and two physicians failed to detect a dangerous dose prescribed by a second-year oncology fellow." This, despite the fact that she had an abnormal EKG, abnormal blood tests, and swelling, and was vomiting. If, in fact, the overdose had been detected earlier, she might well have lived. And Lehman wasn't the only victim of such miscalculation at Dana-Farber Cancer Institute.

Teacher Maureen Bateman, another breast cancer patient participating in the same experimental program, also received an overdose of the medication. While it didn't kill Bateman, it damaged her heart so severely that doctors thought she would die. She survived, but died four years later of cancer, which was unrelated to the error. The Lehman and Bateman cases were two of several sensational medical mistakes reported in the 1990s. In 1995, a Florida man, Willie King, had the wrong leg amputated. The same year, a seven-year-old boy, Ben Kolb, going in for elective ear surgery, died when identical dishes containing different medicines were mixed up by the surgical team. These tragedies ignited outrage and prompted changes in the way the hospitals run. In some cases, such as the Betsy Lehman fatality, the medical mistake was so egregious and received so much publicity that the institution was rocked to its very core, and undertook a painful and exhaustive review of its culture and procedures.

Those deaths created what Reason calls a "fundamental surprise." A fundamental surprise reveals a profound discrepancy between one's perception of the world and the reality, and therefore calls for a major reappraisal. Situational surprises, on the other hand, are localized events requiring us only to respond by solving a specific problem. Reason likens the difference between fundamental and situational surprises to the difference between surprise and astonishment, and quotes this apocryphal anecdote to demonstrate what he means: Noah Webster, the lexicographer, returned home to find his wife in the arms of his butler. "You surprised me," said his wife. "And you have astonished me," responded Webster. Mrs. Webster experienced merely a situational surprise—she didn't expect her husband home at that time. Mr. Webster suffered a fundamental one, forcing him to reanalyze his relationship with his wife.

"The natural human tendency is to respond to fundamental surprises as if they are only situational ones," Reason said. For example, the nuclear accident at Three Mile Island was a fundamental surprise. Before that incident, emergency planning and risk analysis focused on large equipment failures, not on a series of small, technical, and human failures. What happened at Three Mile Island was inconceivable before it happened—the very definition of a fundamental surprise. At first, post-accident investigations at the nuclear power plant focused heavily on what went wrong between the technical systems and the workers at the plant. But then the nuclear industry shifted direction and treated the incident as though it were simply a narrow anomaly, and examined purely technological solutions. If accidents are viewed as unique, "there is little need for change, or at least only local fine tuning steps are needed to address those exact conditions," said David D. Woods, who wrote *Behind Human Error*. Such rationalization "produces a strong incentive to stop at first stories and avoid the work needed to uncover second stories."

But *To Err Is Human* was a rare instance of a fundamental response to a fundamental surprise. It "truly changed the conversation" about medical errors and injuries, said Lucian Leape, a Harvard professor who has studied patient safety for decades. It tore away the pretense that doctors and medicine can be infallible. It lay bare the depth and breadth of the problem and said it was high time—indeed, past time—for it to be addressed. But what else happened besides talk? Well, just to use a few examples, there have been some basic but simple changes that have saved lives. Fewer patients die from accidental injection of concentrated potassium chloride—on the older bottle, the label looked a lot like the one for dextrose, and this resulted in many mix-ups and fatalities. The label was redesigned. Serious infections have decreased as hospitals have tightened infection-control procedures. And if we check in again with my friend Rebecca and her husband, Larry, who is a pulmonary specialist at the same hospital, they say that there is no question that over the past ten years there has been an institution-wide emphasis on reducing errors. That includes everything from prohibiting certain abbreviations of drugs because they can be confused to much greater openness with patients. "About ten years ago, declaring an error was considered the formal policy, but practiced more in the breach," Larry told me. That is not the case anymore—every mistake, no matter how inconsequential, has to be disclosed to the patient.

But far less has changed than those involved in the original report hoped for. To give just one example of a common medication error: Primidone, an antiseizure medication, and prednisone, an anti-inflammatory medication, are still often confused. Such a mix-up led to the death of a teenager in California in 2004, despite the fact that the potential for mixing up the two medications had been identified three years earlier. Confusion caused by similar drug names accounts for up to 25 percent of all errors reported to the Medication Error Reporting Program. And labeling and packaging issues were cited as the cause of 33 percent of errors, including 30 percent of fatalities reported to the program. Perhaps the best-known example of this type of error occurred when actor Dennis Quaid's infant twins were given one thousand times the prescribed dose of the blood thinner heparin in 2007, a mix-up that occurred because the manufacturer packaged different doses of the drug in similar vials; the result was a blast of media publicity and congressional hearings. Fortunately, the babies were not permanently injured.

The culture of medicine is incredibly convoluted, with numerous specialties and subspecialties. "The more complex any system is, the more chances it has to fail," Leape notes. There is a need for better measurements to identify problems, determine progress, and demonstrate improvement. Finally there is simply fear—normal human resistance to change, fear of losing autonomy and status, and an understandable concern that more openness will lead to more lawsuits. As we know, true cultural change, whether it be in a business or in a hospital, is awfully difficult. As research scholar Nancy Berlinger wrote in a briefing paper by The Hastings Center: "The 'hidden curriculum' in teaching hospitals may undermine what residents are taught about their truth-telling obligations; if they never see senior colleagues acknowledge and disclose mistakes, residents may conclude that to do so is not in their career interests, either."

While those working in the medical field face different challenges than the rest of us, and some mistakes can be resolved only in ways uniquely suited to that field, it is still possible to extrapolate much of what has been learned in the health care arena about managing and responding to mistakes to help the rest of us. Those in the medical field discovered that mistakes couldn't be addressed if:

- There are no quantifiable measurements to determine how widespread a problem is.
- Workers feel they can't trust their colleagues or bosses. They won't own up to errors—especially near misses that could easily be swept under the rug.
- There is only lip service, not genuine change, in the culture at the top levels; if the usual approach to mistakes is still to humiliate and punish.
- There is no change at the bottom—that is, in this case, if students in nursing and medical schools are not taught new findings and approaches to handling mistakes.
- Hierarchies remain inflexible and there is no transparency.
- There is no or limited feedback.

While I may not be injecting life-saving medication or measuring blood pressure or cutting into a brain anytime soon—and my tool of trade is a computer rather than a syringe—all these factors are as true in my field as they are in medicine. Let's say I'm a conscientious journalist doing the best I can to avoid mistakes, and I write an article that is published with an error in it. If I feel that admitting it to my editor or colleagues would make me appear to be some kind of screwup and treated accordingly, I'm less likely to do so. And if I am told that it's really okay to admit to any mistakes I make, but in reality I'm demoted to covering dog shows (no offense to dog owners here) or yelled at, then no matter how much I'm told that I should own up to my mistakes, I won't until forced to. And if blanket orders are issued that anyone with errors in more than three separate stories in a year will be fired—without taking into account whether the errors are substantive or minor or what my track record has been in the past—I may work harder to prevent errors, but if I am already a diligent reporter, I will also feel frightened and demoralized. And finally, if there is no systemic way of determining whether many reporters are making the same error—say, misspelling the mayor's name—then no one can come up with a way to resolve that problem, which could be as simple as sending out an e-mail requiring reporters to post the name beside their computers.

But enough about me. Enough about what not to do. What can work? Let's look at how one doctor solved one problem in medicine that cost thousands of lives annually in this country—line infections. Not as dramatic as cutting off the wrong limb or killing a patient through an overdose, but, as I have learned, a really serious problem in medicine. Lines are inserted into various parts of the body to deliver medications and nutrients, to measure activities in the body, and for procedures such as dialysis. Each year what are

known as central lines cause an estimated 80,000 bloodstream infections and, as a result, about 31,000 deaths.

As surgeon and author Atul Gawande has noted, intensive
care units barely existed fifty years ago, but now the critical care
they deliver is an increasingly large portion of what hospitals do.
An anecdote that Gawande tells shows the impact these infections
have: A patient who started to hemorrhage during an operation for
a hernia and gallstones began rapidly going downhill. After intensive efforts, he stabilized for ten days, and just when doctors were
ready to take him off a ventilator, he developed a high fever, his
blood pressure sank, and his blood-oxygen level plummeted. "We
didn't understand what had happened," Gawande wrote. "He
seemed to have developed an infection, but our X-ray and CT scans
failed to turn up a source." They finally replaced his lines with new
ones and sent the old ones off to the lab to be cultured. It turned
out that an infection had probably started in one line, moved to the
other, and in the end they were all "spilling bacteria into him."

So what's the answer? Lines made of a different material? More
staff to constantly monitor them? Or a way of ensuring that providers
avoid infections as much as possible when inserting lines? It was a critical care specialist at the Johns Hopkins University School of Medicine
in Baltimore, Peter Pronovost—who was a medical student when his
father died because of a misdiagnosis—who came up with a decep-
tively simple concept: a checklist to address the problem. Checklists
to avoid harm or death are nothing new in high-risk fields. Pilots have
used them for decades, since airplanes became too complex to fly
from memory alone. And Gawande says medicine has now entered

the phase where many aspects of what doctors do—most notably in ICUs—are just too complex to carry out through simple memorization. But there was resistance. Besides questions about their usefulness, checklists seemed just infantile to many doctors and administrators.

Here is Pronovost's checklist for doctors:

- Wash your hands with soap.
- Clean the patient's skin with chlorhexidine antiseptic.
- Put sterile drapes over the entire patient.
- Wear a sterile mask, hat, gown, and gloves.
- Put a sterile dressing over the catheter site once the line is in.

Guess what? Pronovost asked his nurses in the ICU to observe the doctors for a month as they put lines into patients and record their findings. In more than a third of the patients, the doctors skipped one step on the checklist. But, as Pronovost told me, handing out checklists is only one leg of a three-legged stool. You also need to measure and give feedback on infection rates, and change the culture. Part of that change in culture meant that the administration told nurses that they should speak up if they saw a doctor skipping a step on the checklist and should be able to ask if a line should be removed so it wouldn't stay in longer than necessary. Times are changing, but even now, in most hospitals nurses often aren't sure whether they are allowed to confront doctors, especially for an apparently minor error. But it was now clear that if doctors didn't follow every step on the checklist, nurses would have backup from the administration to intervene.

Here's what's amazing: When Pronovost and his colleagues monitored what happened a year later, the infection rate for patients with intravenous lines for at least ten days had gone from 11 percent to zero. So they followed for fifteen more months, and only two line infections occurred in the entire period. They figured that in this one hospital alone, the checklist had prevented forty-three infections, avoided eight deaths, and saved $2 million. But Johns Hopkins is one of the top teaching hospitals in the country, with staff and Pronovost himself following up personally. Then, in 2003, the Michigan Health and Hospital Association asked Pronovost to try out three of his checklists in Michigan's ICUs, where many hospitals were underequipped and understaffed. The success rate was again phenomenal—the infection rate in Michigan's ICUs decreased by 66 percent. The typical ICU cut its quarterly infection rate to zero, saving the hospitals an estimated $175 million in costs and more than 1,500 lives. And it's been maintained for over four years.

Then the federal government got a whiff of this and wanted all hospitals to use the Pronovost checklist. But Pronovost knew that simply ordering checklists to be used was fairly useless without the other two legs of the stool—without measurement of infection rates and feedback, and cultural change from the top down.

Pronovost, who has since won a MacArthur "genius grant" and is one of government's go-to people on patient safety issues, knows it's going to be a long, long road to substantially reduce medical errors and change medical culture. "There's an expectation of perfection, and when there isn't perfection, there's shame and guilt," he said. And although moving from blaming the individual is a good step, he cautioned that if we're not careful, the upshot can be simply pointing the finger at a group rather than actually trying to figure out solutions. "We've just moved it up—'those dumb insurers,' 'those administrators,'" he said. The sheer complexity of the situation defies black-and-white solutions, and too often policymakers don't realize that. As Pronovost told me, he sits on a number of national health policy committees and he is often the only practicing doctor in the room.

I watched one of Pronovost's safety tools in action while visiting a Johns Hopkins ICU that treats patients just out of heart surgery. Pronovost is an intense yet very cordial man with almost movie-star good looks. He is also not a man to bide his time patiently. Instead of waiting for the slow elevators, he suggested we take the stairs to the ICU. I agreed, and ended up huffing behind him as we rapidly climbed from the second to the seventh floor. When we got there, Pronovost greeted his group with a few questions and lighthearted comments, and then quickly got down to work. He, along with a physician's assistant, nurse practitioner, and clinical pharmacist, stopped by the beds of very sick people, most unconscious and hooked up to what seemed to be dozens of lines. Johns Hopkins differs from many hospitals because it has a clinical pharmacist dedicated just to this ICU, and she can discuss and suggest medications and warn of possible interactions on the spot. Not every hospital can add staff, but Pronovost has put in place something else that doesn't cost money—daily goals. After the physician's assistant, Anne Boyle, updated the team on the patient's status overnight—a five-minute litany of abbreviations and jargon that was completely incomprehensible to me—they all discussed options. Meanwhile, the nurse who was assigned specifically to that patient listened and wrote. In one case, it was a nurse with the great name of Rocky Cogle. After the discussion, a decision was made on the next steps to take in terms of medication and procedures, something Cogle repeated aloud. Before this policy of reiterating the daily goals and having the nurse read them back, it was often unclear what the final decisions were, and, Cogle said, "seventy-five percent of the time, I needed something clarified." Ambiguity is one of the main causes of error.

Just to show how the actions of others can influence us in a very short period of time: On the ICU ward, hand sanitizer dispensers were *everywhere*, and the staff were constantly using them. After spending several hours on the floor, I stood waiting for the elevator to go down. I started reaching for the hand sanitizer as I had seen so many others do that day. Although I hadn't touched a patient—nor was I intending to—I was already acculturated into the clean-hand ritual.

Atul Gawande devotes an entire book, *The Checklist Manifesto*, to telling the history and success of verbal checklists in fields ranging from professional football coordinators to chefs to disaster relief. When he was asked in 2007 to work with the World Health Organization in reducing avoidable deaths and harm from surgery worldwide, the concept of checklists emerged. WHO agreed to try it in a pilot program. Gawande describes how he returned to his hospital, Brigham and Women's in Boston, to give the checklist a try himself. But the checklist they used was too long and ambiguous, and everyone soon got exasperated—including the patient who raised her head after a while and asked, "Is everything okay?"

Gawande went back to the drawing board, researching how

different fields—such as aviation—devise effective checklists. He found that the wording should be simple and exact. It should fit on one page, without unnecessary clutter or lots of different colors. He developed one for safe surgery, which was then tested in eight hospitals around the world based in high-income countries and poorer nations, with all sorts of resources (or lack thereof), serving all types of patients. But they didn't just dump a bunch of forms in the hospitals. Hospital staff were given PowerPoint slides and YouTube videos demonstrating "How to Do the Safe Surgery Checklist" and "How Not to Do the Safe Surgery Checklist." Gawande and his colleagues visited the pilot sites to observe. In October 2008, the results came in from the hospitals that had used the checklists: The rate of major complications for surgical patients in all eight hospitals fell by 36 percent, and deaths dropped 47 percent. Overall, out of nearly 4,000 patients, 435 would have been expected to develop serious complications, on the basis of previously collected data. But instead just 277 did. So the checklist had spared more than 150 people from harm, and 27 of them from death.

In 2009, the results were published in *The New England Journal of Medicine*, and implementing checklists became a nationwide campaign. In a survey of 250 surgeons, nurses, anesthesiologists, and others, some 20 percent said they didn't like the checklists, feeling they were difficult to use, too long, and had not improved safety. But a full 93 percent said if they were having an operation, they would want the checklist to be used. While it can almost sound like checklists perform some sort of magic, as Gawande points out, at the end of the day "just ticking boxes is not the ultimate goal here. Embracing a culture of teamwork and discipline is." One of the requirements on the WHO checklist is that everyone introduce himself by name.

Gawande said at first this seemed kind of hokey to him and he wondered what the point was. But it turns out that several psychological studies in various fields show that people who don't know one another's names don't work together as well as people who do. I have to say I've found that to be true: in small meetings, for example, in which we're all supposed to brainstorm together, I feel less comfortable and connected if I don't know the names of the people I'm talking to.

Here is the WHO Checklist for Surgery, which is intended to be modified to fit local practices:

Before Induction of Anesthesia

- Has the patient confirmed his/her identity site, procedure, and consent?
- Is the site marked?
- Is the anesthesia machine and medication check complete?
- Is the pulse oximeter on the patient and functioning?
- Does the patient have a:
  Known allergy?
  Difficult airway or aspiration risk?
  Risk of >500ml blood loss (7ml/kg in children)?

Before Skin Incision

- Confirm all team members have introduced themselves by name and role.
- Confirm the patient's name, procedure, and where the incision will be made.

- Has antibiotic prophylaxis been given within the last 60 minutes?

Anticipated Critical Events

To Surgeon:
- What are the critical or non-routine steps?
- How long will the case take?
- What is the anticipated blood loss?

To Anesthetist:
- Are there any patient-specific concerns?

To Nursing Team:
- Has sterility (including indicator results) been confirmed?
- Are there equipment issues or any concerns?

Is Essential Imaging Displayed?

Before Patient Leaves Operating Room

Nurse verbally confirms
- The name of the procedure
- Completion of instrument, sponge, and needle counts
- Specimen labeling (read specimen labels aloud, including patient name)
- Whether there are any equipment problems to be addressed

To Surgeon, Anesthetist, and Nurse:
• What are the key concerns for recovery and management
of this patient?

Even at such an enlightened hospital as Johns Hopkins, though, "there is tremendous pressure to perform without mistakes," a junior resident at Johns Hopkins told me. "I live it every single day. There is pressure to never make mistakes. It varies from an unspoken under- standing to people actively yelling at you. I think we should be held to a high standard, but the negative is the shaming, where people are made an example of, rather than looking at the whole process." The resident, who didn't want his name used for fear of standing out in what he called "a very conservative institution," pointed to the morbidity and mortality meetings, which have been around for about a hundred years and are now a common tool at almost every hospital. At this weekly session for all residents, someone—not the people involved with the issue—presents to the group a problem that occurred the week before. The names are withheld, but no one wants to be the subject of that week's lesson. A common joke in sur- gery is, "Don't do that or we'll end up in an m and m." But, the resi- dent said, the sessions play two very important roles: the humiliation reinforces the need to do certain things right and helps you gain a certain sense of responsibility. "I don't know a better way," the resi- dent told me, "but it seems like there should be."

Before the Johns Hopkins resident was even born, Dr. David Hil- fiker, who worked in a family practice in rural Minnesota, published an article in 1984 in *The New England Journal of Medicine* called "Facing

Our Mistakes." In his heartfelt—and highly unusual—confessional, Hilfiker wrote about how unbelievably difficult it was to make mistakes as a doctor, and yet it happens all the time. He opens with an anecdote about a patient, Barb, who has all the symptoms of a pregnancy, yet four pregnancy tests at different intervals come up negative. Hilfiker could order an ultrasound, but Barb would have to travel some distance for the examination, and it would prove costly for her, as she was of modest means. He comes to the conclusion that she is carrying a dead embryo and performs a dilation and curettage, or D&C, to remove the embryo. The only trouble is, as he continues the operation—which is done, at the time, completely by feel—he is surprised by the size of the body parts and the blood. Hilfiker does his best to suppress his rising panic and suspicion that he is, in fact, aborting a live fetus. A pathologist confirms that the fetus was alive—in fact, it was almost eleven weeks old—and there is no explanation why the pregnancy tests were negative. "My meeting with Barb and Russ later in the week is one of the hardest things I have ever been through," Hilfiker wrote. "I described in some detail what I did and what my rationale had been. Nothing can obscure the hard reality: I killed their baby." Hilfiker talks about the grand illusion of perfection that is desired by patients and perpetuated by doctors. "A physician is even less prepared to deal with his mistakes than is the average person," Hilfiker wrote. "Nothing in our training prepares us to respond appropriately. As a student, I was simply not aware that the sort of mistakes that I would eventually make in practice actually happened to competent physicians."

Hilfiker told me that his article generated about 150 responses—a significant number, especially before e-mail—and only two of them told him he must be a lousy doctor for making such mistakes.

Most of the other responses, including many of the letters Hilfiker subsequently received, were surprisingly sympathetic. Many were from doctors telling him about their own mistakes and thanking him for bringing it out into the open. "Even more, however, were from those close to doctors—their spouses, nurses, office staff, et cetera—who told me about the suffering of their doctor because of the mistakes," he added. The article went on to be published in *Harper's* and then became a chapter in a book Hilfiker wrote. As far as Hilfiker knows, it took many years before another article was widely published by a physician on medical mistakes.

Changing a deeply embedded culture, as we've seen, is very tough and an ongoing process. Changing some systems that lead to mistakes can be easier. For example, at McLeod Regional Medical Center in Florence, South Carolina, administrators adapted a number of methods to stem medication errors. Installing automated medication storage and dispensing cabinets in all inpatient units and streamlining the dispensing system—down from seventeen to five steps—was important. So was eliminating the punitive approach to such errors. Instead of the old finger-pointing, health care workers now attempt to figure out how the system failed. Even the terminology changed—instead of an error report, workers fill out an "Improve the Process" form. The no-blame culture initiated a sharp increase in the number of staff-reported medication errors— from seventy a year to two hundred a month. And administrators are pretty confident that those numbers don't mean so many more errors are happening, but that people are more comfortable talking about them.

Another way to encourage more people to come forward is

to alleviate some of the fear that information about errors could be used against someone in a malpractice lawsuit. On the federal level, the government tried to address this by creating the Patient Safety and Quality Improvement Act of 2005, which created Patient Safety Organizations to collect, aggregate, and analyze confidential information reported by health care providers. That information is considered privileged and cannot be used in a lawsuit, but rather to identify patterns of failure and establish measures to correct them. That doesn't mean lawsuits can't be pursued, but that that particular information reported to the Patient Safety Organizations is protected.

As I was writing this book, the name James Bagian kept coming up as an innovator in the field. He has had a unique career—he was finishing his residency in anesthesiology when he was selected by NASA to be part of its astronaut training program. He was with NASA from 1980 to 1995, and in 1986 was the investigator for the *Challenger* space shuttle accident. In 1998, he was chosen as the first director of the Veterans Administration's National Center for Patient Safety, overseeing its 153 medical centers and other types of outpatient, nursing home, and in-home care facilities. The health care industry, he said, is where aviation was fifty years ago, when if something went wrong, the guilty party was fingered and then punished. Or else, when pilots crashed planes, people blamed fate— you know the old saw: "If man were meant to fly, God would have given him wings." But that changed with the introduction of the jet aircraft in the 1950s, and the large number of plane crashes that cost the military and airplane companies not only lives, but valuable property as well. In 1954, the Navy lost 776 aircraft—and those crashes didn't occur in combat. Now, the average is 90 percent less.

Since the money simply wasn't there to continually replace the lost aircraft, aviation experts had to figure out how to reduce the number of accidents.

BACK THEN, there were far fewer standards that defined how to fly or maintain a plane, and that had to change. Although checklists already existed, they became more comprehensive and explicit to avoid needless differences. Bagian stressed needless, because pilots have to have flexibility. You don't want the checklist "to become a cookbook that is blindly and slavishly followed."

Now, there is much less variation in aviation than in health care. Of course, there's always the unexpected, but if you're flying a Boeing 737-400, and then walk over to the next 737-400 and hop into the cockpit, it's going to be essentially the same. That also goes for a car—if you buy two Ford Focuses with identical options, the emergency brake isn't going to be on the left in one car and on the right in the other. But the patient lying on the operating table or recovering in bed may have similar symptoms to a patient down the hall, but she's not a replica. There are not as many bright lines in medicine. That doesn't mean, however, that there aren't any.

Bagian was working on improving patient safety even before the publication of *To Err Is Human*. In 1998, the VA took a survey of health care professionals and their attitudes toward safety. The results were a surprise; although worries about punishment and malpractice lawsuits were a concern, they weren't number one on the list. Rather, it was fear of being embarrassed in front of their peers. "So that changes what you need to address," Bagian said.

Because if your aim is to get doctors and nurses to be more open about events that did or could harm a patient and more willing to learn from them, you can make all the rules you want assuring people that they won't get fired if they make an error—but they're still going to worry about being humiliated in front of their coworkers and patients. So the idea, again, is to look at the problem, not the person, and ask these three key questions: What happened? Why did it happen? What do we do to prevent it from happening in the future?

Here is one way the VA tried to foster such a culture. Ten years ago it instituted a policy in which only an "intentionally unsafe act" could lead to disciplinary action. Such an act is one that is criminal, involves alcohol or other substance abuse by the provider, involves patient abuse, or is purposefully unsafe. Only those events that are suspected of being intentionally unsafe acts would result in an administrative investigation that could trigger a disciplinary action. Of course, not all adverse events or close calls require a root-cause analysis, and Bagian and his team developed a prioritization methodology to help staff decide whether there was a need to take action. This was done by determining the severity of the outcome or the potential severity of a close call and then assessing the likelihood of it happening again. So if something goes wrong, a member of the staff can report it to the facility's patient safety manager, who uses the criteria mentioned above to prioritize and take the appropriate action. And it is privileged information protected by federal law, so it cannot be used in a lawsuit.

In 2000, the Department of Veterans Affairs and NASA jointly set up a federal program called the Patient Safety Reporting System

(PSRS), based on the similar aviation program, which I discuss in chapter 5. PSRS provides a forum where health care personnel at the VA can anonymously report mishaps; it is scheduled to expand to other hospitals in the future. The PSRS attracts far fewer reports than the VA's internal patient safety system—840 between 2000 and 2009, compared with 600,000 internally. Bagian attributed that to the anonymous form, which means it is far more difficult to delve into the systemic cause of a problem or error. Linda Connell, program director of NASA's Aviation Safety Reporting System, who helped develop the PSRS, countered that even if the number of complaints has been relatively small, the information they contained has proved very helpful. For example, one complainant told of the wrong kind of disinfectant being used to clean dentures and causing irritation. Another warned of wall-mounted televisions falling off brackets and onto patients. In both cases, the PSRS issued a system-wide bulletin alerting the entire VA of the potential problem.

"People want to see things go well, but also want to be treated fairly," Bagian said. In an analogy that struck close to home, Bagian presented me with a scenario in which my editor asks me to report all the mistakes I make in my articles. If that figure is going to be used to fire me or dock my pay, or if I know that other people aren't being asked to do the same thing, I might fudge my stats a little. If I feel similar data are being collected from my colleagues and used in a nonpunitive way to figure out a system that would weed out some of those errors, I would be much more forthcoming—if I trusted the system and the editor. Although not perfect, and although it is always extremely difficult to measure the success of such programs, the VA's patient safety system is often cited by both government and special interest groups as groundbreaking.

In trying to classify the severity of mistakes, we need to look not just at the mistake itself, but at the outcome and the reason it occurred. The concept of Just Culture represents an attempt to find the balance between only blaming the individual and never blaming the individual. The model was developed in the 1990s in tandem with James Reason's work on human error. "We were trying to build better systems around the inherent fallibility of human beings and help them make better choices," said David Marx, who was then a Boeing aircraft designer and helped create and disseminate the Just Culture philosophy. An underlying idea in Just Culture is that we as a society are too focused on outcomes and not on choices and behavior; for instance, if a drunk driver hits a car and kills a person, she is punished far more severely than one who hits a car and doesn't kill anyone. They both might have equal amounts of alcohol in their systems, but the justice system acts on the outcome. That is wrong, Marx says.

As we discussed, some institutions take the approach that weeding out one bad actor will resolve problems. In other institutions, especially in aviation, where the goal is to get people to come forward to fix systemic errors, some feel individual accountability has taken too much of a backseat. In an effort to address this tension, Just Culture identified three classes of human fallibility: inadvertent human error, at-risk behavior, and reckless behavior. Let's take the case of a hospital-wide requirement to read a patient's name band to make sure he receives the correct medication. An inadvertent error could be looking at the band but misreading the label. An at-risk behavior would be knowing you should read the band but not doing so because you choose not to wake the patient. Reckless behavior would be simply ignoring the hospital's requirement and choosing not to read the band. But to make it even more complicated, what could be considered an at-risk behavior in one circumstance could be considered reckless in another.

That is why one-size-fits-all punishments don't work. A nurse who misreads a label (unless she does it regularly) shouldn't be punished but helped to figure out a system that will prevent future error, such as larger print on labels. But let's say in one scenario, a nurse chooses to not wake up a patient because a customer satisfaction survey found that sleep interruption was the number-one complaint, and nurses agreed not to wake patients to check name bands too many times. Then suppose the wrong medication is given to the patient as a result of not reading the label, which results in the patient going into shock. But instead of writing up or dismissing the nurse, administrators must figure out if the nurse was aware of the policy to check name bands, if all nurses on the unit do it, and why she mistakenly thought it was better not to. In another scenario, the nurse lets a patient sleep and doesn't check the name band. In this case a strict policy is in place to check name bands before administering care or medication; it was doable, and others were following the policy. Now the nurse's actions would be considered reckless, and reckless behavior should be punished regardless of outcome. "Just Culture judges the behavior, not the outcome," said Alison Page, who was former chief safety officer at Fairview Health Services in Minnesota when the Just Culture concept was adopted there. In 2010, the American Nurses Association formally endorsed Just Culture, saying, "It does much to improve patient safety, reduce errors, and give nurses and other health care workers a major stake in the improvement process."

So the way to create a culture more aware of errors, then, is not to institute an atmosphere where there is zero tolerance for mistakes or to declare an "error-free" zone. First of all, perfection is impossible, and second, it creates an oppressive and fearful atmosphere. Rather, the idea should be to establish an environment where people feel safe to ask questions and experiment. But that is one of the most difficult dilemmas in the medical field. One of the reasons is the strict hierarchy with surgeons and doctors at the top. Things have changed: Avrum Bluming, a clinical professor of medicine at the University of Southern California, recalls a time when nurses stood up and offered their seats when a doctor walked into a room. You probably won't see that much now, but Bluming, who oversees an oncology unit at a Southern California hospital, said some doctors still expect deference from nurses and other health care workers, and are uncomfortable with the perception that their authority is being undermined. On his unit, doctors and nurses address each other by first name, and "the nurses are polite but not cowed," he said. But, he added, "some doctors won't work on our unit because they don't like the nurses' attitude." There is unquestionably a hierarchy in medicine, but it must be "very flexible" to give patients the best possible care. It requires mutual respect, "which is very different than a generation ago," according to Bluming.

The big bogeyman is litigation. If doctors disclose errors that patients wouldn't have even known about because they had little or no effect, then aren't they inviting lawsuits among a minority that will seize upon such mistakes as a road to riches? But on the very human level, we all know that when an error is honestly acknowledged and a sincere apology offered, we tend to feel better, and so many of us might be less likely to sue—depending, of course, on the severity and consequences of the mistake. I can draw on a case from my own family. My sister experienced a very difficult labor, and ultimately had an unwanted cesarean delivery with her first child. In a common domino effect, because many doctors are loath to allow subsequent vaginal births after cesareans, her next two were also delivered by cesarean. In the weeks after the first birth, she suffered severe memory lapses, but fortunately there were no long-term problems for her or her daughter. She suspects, although doesn't know for sure, that she was accidentally given either an overdose of a certain drug while in labor or something she was unknowingly allergic to. She went to discuss the case with her doctor, with whom she had always had a good relationship. The doctor refused to even acknowledge a problem, and certainly did not offer any apology. She, in other words, did what lawyers and insurers often tell doctors to do: "deny and defend." As for my sister, who had no intention of suing, it was a sad end to the relationship with that doctor. "All I wanted was for her to say she was sorry this happened," my sister said.

Even though the pendulum has swung slightly from denial of any wrongdoing to greater openness, a survey of 2,637 doctors in the United States and Canada shows that less than half of harmful errors may be disclosed to patients. In that survey, doctors were first offered different scenarios involving medical error. For example, in one case, a sponge was left in a patient; in another a surgeon accidentally inflicted an internal injury because she was unfamiliar with a particular surgical tool. Overall, 65 percent of those doctors responding said that they would definitely disclose the error, although the language the doctors and surgeons used varied widely—less than half said they would use the word "error," and 56 percent said they would mention "adverse event," but not "error." Although most of the physicians agreed that all the scenarios represented serious mistakes, those who received the scenario with the more obvious mistake were more likely to reveal it to the patient.

But it is not just the patient who suffers from medical mistakes, as another study of almost three thousand American and Canadian doctors who had been involved in errors or near misses shows. Many of the doctors said they felt guilty, depressed, and scared after a mistake, and often even after almost making an error. They reported sleeping difficulties, strained relationships with colleagues, and plummeting feelings of self-worth; these feelings were true across specialties and nationalities. Doctors and nurses often are afraid to talk to their peers about their concerns for fear of appearing inferior, being humiliated, and, particularly in the case of nurses, being disciplined or dismissed. They frequently avoid going to counseling programs set up to address such problems out of concern that the talks won't remain confidential. Although studies have shown that accepting responsibility for errors appears to be an important step in creating healthy coping skills, too many providers keep their feelings bottled up inside. And interestingly, despite the differences in Canadian health care—a nationalized, less litigious system than our American one—Canadian doctors did not appear to be significantly less distressed by mistakes than U.S. doctors. So we see that it is not just the fear of malpractice that creates a defensive medical system, but also culture that perpetuates the myth of perfection that too many struggle to maintain.

"Because doctors do not discuss their mistakes, I do not know how other physicians come to terms with theirs," Hilfiker wrote. "But I suspect that many cannot bear to face their mistakes directly. We either deny the misfortune altogether or blame the patient, the nurse, the laboratory, other physicians, the system, fate—anything to avoid our own guilt." For some doctors, nurses, and other providers, the ongoing emotional impact of an error can lead to post-traumatic stress disorder. My friend Larry told me of an excellent doctor who oversaw his team when Larry was a senior resident. The doctor went above and beyond to take care of a friend's son who had fallen ill. Unfortunately, in that case, the doctor made a calculation error in administering a medication, which ended up temporarily harming the boy. "He would not calculate any medicine after that for about six months," Larry said. "I had to do it all for him."

Doctors, nurses, and other providers work in a very complex and ever-shifting environment. They have to manage details and stresses that I can't even imagine. But at the end of the day, the problems and mechanisms they have for addressing mistakes on both an institutional and an individual basis are not that different from such problems and mechanisms that the rest of us have. As Larry said, "We don't become separate humans when we become physicians, we just carry a different set of responsibilities." Although we strive to do the best we can, perfection is not an option. The cultural barriers to working through and learning from mistakes may be more ingrained in the medical field than in other professions, but the basics are true across the board. First of all, avoid scapegoating; the problem often isn't one of an incompetent worker, but of a systemic failure. We can't deal superficially with problems because it's easier. Otherwise, it's like seeing a tree with sickly leaves. Cutting off the leaves will solve the immediate problem, but unless we get to the roots, we probably won't know why the leaves are dying.

But that doesn't mean that complex problems necessarily require complex solutions. The success of checklists shows how something so obvious—a tool essentially used by anyone who has ever gone to the grocery store with a list—can save lives. But it is also important to remember that the checklist didn't succeed in a vacuum. Deep-seated attitudes and assumptions about working relationships had to change to make it work.

We also know people need to be held accountable for their mistakes—changing the way errors are handled is not a free pass to screw up all over the place. The concept of Just Culture is one that can be brought into any environment to ensure that accountability is fair. Adopting such a culture entails systemically figuring out why the mistake occurred and making decisions regarding potential penalties based on those findings, rather than a one-size-fits-all punishment.

Perhaps one of the best lessons we can take away from this chapter is how important it is to create and put in place methods to establish and enhance good communication. In an ideal world, that would come naturally, but in reality it is an ongoing process that requires insightful thinking about how people work—or fail to work—together. As we saw, simply asking a nurse to repeat a doctor's instructions every time alleviated errors. Putting in place systems and strategies where doctors and patients can discuss mistakes with a minimum of defensiveness and mistrust helped both sides cope measurably better. In or out of the medical field, most of us want to have a clear idea of what is expected of us and to feel safe enough to admit our mistakes, whether it be to our bosses, spouses, friends, or children without worrying about being humiliated. We want, within reason, to accept the mistakes of others and have others accept ours. And what we learn from the body of research that has grown out of addressing medical mistakes is that even in this most complex arena, such change is certainly possible. And that's good news for all of us.

5.

LESSONS FROM THE COCKPIT

AVIATION INITIALLY SEEMED TOO FAR AFIELD FROM MY subject and too specific to be relevant to the general public. But the more I read about it, the more I realized how much has been discovered about why and how people make mistakes—and the best ways to try to prevent them—by studying aviation, and cockpit crews in particular. The research in this field provides the building blocks for understanding error prevention across all fields, and to ignore it would leave a gaping hole.

Robert Helmreich, professor emeritus of psychology at the University of Texas, is known as one of the pioneers in developing systems to make aviation safer. For many years, he was principal investigator of the Human Factors Research Project at the university, where he started by researching how to make the dangerous work of aquanauts and astronauts safer. He became involved in pilot safety in 1979, after a "series of embarrassing aviation mistakes," Helmreich told me. One plane ran out of gas, for example, while another landed at the wrong airport. The pilot of yet another plane shut down the one good engine when he meant to shut down the other engine, which was on fire. NASA decided to look at what the role of human error was in plane crashes and asked Helmreich to be a keynote speaker at a conference examining the issues. Subsequently he and the Human Factors Research Project became the go-to place in aviation safety; one can scarcely read any research in this area without coming across Helmreich's name, and he has received numerous awards for his contributions to aviation safety.

Helmreich approached flight safety in a novel way: rather than look solely at how people interacted with the technology, he and his people looked at the human factors that lead to error. These include poor communication, fatigue, stress, and overwork. The Human Factors Research Project worked on the assumption that preventing accidents—like preventative health care—is the goal, not discovering what went wrong after the fact.

It turns out that what Helmreich and others learned from surveying and observing pilots could be applied to numerous other high-risk fields—and even to medicine. In 1994, physicians at the University of Basel in Switzerland invited Helmreich to adapt his approaches in the cockpit to the operating room, and the Human Factors Research Project began work in the medical field. The results were fascinating.

But first, back to airplanes. Aviation might seem kind of technical and of little consequence to those of us who don't fly planes. But we can all benefit from how what has been learned in aviation safety applies to dealing with mistakes in all walks of life. As Malcolm Gladwell notes, "Plane crashes rarely happen in real life the same way they happen in movies. Some engine part does not explode in a fiery bang. The rudder doesn't suddenly snap under the force of a takeoff. The captain doesn't gasp, 'Dear God,' as he's thrown back against his seat. The typical commercial jetliner—at this point in its stage of development—is about as dependable as a toaster. Plane crashes are much more likely to be the result of an accumulation of minor difficulties and seeming trivial malfunctions." Once again, we look back at the idea of many latent errors leading up to the obvious active errors—and it's the latent ones we need to uncover and fix. What we've learned from studying aviation safety is just as applicable to those of us who sit all day in a cubicle as it is to those who work in a cockpit. Know our own limitations, and when to ask for help. Develop good teamwork, share information, and be flexible. Change the culture from above, so subordinates aren't afraid to question superiors. Collect good data to find out what works in error prevention and what doesn't.

Historically, the statistic bandied about in this field is that human error has caused or contributed to over 70 percent of aviation accidents. However, many aviation experts, like Robert Sumwalt, who flew for US Airways for almost twenty-five years and is now a member of the National Transportation Safety Board, believes that virtually all accidents can be traced back to human error somewhere in the system. "In reality, we'll never get rid of error," he told me.

"The focus has moved from eliminating error to managing error. If you build a system around eliminating error, you're set to fail." What we have to do is figure out what mistakes people are likely to make and try to prevent them or build such a robust system that even if the mistake occurs, it won't be calamitous. For instance, if there is one knob in a cockpit that turns counterclockwise while all the others turn clockwise, someone is eventually going to turn it the wrong way. So either engineers eliminate that one, so all knobs turn the same way, or put up some sort of guard to force the operator to think before automatically turning it.

What has proved successful in aviation is a combination of training programs, observation, attitudinal surveys, and data collection that is constantly evolving and being refined. We think of technical advances improving aviation safety—and they have—but something as low-tech as a survey has also proved invaluable. Such surveys help shed light on how pilots see themselves and what interventions are needed to prevent errors before they happen. The surveys include statements, which the respondents agree or disagree with, such as "Even when I'm fatigued, I perform effectively during critical phases," "A truly professional team member can leave personal problems behind when working," and "Junior team members should not question the decisions made by senior team members." Helmreich noted that most of the 30,000 pilots surveyed said their decision-making is as good in emergencies as under normal conditions, that they can leave behind personal problems, and that they perform effectively when fatigued. "Such inaccurate self-perceptions can lead to overconfidence in difficult situations," Helmreich wrote.

The three main programs that Helmreich and others developed to enhance aviation safety are known as Crew Resource Management (also called Threat and Error Management), Line Operations Safety Audit, and the Aviation Safety Reporting System and Aviation Safety Action Program. Crew Resource Management combines team training, simulation, interactive group debriefings, and surveys. The first comprehensive CRM program began in 1981 with United Airlines, after the National Transportation Safety Board singled out a captain's failure to accept input from junior members (a characteristic sometimes referred to as "The Wrong Stuff," a caustic reference to *The Right Stuff*, Tom Wolfe's opus on the history of the space program) and a general lack of assertiveness by the flight engineer as causal factors in a United Airlines crash in 1978. In that case, an indicator malfunctioned, leading the crew to believe there were problems with the landing gear. The captain had concentrated so intently on the malfunctioning indicator light that he failed to notice that his plane was running out of fuel.

The first generation of Crew Resource Management courses focused heavily on psychological testing and general concepts, such as leadership and teamwork. Advocates quickly realized that CRM trainings shouldn't just happen once in a pilot's career but be ongoing. Over the years CRM has evolved; it is now in its sixth generation. There is no universal CRM training program, because, as in medicine, a one-size-fits-all approach would inevitably fail. Rather, each airline customizes it to best suit its needs. Part of the goal of CRM is to get pilots—often a somewhat macho bunch— to understand how stress, work overload, and fatigue can cause them to make mistakes. One of the changes that grew out of CRM was the institution of a preflight briefing, where, much like in pre-operation briefings, and for the same reason, pilots and crew members get together to discuss the upcoming flight and any possible problems that might arise, as well as contingency plans. "Ultimately it makes a lot of sense, but it was a tough sell," Helmreich remembers. Another key change was that junior crew members are not only allowed, but expected, to speak up to the captain if there is a threat. In the past, Helmreich said, he heard instances on voice recorders from planes that had crashed where captains barked, "Shut up and look out the window—if I wanted help, I'd ask for it."

A classic and tragic example of how the reluctance of a first officer to directly convey his concern can lead to disaster is all too apparent in this recording on January 13, 1982, when an Air Florida Boeing 737 crashed into the Potomac due to excessive snow and ice on the airplane and a frozen indicator that gave the crew a false engine power reading:

FIRST OFFICER: "Look how the ice is just hanging on his, ah, back back there, see that? . . . See all those icicles on the back there and everything?"

CAPTAIN: "Yeah."

There is a long wait following de-icing.

FIRST OFFICER: "Boy, this is a losing battle here on trying to de-ice these things. It [gives] you a false feeling of security, that's all that it does."

They're given clearance to take off.

FIRST OFFICER: "Let's check those tops again since we've been sitting here awhile."

CAPTAIN: "I think we get to go here in a minute."

As they're on the takeoff roll, the first officer noticed something wrong with the engine readings.

FIRST OFFICER: "That doesn't seem right, does it?"

CAPTAIN: "Yes it is, there's eighty [referring to ground speed]."

FIRST OFFICER: "Naw, I don't think that's right. [seven-second pause] Ah, maybe it is."

The flight then crashed into the Fourteenth Street Bridge, which spans the Potomac River, crushing cars and plunging into the icy water. Seventy-four people were killed. It was later discovered that the accident was caused in part by failure to activate the engine anti-ice system.

Two years after that, Captain Al Haynes credited CRM with averting a complete catastrophe when landing his plane after complete hydraulic failure while flying from Denver to O'Hare International Airport in Chicago. The airplane broke up during an emergency landing at Sioux City airport, killing 112 of its 286 passengers and one of eleven crew members. But the fact that more than half of the passengers survived such a crash has been attributed largely to the success of CRM. Haynes himself—who was portrayed by Charlton Heston in the 1992 movie *A Thousand Heroes*—said so in a speech about the accident. (He calls it Cockpit Resource Management, which is what CRM was initially named.)

"There was no training procedure for hydraulic failure," Haynes said. "Complete hydraulic failure. We've all been through one failure or double failures, but never a complete hydraulic failure. But the preparation that paid off for the crew was something that

United started in 1980 called Cockpit Resource Management, or Command Leadership Resource Training. All the other airlines are now using it. Up until 1980, we kind of worked on the concept that the captain was *the* authority on the aircraft. What he said goes. And we lost a few airplanes because of that. Sometimes the captain isn't as smart as we thought he was. And we would listen to him, and do what he said, and we wouldn't know what he's talking about. And we had a hundred and three years of flying experience there in the cockpit, trying to get that airplane on the ground, not one minute of which we had actually practiced, any one of us. So why would I know more about getting that airplane on the ground under those conditions than the other three? So if I hadn't used CLR, if we had not let everybody put their input in, it's a cinch we wouldn't have made it."

The three-member crew recruited a pilot from the first-class section for assistance, and together they devised a technique to steer the aircraft by increasing and decreasing power from the two remaining engines. As Helmreich notes, the crew had to deal with controlling the aircraft, assessing damage, choosing a landing site, and preparing the cabin crew and passengers for an emergency landing. Unlike the 1978 United flight, where the captain didn't notice that the fuel was dangerously low because he was fixated on a single task, the crew coped with multiple issues simultaneously. The cockpit recordings showed that not only were crew members able to keep one another aware of the events unfolding and the decision-making process, but junior crew members were free to suggest alternative courses of action. And even during this highly stressful time, crew members were providing emotional support for one another.

Research shows that highly effective cockpit crews use one-third of their communications to discuss threats and errors in their environment, regardless of their workload, while poorly performing teams spend about one-twentieth of their time doing the same. As data on accidents accumulated, it became increasingly obvious that most accidents were related to breakdowns in crew coordination, communications, and decision making. One important way to reduce those accidents was a shift toward a more open culture that allowed questioning and recognized human limitations.

Robert Sumwalt recalled one report he read years ago that demonstrated how a tragedy like the Air Florida flight almost happened again—and was averted. A de-icing crew failed to take the ice off one entire wing. (I bet you'll never fly in freezing weather again, will you?) The passengers, looking out the window, became concerned and told the two up-front flight attendants, who decided that the pilot would be insulted if they brought up the issue and remained silent. Meanwhile, passengers in the back were frantically telling the flight attendant in their part of the plane, who picked up the phone and called the pilot. He came back to look at the wing. The plane waited to be de-iced. And in case we need any more evidence of the success of Crew Resource Management, Captain Chesley "Sully" Sullenberger, the hero of the 2009 US Airways flight that landed safely on the Hudson River in New York City after both its engines were damaged by birds, was responsible for developing and implementing the first Crew Resource Management used at the airline. It seems to have served him—and his passengers—well.

Observing how pilots work in real situations is a key part of aviation safety initiatives. With the Line Operations Safety Audit, or LOSA, trained experts sit as a team in a cockpit during a flight and watch the pilots, precisely recording how they react to threats to safety and error. All the material collected is confidential, aggregated, and crunched, to see where training can be improved. Over the past decade or so, since LOSA was introduced, thousands of flights have been observed, and an average of two threats—such as mountains or buildings, adverse weather, or aircraft malfunctions—is reported each flight. Interestingly, an average of two errors is also found per flight. These errors can be consciously failing to adhere to procedures, such as doing a checklist from memory rather than using written documents; it can be procedural, such as putting the wrong entry in the flight management computer; it can be misunderstanding something like altitude clearance; or it can be simply not having the knowledge or skill to do something correctly. This whole strategy of looking at errors shows why it is so important in all workplaces—not just in aviation or medicine—to systemically collect information about mistakes, because without that information, no one knows what causes errors or how to resolve them.

And different errors require different interventions; if a pilot lacks certain skills or knowledge, more technical training is needed, while decision and communication errors might mean more team training is needed. Deliberately circumventing protocol could indicate a general culture of noncompliance, or the pilot's perception of invulnerability, or poor procedures in place.

Another way the aviation industry gathers information is with the aid of "lessons learned" databases. These databases can take many forms, but the general idea is that pilots and crew members put their gaffes out there on a company or government site, and they receive some protection for self-confessing. The Aviation Safety Reporting System is a classic example that was initiated by a tragic error: in 1974 TWA 514 heading from Indianapolis to Dulles Airport crashed into a mountain. All eighty-five passengers and seven crew members were killed. Investigators later found out that air traffic controllers had told the crew, "You are cleared for approach," a new phrase for the crew and one that was relatively ambiguous. Did it mean that the plane could start landing immediately, or did it mean once it reached a navigation fix—that is, farther beyond the mountain—it could begin landing? Recordings show that the pilots weren't exactly sure what the controllers meant, and in hindsight, it is not clear why they didn't just radio, "Does that mean we go down?" But they didn't ask, to horrific effect.

"When the National Transportation Safety Board investigated, it found out that crews from United said, 'The same thing happened to us, but we missed the mountain,'" Linda Connell, program director of NASA's Aviation Safety Reporting System, told me. "The FAA had also reported other near misses. The FAA administrator said he was tired of going to the site of accidents and hearing people say, 'We knew this was going to happen.'" So the FAA decided to establish a system for anyone involved in aviation to report problems in an effort to avoid another TWA tragedy. The only problem was, after six months, there were no reports. "People said, 'Are you crazy? You're the cop. No one is going to report to you,'" Connell said. NASA came into the picture, bringing together experts in various fields, including psychologists and doctors, and in four days developed the concept of the Aviation Safety Reporting System, with limited immunity as part of the deal. In the following decades, the system has been tweaked but has pretty much remained the same; now pilots can use the Internet—and about 50,000 reports come in annually—but in the pre-Internet days (remember those?) pilots could get a paper with government postage and were told to mail it in if something occurred.

What has been so effective about the procedure is that the developers really thought out how to best use mistakes to solve problems by going down two different tracks: a learning track and an accountability track. The Aviation Safety Reporting System does not report incidents to the FAA, but if a problem is discovered separately by the FAA or the National Transportation Safety Board, it can go all the way to a disciplinary hearing. If the pilot is found to have violated an FAA regulation, then a punishment might be recommended—say a sixty-day license suspension—*and* if the pilot self-reported within ten days of the incident, he could claim immunity. But the immunity is good only once every five years. "If we make accountability part of learning, then we will not hear any more about learning," Connell said. Experts are also constantly trolling through the reports to discover if the same trouble is reported multiple times. For example, there was a problem with cockpit seat lock failure. As pilots were thrusting forward, their seats were flying backward. Through the system the FAA, the seat manufacturer, and those who might be affected were notified. The lock was fixed.

Selective incidents are published anonymously in a monthly online bulletin titled *Callback*, to be shared with anyone who wants to log on to the website. Some examples: A pilot thought he was becoming ill while cruising at 26,000 feet, but in fact, the aircraft wasn't maintaining cabin pressure. He had sunglasses on, so he couldn't see that the cabin altitude warning light was on. After some confusion and use of an oxygen mask, he discovered that he had pulled the wrong valve with his pant leg, leading to the problem. Two other pilots offer stories that warn what a disorderly cockpit can do. One recounted that because some procedure publications were wedged between the landing-gear extension and the floor, a landing-gear circuit was tripped. Another told of a tissue box that slid under his foot and the rudder pedals, causing the rudder to jam. Oops.

Critics say that with ASRS, the information is not identified in the databases and doesn't come directly back to the airline or the control center. Therefore, it cannot be acted on promptly and is not as effective as it could be. In response, in the late 1990s, American Airlines started a voluntary private-public program called Aviation Safety Action Program, or ASAP; it soon was adopted by other airlines and now more than seventy carriers participate. It is another way to get information confidentially in hopes that further accidents can be avoided. With ASAP, when a problem occurs—a possible violation of FAA regulations or any general safety concern—and is reported, a three-person tribunal, comprising a union and company representatives and someone from the FAA, reviews the issue. If needed, a pilot can be called in for further training. And other professions have instituted similar programs: NASA, along with the Department of Veterans Affairs, as I noted before, established a Patient Safety Reporting System; NASA and the FAA helped design the National Firefighters Near Miss Reporting System; and,

Connell proudly told me, the newest program, the Confidential Close Call Reporting System for railroad workers, was just set up in 2010. Everything from poor communication that led to injuries or assumptions about responsibility that could have gotten someone killed are reported, along with how they were handled and what lesson was learned.

Such systems are, of course, not a panacea. Jerry Wellman, who has worked for thirty-two years as an engineer and teaches at Embry-Riddle Aeronautical University, critiques the lessons-learned databases, saying they involve so many variables that it is hard to make them effective. The choice of the lessons included in a database, how they are written about, and the time element— if they are reported immediately or six months later—all affect how a mistake is viewed. Too often such databases "capture current anxieties rather than lessons learned," Wellman said. They are good for single-loop learning, perhaps not much for double-loop learning. But as we know, in many cases, single-loop learning is what is needed—I don't want to dive into the psyche of why a pilot might have a messy cockpit; I want it cleaned up so a stray tissue box doesn't cause the plane to crash.

So has this worked? While it is impossible to draw a direct line between cause and effect, data from the National Transportation Safety Board show that between 1975 and 2008, the number of accidents per 100,000 flight hours for U.S. carriers (that is, scheduled airliners) dropped from 0.53 to 0.0025. It may be easier to understand this way: in 1975, there were twenty-nine accidents—with 122 people killed—per about 5 million hours flown by American carriers. In 2008, there were twenty accidents per 18 million hours flown, and no fatalities. Now, that doesn't mean, of course, that the accidents dropped in a nice linear fashion. The years 2007 and 2008 were the first in aviation history without a single airline passenger death in a U.S. carrier crash. But then in 2009, forty-nine people were killed when a flight from Newark to Buffalo crashed. This is not to diminish such tragedies, but the general trend is in the right direction. In addition, observation and data collected about attitudes from a number of organizations indicated that CRM, with certain limitations, has had a positive effect in changing aviation culture.

What can we learn from aviation's lessons? That in developing systems to avoid errors we can't just go on assumptions, but need to closely observe and collect all sorts of information to truly understand how people involved think and operate. If, as we saw, many pilots believe that fatigue and stress don't adversely affect their ability to fly a plane, then it will certainly be difficult to get them to change their ways or seek assistance when needed. In any workplace, the first step in identifying why mistakes happen and attempting to prevent them is to pinpoint these kinds of embedded beliefs—and the corresponding values, such as it's not manly to admit exhaustion—and then use hard data to show why such beliefs and values can be harmful. The next step, as Crew Resource Management has shown us, is to find ways to solve those problems, not in a cookie-cutter fashion, but with a flexible and ever-evolving approach. And these types of tools aren't just limited to companies with human resource departments and consultants. Even at home, in our little corporations—our families—we can use these lessons to try to avoid misunderstandings and mistakes.

"We have to believe we are going to commit errors and develop systems to address them," Robert Sumwalt said. "I screw up all the time, but I'm hypervigilant. If I know I'm going to take the laundry to the cleaner and I might forget it, I hang it on the door." His wife, on the other hand, he bemoaned, has not learned from certain experiences. While leaving from a vacation at Hilton Head, his wife packed all the dirty clothes in garbage bags. Being the helpful husband . . . "you can see where I'm going," he said. He, of course, threw them out, and there went their nice clothes. But his wife *still* puts their dirty clothes in garbage bags after a vacation. "She's of the mentality that she won't commit errors," he said. "I believe what Ralph Waldo Emerson said, 'Learn from the mistakes of others, because you can't live long enough to make them all yourself.' "

6.

BLAMING YOU, BLAMING ME

AFTER EXAMINING MISTAKES THAT AMPUTATED WRONG limbs and crashed planes, it's hard to remember why I've felt so bad about the relatively minor professional mistakes I've made. But I know I've felt really awful, because after I began writing this book, I made another error in an article and ran a correction (a small public embarrassment). Unfortunately, there had been a slew of such mistakes recently in my section of the newspaper, and a senior editor was not amused. He sent out a terse e-mail to me and other writers who had goofed recently, demanding an accounting. I explained how it had happened, apologized, and said I would do all I could to prevent it in the future. No big deal. Except for me. Upon reading the message, I felt devastated. I was sick to my stomach, sure I would lose my job, terrified that I would make a mistake in my next column. I didn't want to write again, so I would never have to go through this again. I know this for certain, because I wrote down those feelings, thinking it might be helpful for this book. And it was, because although my self-flagellation passed pretty quickly, it's surprising to see how deeply I was wounded at the time.

Yet I know I am not alone in such reactions. When I mention to people that one aspect of mistakes that I am researching is gender differences, most people—okay, to be honest, most women—nod knowingly. There is a general consensus that women agonize more and blame themselves more and that men get over their blunders faster and tend to point their fingers at others. But is there any research to back up the belief that men and women actually respond differently to their screwups?

As I started investigating this and asked experts in the field about research on gender differences in reacting to and learning from mistakes, I kept getting the same response: basically, "I'm not aware of anything, but it sure sounds interesting." So I started piecing together material that might not pertain directly to the issue but would help illuminate it. Much (*much!*) has been written generally on how men and women talk about and react to the same events in very dissimilar ways, and why that might be; how men and women are influenced differently by tentative or by aggressive tones; how they react differently to feedback and criticism; and the dissimilar ways they view transgressions and forgiveness. Even the distinctive ways men and women use computer software reflect their attitudes toward mistakes.

Now I know that discussing differences between men and

women can be as perilous as talking about racial or ethnic distinctions. It is so easy to wander into the realm of stereotype, to, even with the best of intentions, sound patronizing and make one gender, race, or culture sound "good" and another "bad." First let me state that while the research is very interesting and enlightening, of course it does not apply to *everyone.* I often found myself thinking, *Oh, how true,* but then also noting that *Wow, John isn't like that at all—or Margaret—or Nancy.* I emphasize what seems to be obvious because I'm always amazed, in the responses to my column, how many people skip over the words "tend to" or "in some cases" and blast away at me as if I were declaring scientific research to be the Ten Commandments.

Views on gender differences have evolved—and still are evolving. Before the 1970s, common wisdom was that women are more able to express and share their emotions than men, they're more intuitive and empathetic, and they put more importance on relations with each other. In general, these differences were not considered positives, particularly in the business and political arenas. Women may be "natural" caretakers, but they were also seen as weak and irrational. In the 1970s and 1980s, some of this changed, particularly with the 1982 publication of *In a Different Voice,* by Harvard professor Carol Gilligan. Among other things, "feminine" characteristics were reframed in a positive manner—women were caring and connected, a welcome difference from the more aggressive and combative male.

Gilligan's writings have had a powerful impact on gender studies, "turning female difference into superiority," say Myra and David Sadker in their seminal book *Failing at Fairness: How Our*

Schools Cheat Girls. Men and women were still vastly different, according to this thesis, even if who was better had shifted. In the 1990s, books like *Men Are from Mars, Women Are from Venus* reinforced this idea that the two sexes are virtually alien to each other. And more recently, using, and sometimes misusing, studies of gender differences, a vocal minority insists that girls and boy are so genetically diverse, from their hearing ability to their activity levels, that they shouldn't even be educated together.

But now, in the second decade of the twenty-first century, psychologists and neuroscientists are far less willing to draw such a bright line separating the two sexes. As neuroscientist Lise Eliot states: "Scientists themselves no longer pit nature and nurture against each other as distinct, warring entities, but appreciate that they are intricately interwoven. Obviously boys and girls come into the world with a smattering of different genes and hormones. But actually growing a boy from those XY cells or a girl from XX cells requires constant interactions with the environment, which begins in the prenatal soup and continues through all the dance recitals, baseball games, middle-school science classes and cafeteria dramas that ceaselessly reinforce our gender-divided society."

Not all would agree we are that gender-divided a society anymore; many would say that male/female stereotypes are rapidly disappearing. When more women than men are enrolled in colleges, when we've seen the campaign of the first electable woman presidential candidate, when women are routinely members of cabinets and Supreme Court justices and CEOs (all right, not anywhere near in the numbers that men are), is it useful or even true to still talk about "masculine" and "feminine" attributes? Jean Twenge, author of *Generation Me*, for example, gathered over one hundred samples of 28,920 college students on two questionnaires that measured stereotypically masculine and feminine traits. The "masculine" scale items included words like "competitive," "independent," "self-reliant," "forceful," and "ambitious." The average 1990s college woman reported that she had more "masculine" traits than 80 percent of Boomer college women in the early 1970s. The change was so large that by the early 1990s men's and women's scores on the scale of so-called "masculine" traits were indistinguishable.

There is no doubt that girls and women in their teens and twenties are far different from their mothers and certainly from their grandmothers. But we all know what hasn't changed. Far more women than men are the stay-at-home or primary parent in nuclear families. Single-parent families are overwhelmingly headed by women. For those who work, statistics show that one year out of college, women earn 80 percent as much as men; ten years later that drops to only 69 percent. That's controlling for hours, occupation, and parenthood. It is also important to note that women in Twenge's research are self-reporting how assertive they feel personally. That's quite different from how others perceive their assertiveness. "Although people may be more accepting of women's assertiveness than they were decades ago, they are still likely to penalize this more from women than from men," said Amanda Diekman, a psychology professor at Miami University who has researched and written a great deal on this subject. Also, "women, or at least some women in male-dominated contexts, may have a sense that their position or success is still somewhat fragile. They may have some awareness that their mistakes might actually be more costly than similar male peers' mistakes."

In addition, men and women—at least in the heterosexual arena—are expected to act a certain way, whether or not they actually feel that way. I think most of us are more accepting, or at least less surprised, when a woman cries than when a man does. We expect women to sympathize more or at least act more sympathetic than men. And yes, while women are caught in the double bind of either being too aggressive or not aggressive enough, men have their own double bind—it is more acceptable for a girl or woman to act and even dress similarly to a man than for a man to display overt feminine qualities.

Where does all this leave us? Confused as usual? So let's see if we can sort some of this out by looking at what research does exist. I've mentioned Patricia Bryans's work before; now let's look at it more in depth. Bryans, when working at Newcastle Business School at Northumbria University in England, researched management development, gender and emotion, and women in management, and conducted one of the few studies directly looking at how men and women react to mistakes in the workplace. Although by no means comprehensive, it does provide some interesting insights. At first Bryans surveyed forty-five men and forty-five women from thirty to fifty years old and in professions including teachers, social workers, managers, police officers, human resources managers, and health professionals. She then talked in depth with twelve of those surveyed. Interestingly, Bryans did not set out to study gender differences in mistakes, but rather the distinctions emerged from a more general study investigating mistakes made by individual professionals at work. As she looked more closely, she found that "women tend to internalize and personalize the experience of their mistakes, taking them 'to heart' and continuing to live with them long after the event. Rather than looking to find fault externally, women blamed themselves. For men, by contrast, feelings were more likely to be externalized, directed outwards through anger at others, blaming 'pressures' of the system or emphasizing the particularities of the context in which they were operating." Men were also less likely to retain strong emotions after making a mistake.

"Throughout the data, men told 'tidy' stories; generally they found mistakes difficult to recall and were certainly brief and more concise in their responses," Bryans wrote. "Through their stories they were able to rewrite their biographies to show themselves in a better light and produce a 'retelling' of their mistake which is balanced and acceptable. However, the women told 'messy' stories in which they continued to blame themselves and to speak emotionally about their mistakes." For example, typical responses from men when asked about their past mistake were, "I feel philosophical about it now—a learning experience. It seemed like a good idea at the time, was probably years ahead of my time in some ways, but misjudged the organizational culture." In contrast, one woman stated that "although it happened some years ago, it is probably the worst mistake I have made at work. I am usually careful to avoid mistakes so I was particularly upset about this one at the time and it has remained in my memory." Not all women fell into neat categories, of course. Kristy, a retail manager who left some cash unsecured during a busy period, even years later feels terrible: "I knew I should not have done it. I should be perfect, set an example. I felt I was slipping, making too many mistakes. It did not occur to me to question the number of hours or the pressure." But Annette, a health professional who made a mistake in the type of treatment she gave a patient, did not speak of strong emotions, but said the mistake certainly affected her current practice in a positive way; Annette uses the story of her own mistake to teach her junior doctors the importance of honesty.

In the questionnaires, twenty-two women—but only four men—said they were still living with their mistakes. And when responding to the question "How did you feel about your mistake?" there were sixty-four mentions among women of feeling stupid, silly or foolish, embarrassed, mortified, devastated, gutted or terrible, and losing weight or sleep. Only twenty men used the same terms. "These findings reflect women's understanding of mistakes as 'doing wrong,'" Bryans wrote. In contrast, twice as many men were angry at others as were annoyed or angry at themselves. And among the women respondents, there were twenty-three mentions of owning up to the mistake and ten mentions of apologizing. Only four men mentioned acknowledging the error, and two said they apologized. Of course, it is possible that at least some of the men actually felt worse about a mistake than they let on, but felt it was unmanly to expose their feelings so baldly.

While, as I said, it is difficult to find gender studies related directly to mistakes, research that focuses on how men and women differ in responding to feedback provides another way to gain insight into this area. If we fear negative feedback, we'll fear making mistakes—and likewise, if we want only positive feedback, we'll avoid blunders at all costs. One study asked undergraduates—149 women and 62 men—to complete a self-esteem survey. They were then provided with hypothetical performance feedback from two professors, one for a computer program and one for an English paper. Remember, the participants did not write the computer program or English paper—they were by unknown sources. But the undergraduates were asked to imagine that they had received the feedback for their own efforts. In some cases the work was praised by the professor (such as "Your paper gets at the heart of the issues at hand. You have presented a well-reasoned analysis. Your ideas are clearly focused"), while in others it was criticized ("This is a poorly written paper. It does not get at the heart of the issues at hand. You have presented a poorly reasoned analysis. Your ideas are very unfocused"). The participants were then asked to imagine that they had received the feedback and to assign a letter grade to the work. Some of the findings? While there was no gender difference in happiness after receiving positive feedback, women were unhappier and less confident than men when they got the negative feedback. But, interestingly enough, there was no evidence that women perceived the feedback as more accurate than the men did. Nonetheless, women, research has shown, tend to be more dejected by negative feedback than buoyed up by positive responses.

What about how women are viewed by others? Women are often more tentative in presenting their views, often adding caveats like "I think . . ." or "Maybe I'm wrong, but. . . ." They also tend to sound more questioning even when making a flat statement. This research, authored by Linda Carli, a psychology professor at Wellesley College in Massachusetts, used fifty-nine women undergraduates and fifty-nine men undergraduates. (By the way, one researcher told me that, in general, way too many college students are used in research studies—but they're just so darn convenient for professors.) The participants had been surveyed on whether they agreed or disagreed with the statements "The drinking age should be lowered to eighteen in Massachusetts" (where they lived) and "The federal government should provide free day care for working parents." Half were given one topic, half the other, and the two groups were broken into pairs—some women only, some men only, some mixed—in which one person agreed with the statement and the other disagreed. Each pair was asked to discuss the issue for ten minutes. Then the members of each pair were separated and asked to indicate their opinion on a 10-point scale from "completely agree" to "completely disagree."

Researchers videotaped the discussions (although the participants were unaware of it), and a man and woman who didn't know the purpose of the study analyzed all the videotapes and recorded each person, noting how many times he or she interrupted, used disclaimers like "I'm no expert" or "I guess" or "I may not understand this," or tag questions such as "Many teenagers die in drunk driving accidents, *don't they*?" and other phrases. It turned out in this experiment that women spoke more tentatively when interacting with men than when interacting with women. And that proved to be more useful in convincing men. Huh? Well, men were more influenced by women who spoke cautiously than by those who spoke assertively. But women were more influenced by other women who were more forceful rather than hesitant.

Carli's study is from 1990. Hasn't a lot changed over the past two decades or so? Of course it has, but maybe not as much as we think. A 2004 study found that women are much less likely to be viewed as experts than men—even when they have the requisite knowledge.

In an experiment, 143 undergraduate business students completed a questionnaire in which they had to rank twelve items based on their importance in surviving an Australian bushfire. The participants read the information provided about the situation and watched a videotape simulation of the bushfire, which set the context, showing a group of consultants considering the very same situation. The students were told to think about themselves as one of the members of the consulting group shown on the videotape and rank the items needed for survival in terms of most important to least important. The information was compared with what experts have determined is most needed to survive in a bushfire.

The participants were then randomly assigned to groups of three to five individuals, most of them mixed between men and women, with some majority men and some majority women. The group member with the best individual score prior to the group discussion was identified as the expert. The researchers found that not only were women's opinions more often disregarded than men's, but women who had no particular know-how in the area were viewed more favorably than women with greater capability—because the women without expertise tended to go along with the status quo rather than challenge it. "When women contribute unique information that is not demonstrably correct, they are likely to be viewed as less competent than men contributing similar information," the researchers said. Finally, women tended to evaluate themselves more negatively than men even when their performances were equal. "It is not actual expertise but perceived expertise that conveys power and status," the researchers said.

So what have we learned here? Yes, women tend to agonize more about their mistakes, at least in the workplace; women often speak more hesitantly to men than to other women, and in fact women who communicate tentatively are often received better by men than those who speak assertively; men tend to listen more to women who agree with rather than oppose the status quo. So there is less room for women who speak up, who demonstrate their expertise, who are willing to disturb the status quo, who take more risks and therefore make more mistakes. And women, fearing their mistakes may be judged more harshly then men's, are far more reluctant to risk them. In addition, women may steer clear of the possibility of making mistakes because they tend to be more affected, more cast down by them than men. If something causes you pain, you'll do a lot to avoid it.

Of course, the question of where the mistake happens and in what context makes a difference. The workplace or classroom is one thing, but what about at home or in a venue where women are expected to rule? Does a man feel bad if he forgets the diaper bag? If he lets the rice burn? Maybe yes and maybe no, but how bad people feel about their mistakes also depends on whether they're *expected* to be the experts or not—and going back to gender, if it's something a man or woman is "supposed" to be good at. It depends on how central the issue is to your self-concept, according to author Carol Tavris, who also wrote *The Mismeasure of Woman*. Men "are okay feeling stupid about dance lessons, but not about making a bad investment."

But it is not enough to say that, yup, men and women are different. The question is why, because without knowing why, how can we bridge the gap? Are these masculine and feminine traits something the sexes are born with? (How many times have I heard a mother say, "I give my son a Barbie doll and he turns it into a gun"?) I remember volunteering at a lunch activity in my son's classroom where we did a craft project. The girls sat at one table, dutifully coloring and folding their papers, while the boys were loudly throwing paper and crayons at each other. One boy even started an auction, offering to sell his project to the highest bidder. Being the mother of boys, I was fascinated. Aha—boys and girls really *are* different. But we also know that socialization and the messages society sends—even liberal, "I let my boy have a doll and wear pink if he wants" parents—tend to reinforce these differences. A 2000 study, for example, asked mothers of eleven-month-old babies to estimate their child's crawling performance down ramps and slopes. The mothers could adjust the ramp to the level they thought their baby would be comfortable with. Mothers of girls underestimated their babies' performance, while mothers of boys overestimated their abilities. In truth, girls and boys showed identical levels of motor performance.

I am not going to lay these arguments to rest (if I did, I could move on to the Middle East). But I know it's important to walk the line between acknowledging that differences do exist, yet not drawing exaggerated distinctions. As Tavris writes, we need to "resist the temptation to see the work in opposites. Western ways of thinking emphasize dualisms and opposites and pose many questions of human life in fruitless either-or terms. Are we rational or emotional creatures? Will we win or lose? Is this decision good or bad? . . . Are we shaped by nature or nurture, mind or environment? Are we masculine or feminine?" I will not get bogged down in the question of how big a role nature plays versus nurture, but it is pretty clear that both biological differences and culture play parts in developing gender differences and, even more important, that those attributes that we identify as gender are constantly shifting.

Lise Eliot, associate professor in the Department of Neuroscience at the Chicago Medical School, takes a hard look at many of the realities and myths surrounding gender differences in her fascinating book *Pink Brain, Blue Brain.* Her point is that there are innate genetic differences in boys and girls from birth—such as maturation rate, sensory processing, activity level, fussiness, and toys with which they like to play—but these differences are not as great as we think, and by emphasizing them or assuming they can't be changed we create divides where they don't have to be. "The male-female differences that have the most impact—cognitive skills, such as speaking, reading, math and mechanical ability; and interpersonal skills, such as aggression, empathy, risk taking and competitiveness—are heavily shaped by learning. Yes, they germinate from basic instincts and initial biases in brain function, but each of these traits is massively amplified by the different sorts of practice, role models and reinforcement that boys and girls are exposed to from birth onward." Boys and girls are different, but, Eliot says, we inevitably stereotype them when they're fresh out of the womb. Some of the interesting studies Eliot mentions are gender-disguised: baby boys are dressed as girls and vice versa. In one study, girls were described as angry or distressed by adults who thought they were boys more often than they were by adults who knew they were really girls. Also when adults thought they were looking at girl babies (really boys disguised as girls), they more often saw them as more joyful or interested than when they viewed them as boys.

Dozens of other gender-disguised studies also show that people interact differently with babies based on what they think their sex is—such as in more physical ways with boys and more nuanced, verbal interactions with girls.

What start as innate differences lead us to treat boys and girls differently, which then exacerbates the divide. For example, Eliot notes that newborn boys tend to be fussier than newborn girls, more emotionally fragile. So parents often respond more positively to girls, who are a bit happier, but more negatively to boys, shushing them or ignoring them. The point might not be to dampen boys' expressiveness and contribute to suppression of emotion later on, but that might be the result. Rather than acknowledge the different weaknesses of each sex and work to overcome them, we embrace them, and thereby create even greater divides. Eliot writes: "Unlike a generation ago, when parents actually worried about stereotyping their children, the new focus on nature seems to be encouraging parents to indulge in sex differences even more avidly. The more we parents hear about hard-wiring and biological programming, the less we bother tempering our pink or blue fantasies." We "start attributing every skill or deficit to innate sex differences." For example, if we say, "Your son's a late talker? Don't worry, he's a boy," or "Your daughter is struggling with math? It's okay, she's very artistic," we are not simply mouthing innocuous platitudes. "There's enormous danger in this exaggeration of sex differences, first and foremost in the expectations it creates among parents, teachers and children themselves," Eliot warns. She emphasizes the amazing plasticity of the brain, which is another way of looking at Carol Dweck's growth mindset concepts. "Both sexes have their strengths and vulnerabilities, their easy and troublesome periods while growing up. The reason for studying sex differences is not to tally up who's winning or losing, but to learn how to compensate for them early on while children's brains are still at their most malleable," Eliot writes. The real metaphor for men and women, she suggests, should not be living on two different planets, but the more prosaic—yet infinitely more comforting—idea that men are from North Dakota and women are from South Dakota.

So how do we exacerbate these differences? Take something as simple as sports. While a greater number of girls play on sports teams now than in the past, it's still more the purview of boys. Community and school sports, whatever their drawbacks, teach children about losing and rejection pretty quickly. My sons have been chosen for some teams they tried out for and not for others. They've had great seasons that showed what can be achieved when a team pulls together, and seasons where their teams couldn't win a game. When my older son, Ben, was six and seven, he was devastated by loss. I dreaded the after-game tears. But as he grew older, he took it more and more in stride. Some of that is maturation, I know, but some of it is just learning to understand that sports—and life—are all about the ups and downs.

The way boys and girls are treated in classrooms throughout their school years also no doubt has an impact on their willingness—or lack thereof—to speak out, take risks, and make mistakes. In their 1994 book, Myra and David Sadker look at the largely subconscious ways teachers—even good, thoughtful teachers who are very aware of overt sexism—treat boys and girls differently. While some of this has no doubt changed, much is still relevant. Through extensive research, the Sadkers show that teachers spend more time with boys than girls, call on them more, and give them more precise and helpful feedback. Even the fact that boys tend to be criticized more than girls is not a negative—boys learn to handle it better than girls. Also, criticism is often subtly different for the sexes. The Sadkers point out that when boys are chastised, it is often for behavior, or for lack of effort—such as, "If you tried harder, you could have done better." Girls, on the other hand, tend to be criticized for their performance, such as, "I'm afraid you didn't do well on that math test." Missing, they write, "is the vote of confidence, the attribution to effort, the suggestion that girls have the brain power and can do it if they try a little more."

In case we think that's all in the nasty old past of the twentieth century, that great cultural mirror *The Simpsons* says it ain't so. In a 2006 episode of the animated television program, Lisa and Bart's school is segregated after Principal Skinner says publicly that boys are better than girls at math and science (a not coincidental reference to former Harvard University president Lawrence Summers's comment in 2005 that boys may have more innate ability in math and science than girls). The girls' math lessons consist of gentle music playing with images of mathematical symbols floating by; the girls don't do actual mathematics but discuss feelings, such as whether the number seven is odd or just different. Lisa abandons the girls' side and sneaks over to the boys' section, which looks like a prison in the middle of a riot. Excited by seeing a class with real problems, she disguises herself as a boy the next day and goes to the boys' class. She is even pleased when the teacher bluntly tells her she is wrong about a certain math problem, and she thinks, *Oh my God, I was wrong. And by being corrected, I learned.*

Another reason for these differences between men and women? One that is somewhat uncomfortable to acknowledge but is still true—the status disparity between the two sexes. A number of experts in this field argue, and I would agree, that many of these "female" tendencies—speaking tentatively, picking up on nonverbal messages, cooperating rather than competing—come from the long-standing status difference between the two sexes. Women, subordinate for so long, learned the language of subservience. What would happen to your language if you played a subordinate role in society? Carol Tavris asks. "You would learn to persuade and influence, rather than assert and demand. You would become skilled at anticipating what others wanted or needed (hence, 'women's intuition'). You would learn how to cultivate communication, cooperation, attention to news and feelings about others (what men call gossip). In short, you would develop a 'women's language.' But the characteristics of such a language develop primarily from a power imbalance, not from an inherent deficiency or superiority in communication skills, emotion or nurturance. They develop whenever there is a status inequity, as can be seen by the languages of working-class Cockneys conversing with their employers, blacks conversing with whites or prisoners conversing with guards." And such difference persists in the twenty-first century, where jobs traditionally held by females—nurses, teachers, social workers—are considered lower status and are often lower paid than traditionally male jobs.

This ties into Linda Carli's work, where men listened more to women who spoke tentatively; she postulated that status differences played a role in why a woman speaking to men was considered more influential if she spoke tentatively, even if she was less knowledgeable and competent than a woman speaking assertively. "The low status [people] must first demonstrate they have no desire to compete for status before their ideas will be considered by higher status individuals," she wrote. "In this study, men perceived a tentative woman to be more trustworthy and likable than an assertive woman, whereas women judged her to be less likable and trustworthy." And just to reinforce what I mentioned before, the opposite was true if a woman was speaking to an audience of women—they viewed a more faltering speaker as less trustworthy, less likable, and less competent than a more self-assured speaker.

Now I think it's clear, from reading research and just from my own observations, that some of the lines between the sexes are blurring: the teenage girls and young women I meet are often confident, capable individuals who would laugh at the idea of feeling inferior to boys. They play sports intensely and they pursue their studies and career goals aggressively. My local public high school proudly boasts being home to state championship teams in both girls' field hockey and boys' baseball. But the boys got a town parade; the girls didn't.

While society is changing, the elusive goal of being the good girl, the nice, smart, flawless girl, is still alive and well. Rachel Simmons, who runs the Girl Leadership Institute, talks about a certain segment of teenage girls today terrified of not being perfect, of, yes, making mistakes. In *The Curse of the Good Girl*, Simmons writes: "For many girls, criticism is the knowledge that you failed not just some*thing*, but some*one*." Zandra, a sophomore, is quoted as saying that criticism from an adult makes her "feel like I've made [someone] unhappy in some way and that I've upset them, and I, like, take it personally as something I'm doing wrong, and, like, I don't take it as I can do better. I take it more as, like, 'Oh, I did this wrong, how am I ever going to fix it?' type thing." And, worse, their fear of disappointing others means they can't acknowledge mistakes. Isabel, another teenager, says, "You don't ever want to admit to yourself that I'm wrong. . . . Like, disappointing other people around you makes you so upset that you can't even handle it, so you just . . . can't admit you're wrong." The Good Girl persona, Simmons writes, is fixated on projecting an image of faultless performance and appearance. Further complicating matters, she adds, is a peer culture obsessed with cell phones and Facebook, which can record and magnify even the smallest slipups.

What are some of the ways to address these issues? One is to work against some of the natural tendencies of boys and girls. Starting when children are infants, be aware if you are apt to hover more over your girl, warning her to be careful on the playground while letting your boy race around heedlessly. As they get older, talk about feelings and teach empathy, especially with boys. People assume that empathy comes naturally, but it has to be learned and practiced. Don't push the boys out when company comes because they're disruptive, but have them practice their social skills. They don't have to sit through a whole evening, but what about coming in, shaking hands, making eye contact, and exchanging a few words? Encourage activity and some sort of fitness, particularly among girls. In fact, I am a big believer in team sports; I played on my high school volleyball team. I worked my way up from junior varsity to varsity, and while not a star, I contributed and felt part of a team. We lost and we won, but mostly I remember the high-fives after a particularly good spike.

One question that often comes up when discussing this issue is whether girls and boys would be better off if they were educated separately—particularly if we focus on the idea that part of women's fear of criticism and mistakes stems from the different ways teachers react to blunders by each sex. It won't surprise you if I tell you that the debate around single-sex schools is almost as heated as the gender discussion in general, but there is no doubt that the idea is growing in popularity. In 2002, there were eleven public schools in the United States offering either complete single-sex education or segregated classrooms in the same building; by 2009 that grew to 547. Remember, I'm not talking about private schools, but publicly financed ones. So clearly some people think it's a good idea, but not always for the same reasons.

There are those who promote single-sex schools based on exaggerations of minor—and not even proven—biological differences, such as that girls hear better than boys and so need an environment where teachers speak softly, or that boys are better at seeing action while girls are better at seeing color and texture. Then there are those, like Rosemary Salomone, a law professor at St. John's University in New York, who say that, particularly in low-income communities, single-sex schools provide a safe haven that helps students develop greater self-confidence and broader interests. In addition, research has shown that such schools and classes promote less gender-polarized attitudes toward certain subjects—that is, girls are more willing to pursue math and science interests and boys language arts and foreign languages. On the other side of the argument are those who contend that boys and girls grow up to be men and women who have to live and work together in the real world; creating an artificially segregated environment does no one any good. Often, I find, our sympathies—or prejudices—lie with how we ourselves were educated as children.

It's worth noting that even in coed environments, there are ways of addressing the issue of how boys and girls learn and react differently. Rachel Simmons has developed a curriculum called "Nobody's Perfect"—not yet in use—to address some of the fears girls have acknowledging mistakes. Here is one lesson she has prepared for teachers:

THREE REACTIONS TO CONSTRUCTIVE CRITICISM

Explain that you will now explore some of the most common ways people react to constructive criticism.

Ask for a student volunteer to role-play three brief scenes with you. The student will play the part of a soccer coach telling a student (played by you) respectfully that she needs to hustle more and give more time to the team. The coach's comments will be the same in each scene; your lines will change.

REACTION 1: (deny) "What? I have been working *so* hard. I am hustling more than anyone else on the team.

I am constantly backing up the right wing. She never moves!"

REACTION 2: (accept) "You know, I think I've been really distracted. I will see if I can push myself a little more this afternoon."

REACTION 3: (exaggerate) "Fine. So I guess you're saying I'm pretty much the worst player on the team. Whatever. Why should I bother playing, anyway?" (Pretend to cry and storm off.)

Distribute and review the Three Reactions to Constructive Criticism handout. As you go over each reaction, ask girls to match their reaction to one of the role-plays you did.

TALKING POINTS

- *Acceptance is only appropriate when criticism is constructive. If you are being attacked, it's hard not to defend yourself (denial) or take it hard (exaggeration).*
- *Most people do not exclusively react in one way, but they do tend to exhibit one type of reaction more than another.*

PRACTICE

Assign each student a response of "Acceptance," "Denial," or "Exaggeration." Read the examples below and ask different girls to respond to you "in character" as assigned. Make sure to request each of the three responses for each instance of criticism.

EXAMPLES:

- Your teacher says your side conversations during class may bring down your grade.
- Your parent says you were impolite when you texted your friends during dinner.
- Your teammate says you are distracted during the game.
- Your friend says you are often late and she ends up waiting for you.
- Your sister says you borrowed a shirt without asking and she really needed that shirt.
- Your friend texts you that you haven't been there for her. (Speak your response as if you were writing a text message reply.)

Simply understanding that someone of the opposite sex—be it a colleague or spouse—has the tendency to react to mistakes differently can help us. Research has shown some very interesting ways this can work. Take the area of forgiving someone for mistakes or deliberate transgressions. Julie Juola Exline of Case Western Reserve University in Cleveland and three colleagues conducted a number of studies looking at whether people tend to be more forgiving of others if they can imagine themselves capable of committing a similar offense. Exline, like other researchers, wasn't looking for gender differences, but they cropped up. For example, in one study men and women were asked to read a scenario about a hypothetical offense by a college student. Cleverly, the people in the scenario are given ambiguous names—Lee and Chris—so the participants are asked to imagine both people as being of the same gender as the reader. Lee and Chris are roommates, and one night Lee confides in Chris about some very painful childhood memories, but swears Chris to secrecy. A few weeks later, Chris is with some friends and they start gossiping about Lee, and one friend turns to Chris and asks, "Well, you're Lee's roommate, what dirt have you picked up?" Chris then blurts out Lee's secret, and everyone laughs. Inevitably, word gets back to Lee that Chris spilled this information.

Some participants were then asked to recall a similar situation where they revealed something negative and private about someone else. In the control group, the participants simply read the scenario and answered questions about it; in that case men and women did not differ in how forgivable they thought Chris's offense was. Yet men recalling similar misbehavior of their own saw Chris's offense as much more forgivable, "suggesting that the prompt to consider their own misdeed made them less harsh toward the hypothetical offender," Exline said. For women, in contrast, recalling a similar transgression of their own had no effect on forgivability ratings. This was true in other experiments using real-life offenses and in another study where various scenarios were presented, including failing to drop off an urgent job-related letter for a friend at the post office and a babysitter's carelessness that led to a child drinking cleaning fluid. The follow-up experiments all revealed that in general, men tend to feel as vengeful as women, if not more vengeful, if they don't compare the offense they were reading about with their own wrongdoing. Once they did compare their wrongdoing, they became as forgiving as women, but not more so. For women, recalling a similar offense did not make forgiveness more likely. In fact, some studies suggested that for women, recalling a similar offense could have the opposite effect—it sometimes made the women feel bad about themselves, and therefore they judged more harshly. In men, however, the ability to put themselves in another person's shoes seemed to prompt empathy and facilitate forgiveness.

Although Exline's study didn't focus on why men and women react differently, she said one possible explanation is that, "for men, a prompt to empathize tends to be something relatively novel, and it can be really helpful." For women, as we've seen, who tend to empathize more anyhow, "a prompt to empathize may not help if empathizing means focusing attention back on our own transgressions. It might push women into self-focused rumination patterns—which tend to lead to bad moods and not toward transcendent activities like forgiveness."

And here's something concrete that shows that something as seemingly unbiased as software can be changed if the different ways in which men and women react to and learn from mistakes are taken into account. Laura Beckwith, while a graduate student at Oregon State University, discovered that men were more likely than women to use advanced software features, specifically ones that help users find and fix program errors—known as debugging. After looking at thirty years of books and economic papers about gender differences in problem solving and computer use, she focused on one relationship—that between high confidence and success. Many women have less confidence than men in their computer skills. So Beckwith delved into the conundrum in her Ph.D. dissertation, trying to pinpoint and solve the differences. She focused on men's and women's use of debugging tools when writing programs. That sounds pretty advanced to someone like me—I think of programmers as computer professionals—but apparently even amateur users like me write a program when we do something like set up filters for e-mail.

After numerous experiments she found that men's confidence levels didn't matter—some with high confidence avoided the automated debugging tools and relied instead on the system they were more comfortable with, such as editing formulas one by one, while some with low confidence did use them. But with women, only those who were very confident that they could complete the task successfully used the automated debugging tools while those with lower confidence didn't. Ironically, women were often afraid to take the time to learn how to use the tools, thinking it would take too long; however, the amount of time they took editing the problems one by one instead of using the automated system eclipsed any time saved. And studies showed that in reality men and women learned the new features at about the same rate. The problems became a self-fulfilling prophecy, as the women who lacked confidence to use the debugging tools had even more trouble with the programs because they failed to benefit from the tools at their disposal. Beckwith isn't a psychologist, so she wasn't aiming to raise women's confidence levels. Rather, as a computer scientist, she wanted to change the software to make it more appealing to insecure women without alienating others. For example, instead of offering only two choices in the debugging tools—right or wrong—she offered two more choices: "seems right maybe" and "seems wrong maybe." She also used softer colors. Beckwith says that while there is a relationship between the features she developed and increasing some women's computer confidence, whether these are short-term or long-term confidence changes is still under investigation.

While boys and girls and men and women tend to react to mistakes differently, neither sex has a monopoly on the "right" way to cope with mistakes. (I can hear the protests from here.) Rather, we could each take something from the other's playbook. Women, as we see, tend to be more emotionally devastated by errors they make, and dwell on them far longer than men. This can occur for numerous reasons, but in general women—certainly in the workplace—have to face prejudice about their expertise and are more harshly judged if they do something wrong. This can make them more compassionate and understanding when mistakes are made by others and more willing to talk through and learn from blunders. On the other hand, if a great deal of energy is spent in beating oneself up, then there is not much left over to actually learn from mistakes. I'm not advocating blaming "the system," but being able to depersonalize mistakes helps us to view them more objectively and learn whatever lessons can be learned from them. And we can help ourselves by being less self-deprecating and tentative in asserting our thoughts and opinions—even though research has shown that men often react more negatively to women who are self-assured, there is no time like the present to change this pattern. Men, on the other hand, tend to find others at fault and then leave the error hastily behind— or at least appear to. The upside is, they aren't as shaken up by mistakes and thus can be more willing to take risks. The downside is that not much learning can take place if one doesn't realistically look at how the problem occurred and what can be done to prevent it in the future.

We've seen, however, that in response to these differences, we don't have to throw up our hands and fall back on that old cliché of Mars and Venus. We can start as parents, coaches, and teachers by working hard to avoid even the most benign stereotypes. I'm not advocating some culture of oppressive political correctness, but rather a greater awareness of how we respond to boys and girls differently, especially when correcting mistakes and criticizing. Are we subconsciously encouraging our girls to fall into the trap of wanting to appear perfect? Do we assume, without even realizing it, that our boys just can't be as caring and social as their sisters?

In the workplace, we can use some of the findings from research to create a more empathetic dialogue. Julie Exline's experiments, for example, demonstrate that men, when confronted with another's error, tend to judge others less severely when asked to recall a similar mistake that they themselves made. We can acknowledge that men and women often have different mistake-handling skills. The point, however, is not to underscore them, but—through some understanding of what they are and why they might be there—to diminish them. To create a world in which it is safe for both men *and* women to make mistakes.

7.

You Say Mistake,
I Say Lesson

It is easy to assume that our approach to mistakes—whatever that may be—is universal. But that's not true. Our response to errors grows out of deeply embedded cultural beliefs and values—beliefs and values we're often not even consciously aware of. I've always found cultural comparisons to be fascinating, largely because they teach us that there are so many different ways to view things that we often consider immutable. Even now, in an era of increasing globalization—which often translates as Westernization—and the far-reaching hand of the Internet, cultural differences are still deeply embedded.

Geert Hofstede, an influential Dutch psychologist whose work has helped shape cross-cultural research, notes that we shouldn't confuse *practices* and *values*. A young Turk may drink Coke and text his friends on his cell phone just like his American counterpart, but that doesn't mean his basic values—his fundamental feelings about life and about other people—are necessarily similar. Hofstede talks of an "onion" model in which practices are the outer layer or visible part of the culture while values are the core—more difficult to see and much more difficult to change. These values are shaped at many levels: national, regional, ethnic, religious, language, gender, social class, generation, and, for those who are employed, by organizations and corporations. And even though people in different countries may appear to be pretty much the same as we are, if we dig a little deeper, we may find more dissimilarities than similarities.

While researching this chapter, I found that most of the comparative work available relating in any way to errors and mistakes compared North American and Asian—primarily Japanese—cultures. This is for a few reasons: Unlike people in most countries (the United States and Canada excepted), the Japanese have already done quite a bit of research on psychology, so it is much simpler for researchers to build on those theories and ideas, rather than start from scratch. It's also, for logistical reasons, easier to study Japan because it is a highly industrialized society with an extensive university system, and students make up the vast majority of subjects in all psychological studies. In addition, North Americans are very interested in emulating the success of Japan's education system, or at least Japanese success on international standardized tests.

I also realize that strikingly different cultures exist not only outside the United States, but inside it as well, and that identifying one group as Americans diminishes the wide variations of religion, class, race, and ethnic origin within this country. Unfortunately, however, I found very little research comparing responses to mistakes among different American strata, and therefore, as important as I believe these distinctions might be, they aren't something I was able to pursue. That said, I also don't want to imply that comparing Asian and North American cultures isn't useful. While Asian societies may adapt certain aspects of culture that we're so happy to export, they often mold them to fit their own customs and philosophy. For example, although baseball is wildly popular in Japan, when looked at closely, it is played with a radically different philosophy. In terms of individualism, community, and perceptions of success and failure, Asian society is very distinct from ours—unlike, say, most European countries—and provides a valuable framework to look at these issues outside our normal prism.

One of the main differences, broadly speaking, is that Japan is oriented toward the community and the group, while the United States is a highly individualistic society. Hazel Markus, professor of psychology at Stanford University, explained it to me this way: "You don't feel your performance is a function just of you and what's inside you. [In a Japanese school] the reality is interdependence of people—my behavior is a function of you and yours of mine." Making a mistake, therefore, isn't a reflection of your lack of ability or intelligence, but simply that you haven't learned something yet. "You have to show you're trying hard—they have this expression for 'facing the desk,'" she says.

This approach to mistakes reveals itself very early. In her book *Educating Hearts and Minds: Reflections on Japanese Preschool and*

Elementary Education, Catherine C. Lewis recounts feeling uncomfortable at first "when children's mistakes were bared for all to see. Don't children feel humiliated when they put an incorrect math solution on the blackboard? Or when their drawings are singled out as looking like stick figures?" But Lewis noted that there was a reason this wasn't considered mortifying—the community sense of cooperation that dominated classroom values. "Often teachers asked for a show of hands from students who had obtained correct and incorrect answers to a problem and the show of hands for incorrect answers was often substantial. Students who criticized their own thinking were warmly acknowledged, as were students who explained the thinking behind their mistakes, so that, as one teacher said, 'Everyone in the class can learn from the students who tried to solve the problem this way.' Mistakes became opportunities to help classmates rather than failures to be hidden."

James Stigler, a UCLA psychology professor who has written extensively on Asian and American teaching practices, says that "for Americans, errors tend to be interpreted as an indication of failure in learning the lesson. For Chinese and Japanese, they are an index of what still needs to be learned." So in Japanese culture, children can be asked to work out, say, a math problem on the board for a healthy period of time, and the teacher might see the mistake that's being made and yet have the student continue with the problem for a while to try to figure out where it went wrong. "I've seen videos where a student spends twelve minutes explaining why he added denominators and the teacher never said, 'That's a mistake.' The teacher would say, 'I don't understand, why is this the answer?' And the student would try to explain and couldn't.

Making a mistake doesn't make you better but examining what happens makes you better." In an American classroom, far less is done in front of the entire class, and if it is, an American teacher would be much more likely to rush in and try to correct the error so the child will not be embarrassed. "The whole assumption with American classrooms is not that there is some underlying understanding that you're trying to achieve, but getting the right answer," Stigler says. There is a real fear in this country, he said, that if students are allowed to pursue the wrong path in figuring out a problem, they might, in fact, learn the subject matter incorrectly. So teachers tend not to leave a mistake uncorrected for even a short period of time. That is not true in Japan.

"We translated some textbook pages from a Japanese math textbook," Stigler told me, sitting in his office in the rabbit warren that is the UCLA psychology department. "There was a really interesting note in the teacher's edition, and it said: 'The most common mistake students will make in adding fractions is that they will add the denominators.' Then it said: 'Do not correct this mistake. If you correct it, they will immediately stop doing it. But what you really want is for them to take several weeks to understand the consequences of adding the denominators and why that does not work.'" The expectation, according to Stigler, is that by focusing on the mistakes and why students make them—rather than simply telling the students that they're doing the probems incorrectly—they will not simply attain a superficial knowledge of math, but truly understand the underlying concepts.

It is important to keep in mind, when talking about education, that most countries have a national education curriculum, rather than the diffuse system we have; we're a nation full of immigrants with a vast variety of languages and needs, while most East Asian countries are far more homogeneous; and elementary and secondary school teachers in the United States are generally not valued—either in social status or through salaries—the way their colleagues are in many other countries.

Nonetheless, the varied approach to mistakes isn't simply a different teaching style or curriculum; it grows out of a fundamental difference between North American and Japanese culture. To understand this, we have to first back up and look at the difference in concepts of self-esteem. We looked at the changing concept of how we attain self-esteem in earlier chapters, but overall, the idea is to feel good about yourself from within. Steven Heine, a psychology professor at the University of British Columbia, calls it self-enhancement, which emphasizes what is good about the individual. On the other hand, the Japanese culture tends to focus on self-improvement, which stresses what is *not yet* good enough. A great deal of research has found that North Americans (and I include our fellow Canadians, since much of this type of research has been done in Canada and with Canadians) tend to be encouraged by success—if they do something right, then they want to keep doing it right, but if they fail, they're less likely to persevere. On the other hand, the Japanese are more likely to see failure as an impetus to improve themselves.

In one study that Heine conducted with Canadian and Japanese undergraduates, the students were asked to take a test they were told was to assess the connection between creativity and emotional intelligence. After it was over, some students were randomly told that they had failed, and some that they had done very well. The experimenter then explained to the participants that the next phase of the study involved an emotional intelligence test on the computer. However, the computer then crashed (this was planned). The experimenter said he or she would have to find a professor to get a new file to make the computer work, and the students were told they could work on another set of test items similar to the one they had just taken, although this would not count—it was just a way to kill some time. The experimenter then went to an observation room to watch the participants without their knowledge through hidden cameras. After a while, he or she went back in and told the participants that the computer couldn't be fixed and they were dismissed.

The results: The Canadians who had scored well on the first test—in effect, those who were successful—persisted significantly longer on the second task than those who had failed. In stark contrast, the Japanese who had succeeded were far less persistent on the second test than those who had failed. Further studies along these lines with other variables thrown in demonstrated that failure tends to serve as a motivating factor for Japanese, while Canadians are more inspired by success. The Japanese want to focus on their areas of weakness and therefore improve themselves; they tend to concentrate on the process rather than the product, while Canadians (and this has proved true for Americans as well) would much prefer to maintain a positive self-image by avoiding tasks that they feel reflect badly on them. This idea, backed up by studies, sums it up pretty neatly for me: Americans are motivated to achieve success, while Japanese are motivated to avoid failure.

Some of this goes back yet again to Carol Dweck's concepts of fixed versus growth mindsets discussed in chapter 2. In one survey, Americans of European descent estimated that 36 percent of intelligence comes from one's efforts, Asian-Americans estimated 45 percent, and Japanese 55 percent. Chris Arnold, a former San Francisco Giants baseball player who went to play in Japan for the Kintetsu Buffaloes, said, "I'll tell you the big difference between Japan and the U.S. In the U.S. we believe that a player has a certain amount of natural ability, and with practice he reaches a certain peak point— no amount of practice will make you better because after a certain point your ability reaches its limits. But the Japanese believe there is no peak point. They don't recognize limits." This may be good in some ways but counterproductive in others. In the charming book *You Gotta Have Wa*, about the clashes that occur when Americans go to Japan to play with Japanese baseball teams, the author, Robert Whiting, describes a pitcher, Choji Murata, who threw a hundred or more pitches every day in practice, and in games he would throw every pitch as hard as he could. This was contrary to standard practice in the United States, where pitchers take three or four days off between starts. Eventually his arm started giving out, but he pitched through the pain. He ended up, after many efforts to resolve the problem in other ways, having to have what is known as Tommy John surgery, which meant taking a tendon from elsewhere in his body— in his case, his left wrist—and using it to repair his right elbow.

The emphasis on making the effort is so strong that many people believe that how hard a man tries to accomplish a task is the ultimate measure of his worth: results are almost secondary. Interestingly, the words *doryoku* (effort) and *gambaru* (persistence) have been rated as the first and second most popular words, respectively, in surveys in Japan. These traits are also highly prized in China; I was thinking about this when I heard a young Chinese pianist, Xiayin Wang, recently interviewed on the radio. When asked how she managed to stand out from so many talented pianists in her country, she talked about working hard and trying her best and step by step getting to where she wanted to go. The North American interviewer tried to pin her down, asking what made her, specifically, so special. The young woman hesitated, then admitted that she was not used to talking about herself, but she would try. She then proceeded to talk in abstract terms about what makes a good pianist, never once saying, "This is what *I* do well." The interviewer gave up.

While North Americans also value hard work and perseverance in the face of obstacles, they—to an even greater extent, I would wager—like the image of greatness that is accomplished with ease. I would agree with Heine, who presumes that if we had a similar national survey (a little hard to imagine), we would vote for the word "effortless" over "effort." In case you think I'm just picking on Americans, note what French executive Pierre Chevalier says: "We are not a nation of effort. After all, if you have *savoir-faire*, you do things effortlessly."

Here is another interesting difference. Most of us have heard the phrase "cognitive dissonance," even if we're not 100 percent sure what it means. It's when we have two ideas, beliefs, or opinions that are at odds with each other, such as "smoking is a dumb thing to do because it could kill me," and "I smoke two packs a day." Or for those of us who don't smoke: "I don't need any more black shoes" but "I really want those cute little numbers on sale." We spend a lot of our mental energy trying to reduce that tension or dissonance ("The shoes are such a good deal, it's practically like *saving* money"). So, what does this have to do with mistakes? Well, when we make mistakes, we often try to convince ourselves (and others) that it wasn't really a mistake by reducing dissonance—and this isn't necessarily bad. We want to sleep at night and we want to feel okay about how we live. I had a neighbor who moved to the next town and then started telling people how poor our local schools were—schools she never had a problem with before. She was unsure if the move was the right thing and she was trying to justify it to herself and us. However, cognitive dissonance is a real problem when we're so tied up in believing that we're right that we refuse to acknowledge facts before our eyes. Remember weapons of mass destruction?

Reducing dissonance is often crucial to keeping our self-esteem high, because we all want to have a positive self-image as good, moral people. Once I pulled out of a parking spot and brushed the car next to me. It was dark, and I couldn't really see if there was any damage. I should have left a note. But I told myself I probably hadn't scratched the car. And anyhow, people do this all the time—haven't I come back to my parked car and seen a dent in my side door more than once and no note on the windshield? Okay, maybe this was worse than a ping, but probably not. What if the other driver claimed there was damage when there really wasn't? I worked mightily to reduce dissonance—I'm the kind of person who likes to see herself as honest and someone who acknowledges her wrongdoings but I didn't want to pay for the potential scratch. Ultimately, I did drive off without leaving a note. I felt so bad, though, that I drove back about ten minutes later. The car was already gone.

"Dissonance reduction operates like a thermostat, keeping our self-esteem bubbling along on high," Carol Tavris and Elliot Aronson write. "That is why we are usually oblivious to the self-justifications, the little lies to ourselves that prevent us from acknowledging that we made mistakes or foolish decisions." But since the Japanese emphasis is not on making themselves feel better but on improving themselves vis-à-vis a group, cognitive dissonance is far less necessary. In one study, Japanese and Canadian participants chose between two compact discs, and evaluated them before and after making the choice. Typically, the North Americans evaluated the CD they chose more positively and the one they rejected more negatively after making their decision than before making the choice—like my neighbor and the schools, the participants wanted to convince themselves they had definitely made the right decision. The Japanese, on the other hand, did not change their evaluations of the CDs. This would further indicate that the Japanese have less stake in being "right" than North Americans.

This is not to say that people from Japan don't want to feel good about themselves, but rather that in their culture, individual self-esteem is not necessarily the road to satisfaction. It is more about maintaining face, which has been explained as "the respectability and/or deference which he occupies in his social network and the degree to which he is judged to have functioned adequately in that position." In North America, although other people's compliments or criticisms play a role, ideally our self-esteem comes from within. In Japan, face is claimed from others. Individuals can't determine how much face they can have; rather, they must earn it from others. They must perform their role well within a group and work toward the shared aims of the group; shame arises when they are unable to perform to the standards necessary to maintain harmonious interactions within the group.

I asked James Stigler a question he had heard many times before: Is it possible that the Japanese education system, while laudable, doesn't encourage individual differences enough? Does it help or hinder the exceptionally brilliant and uniquely talented in achieving their highest potential? "That's an objection people always make to me—how many Nobel Prizes come from Japan? Well, Japan doesn't see its education system as a method of producing Nobel Prizes. It wants to educate everyone to a higher level. We actually do a pretty good job on the geniuses, but we do a really terrible job with everyone else," he answered.

Here's where I bumped up against what seemed to be a paradox. How does the Japanese apparently greater acceptance of mistakes and failure fit with this idea of shame and saving face, which is such a large part of the culture? Robert Whiting writes about the slow and cautious pace of Japanese baseball games in his book, and about the desire of players not to do poorly or reflect negatively in the eyes of the team and the fans. The game, he says, "was designed to avoid unpleasant confrontations and embarrassing mistakes. Nobody wanted to look bad. Nobody wanted to be the one who fouled up and threw a home run pitch." This seems contradictory to everything I've been saying.

But if we look at making mistakes in private versus public life, it begins to make more sense. Let's use an analogy of putting on a play. Most of us would agree that rehearsals are the time to make mistakes, to learn, and to improve, while we want the performance to be as flawless as possible. If we view team practices or classrooms as rehearsals for the public forum, then that is the arena where mistakes are welcomed and used in Japan, far more than in North America. In the classroom in the United States, for example, the emphasis is much more on the product—the A's and B's—than the process, while the Japanese are more interested in the process. But in a public forum, the Japanese fear failing more than we do. If we screw up publicly, "it's our personal reputation, but in Japan, it's letting everyone else down," Steven Heine said.

So are other cultures doing everything right and we're doing everything wrong? Of course not. It's useful, however, to see the differences and reflect on how we can change. For example, Rossella Santagata, an assistant professor in the School of Education at the University of California, Irvine, compared American and Italian teachers' use of mistakes in teaching. Looking at videotapes of thirty Italian and thirty U.S. eighth-grade mathematics lessons, she found that mistakes are discussed publicly twice as often in the Italian classes as in the American ones. Also, while American teachers would encourage students who were having trouble working out a problem on the board with phrases like, "You're on the right track," "That was tricky," and "You're almost there," Italian teachers were much harsher. When a student wrote the wrong thing, the teacher would ask, "Giacomo, are you joking or are you sleeping?" Or comment that her student was *di coccio*—a blockhead.

I read this research and thought, *I'll stick with American schools—who wants to be called a blockhead, either publicly or privately?* But there was one part of the experiment that resonated with me: When Italian and American students were separately questioned in focus groups, the Italian students took responsibility for doing their homework and studying, and justified as necessary the teacher's negative and sometimes even unkind remarks. As the students put it: "The teacher is doing her job . . . and she gets angry. It's her job to say, 'Look, you made a mistake.'" American students, when interviewed in the focus groups, were much more likely to deflect the responsibility for doing well off themselves and onto the teachers. When asked what they do when they make a mistake, the students said things like, "I try to do it over, but if I can't, I call the teacher." Another student suggested looking at the notes, but the first student said, "Yeah, look in your notes, that doesn't help me and it gets me mad 'cause she's supposed to teach us and show us." Another chimed in, "She doesn't know how to explain it really. She just gives the examples and expects us to know it."

This really struck close to home, because I have a teenager, and foisting blame onto others is his preferred method of addressing mistakes—and it drives me crazy. Are the Italians doing something right, then, if they're raising kids who own up to their own errors? I put the question to Santagata, a vivacious young professor, who thought about it and said, "I don't think the Italian way is good either. I think the Italians and Americans are on the two extremes. The Italians always blame the students, while Americans don't talk about mistakes." Not surprisingly, each mode of teaching reflects the corresponding country's culture as a whole, she noted—Italians are more direct and tend to use irony and sarcasm liberally, while Americans are worried about ensuring that others, especially children, don't feel bad about themselves. There's a great fear that making mistakes—and having others know—will create anxiety, "and it does," Santagata said. "But what's wrong with optimal anxiety?

You also learn from suffering. If you experience failure or mistakes, you may not fear it as much. Italians are less concerned that the mistakes kids will make will harm their emotional development."

Now, education isn't the only field that has been studied intensively for cross-cultural differences. Interestingly enough, aviation—which we all now know has played a crucial role in highlighting and teaching about safety and error prevention—has also proven a fertile place to observe such distinctions. Aviation, if you think about it, is a natural arena; there is already a great deal of available research on safety, and different cultures are constantly bumping up against one another, whether it be with passengers, ground-to-air communications, or multicultural crews. One area that has been looked at is our old friend Crew Resource Management from chapter 5—working in various ways to increase and improve team communication among airlines' crews—and how well such a program adapts across cultures.

First, let me back up a moment to expand on the research that Geert Hofstede, the Dutch psychologist, has done over the years to identify and explain variations among societies. His initial large-scale research, first published in 1980, used data collected from surveys of national and cultural differences of IBM subsidiaries in sixty-four countries, and was later expanded to other countries and other professions by himself and others. Hofstede has updated his work several times, and over the decades it has been widely used as a framework for comparing cultures. It is best known for developing a method to compare national cultures by using five different dimensions. These include:

- *Power-distance index:* How much subordinates believe they can speak up to and question those above them and how much a culture values and respects authority. It also is an indication of how much less powerful members of institutions and organizations accept and expect that power is distributed unequally.

- *Individualism versus collectivism:* The relationship between an individual and other individuals around him or her. It is bred in the family, where children are taught to think in terms of "I" or "we." In individualist societies, ties between individuals are loose, and everyone is expected to look after himself or herself and immediate family. In collectivist societies, people are integrated into strong, cohesive groups from birth, which support and protect them in exchange for strong loyalty.

- *Masculinity versus femininity:* Hofstede defines a society as masculine when emotional gender roles are clearly distinct: men are supposed to be assertive, tough, and focused on material success while women are supposed to be more modest, tender, and concerned with relationships. A feminine society is one in which gender roles overlap, and both men and women are expected to be modest, tender, and concerned with relationships. For instance, in a feminine society, careers are optional for both genders, there is a higher share of working women in professional jobs, women and men teach young children, children are socialized to be nonaggressive, and competitive sports tend to be extracurricular. In masculine societies, on the other hand, careers are compulsory for men and optional for women (rather than optional for men and women), only women teach young children, aggression by children is accepted, and competitive sports are part of the curriculum at school.

- *Uncertainty avoidance:* A society's tolerance for ambiguous or unknown situations, which is related to the control of aggression and the expression of emotions.

- *Long-term orientation versus short-term orientation:* How much a society prizes virtues oriented toward future rewards—such as thrift and perseverance—as opposed to fostering virtues related to the past and present, such as respect for tradition, saving face, and fulfilling social obligations.

There is a danger in reducing comparisons to little more than stereotypes, and Hofstede's dimensions have been critiqued for failing to take into account minority societies within a dominant culture. Nonetheless, his work has proved very useful, and has withstood the test of time, in helping understand important cultural differences.

Now, if we're talking about mistakes and failure, the dimensions of power-distance index and individualism versus collectivism are key. First the power-distance index dimension: Hofstede measured this with three survey items: (1) Answers by non-managerial employees to the question: "How frequently in your experience does the following problem occur: Employees being afraid to express their disagreement with managers?"—on a scale of 1 to 5, ranging from "very frequently" to "very seldom." (2) Subordinates' perception of their boss's actual decision-making style—four possible styles ranging from autocratic to paternalistic plus "none of these." (3) Subordinates' preference for their boss's decision-making style, such as paternalistic, autocratic, or on the contrary, a majority vote. In comparing seventy-four countries,

Malaysia, Slovakia, Guatemala, Panama, and the Philippines were in the top five—meaning greatest respect for authority and hierarchy—while the German-speaking part of Switzerland, New Zealand, Denmark, Israel, and Austria were in the bottom five. The United States ranked seventeenth from the bottom, right between Luxembourg and Canada as a whole (Quebec was also measured separately). The Arab-speaking countries and Latin American, Asian, and African countries tended to show high power-distance values.

An interesting note: Hofstede found that if a country as a whole scored higher in power distance, this proved true for all employees, both low- and high-status. But in countries with lower power-distance indexes, lower-rank workers often had more respect for (or fear of) those above them than did their higher-status compatriots. As he writes, "the values of high-status employees with regard to inequality seem to depend strongly on nationality; those with low-status employees much less."

I was told an anecdote to demonstrate how different our notions are of what a boss not only does but is *supposed* to do in countries with lower versus higher power-distance indexes. An American goes over to Belgium (pretty high in power-distance values) to become managing director of a manufacturing plant. After a few days he goes out to the shop floor to talk to the workers about what they see as the future of the company. This is something seen in the United States as a good thing—a sign that the boss respects the input of those below him. But the Belgian workers lost all faith in his leadership. "Why is he asking us?" they wondered. "Doesn't he know what he's doing?"

Individualism versus collectivism was measured using a set of fourteen work goals. People were asked to think what factors would be important to them in an ideal job, followed by fourteen items, which the participant could score from 1 (of extreme importance) to 5 (of very little importance). Those on the individualist end valued personal time, freedom to adopt your own approach to the job, and challenging work, which can provide a personal sense of accomplishment. Those on the collectivist side sought training opportunities, good physical working conditions, and full use of their skills and abilities on the job. The individualists stressed independence from the employer, while the collectivists valued what the organization could do for the worker and the employees' dependence on the company. As Hofstede points out, individualist countries tend to be richer than collectivist countries, and therefore in wealthier nations, training, physical conditions, and use of skills may be taken for granted. In poorer countries they are essential in distinguishing a good job from a bad one.

Now, it probably won't surprise you that the United States is *número uno* on the individualistic scale, followed by Australia, Great Britain, Canada, and Hungary. Down at the bottom are Colombia, Venezuela, Panama, Ecuador, and Guatemala. Of the seventy-four countries listed, Japan fell more or less in the middle. Those countries that scored high on the power-distance index tended to also score low on individualism, and vice versa. There are exceptions, though: France and Belgium combined medium power distance with strong individualism. For a fun exercise, you can go to www.geert-hofstede.com and compare your country's cultural dimensions with those of any other country.

Robert Helmreich, the aviation expert from chapter 5, and his colleague Ashleigh Merritt used Hofstede's dimensions to see

whether and, if so, how they were replicated in the culture of aviation; the most pertinent ones were power-distance individualism
versus collectivism. Why do we care about this in terms of mistakes? Because, as we know, a crew member's fear of questioning
the captain or even alerting him to dangers can be fatal. And an
unwillingness to let down the group by admitting to personal vulnerabilities, such as fatigue, can lead to tragic consequences.

Eighteen hundred pilots and flight attendants from the United
States, Hong Kong, Japan, Korea, Thailand, Singapore, and Taiwan
took a twenty-question survey. The pilots were overwhelmingly male;
the flight attendants largely female. The survey included statements
such as "Captains should encourage crew member questions during
normal flight operations and in emergencies," "Even when fatigued, I
perform effectively during critical times in a flight," "I let other crew
members know when my workload is becoming (or about to become)
excessive," and "Crew members should avoid disagreeing with others
because conflicts create tension and reduce crew effectiveness."

Helmreich found that pilots from countries with a high power-
distance index and an emphasis on collectivism believed that the
captain is the unquestioned leader and that he or she can overcome
any personal or situational problems to ensure that group members
aren't let down. Those from cultures with a moderate power-distance
index and moderate individualism still believed that the captain is
unquestioned, but with the caveat that a good captain invites questions from the crew. In this group, there was not much disclosure
about stress and personal problems, and crew members worked
more as individuals with specific jobs than as an interconnected
team. Those with high individualism and a low power-distance

index believed that the captain's views are not absolute, and had a greater recognition that one's performance can be affected by emergencies and personal problems. There was more stress on self-reliance and personal responsibility for success and failure.

Helmreich indicated high power distance as one factor in the 1990 crash of an Avianca airliner flown by a Colombian crew. The plane ran out of fuel following a missed approach to JFK, and seventy-three people died in the accident. Although there were many factors leading up to the tragedy, one that Helmreich identified was the interaction between the junior officers and the captain, as well as air traffic controllers and the cockpit crew. The flight recordings after the crash show that the Colombian captain—from a high power-distance culture—did not solicit advice or suggestions from his crew, nor did the crew attempt to interject, even when the situation got very serious. And the Colombian pilot seemed hesitant to forcefully communicate his increasingly dangerous dilemma to the New York air traffic controllers.

The point, as with gender comparisons, is not to argue that one culture is better than another—each has its weaknesses and strengths. For instance, Helmreich and Merritt write, when the idea of teamwork and all it entails was introduced into U.S. aviation, "the highly individualistic U.S. pilots were asked to forgo their romantic image of the solo flyer/hero and to value more working as a team. By comparison, collectivist cultures, such as those found in Asia and Latin America, already value team interdependence and communication. However, given the high power-distance norms, free and open exchange of information in the cockpit may be difficult. Formalizing communication via checklists may be one way to facilitate the desired end goal without disrupting the higher power-distance norms."

Understanding cultural differences can help us tackle problems in appropriate ways, rather than in a one-size-fits-all approach. Take the example of the willingness to admit that fatigue, stress, and personal problems can have an impact on one's abilities. If pilots (or any of us, for that matter) believe or pretend to believe ourselves invulnerable, then we won't recognize our own depleted resources and can't reach out when help is needed. Teaching airline crews that they should acknowledge such worries, not out of weakness or disrespect but out of concern for the safety of the flight, would seem to be a fine approach. But it should be done differently depending on the culture. In individualist countries there should be an emphasis on individual awareness and responsibility. For instance, a captain who says in his briefing to his crew, "This is my last leg of a long trip. I know I'm more likely to make errors today because I'm very tired and I can't wait to go home, so we need to be extra careful to watch out for each other," is sending a message to his crew that a true professional is aware of his performance limits and adjusts his work accordingly.

But in more collectivist countries, encouraging pilots to consider their personal reactions to stress may only serve to heighten their sense of shame for not meeting the group's professional standards. A broader approach is necessary in order to change the group norm, such as senior management's need to emphasize that true professionals are not those who deny vulnerability but openly acknowledge it. Even training should differ—those nations with a lower power-distance index might train captains and first officers together, while those with a higher power-distance index might want to train the captains first and then use them to help the junior crew, in order to honor the established hierarchies.

Hofstede's masculinity/femininity dimension provides interesting insight into some American workplace cultures and why people may be hesitant to share their mistakes and problems publicly. The United States is on the high end of the masculinity scale, while the Netherlands is third from the bottom—making it pretty darn feminine. A Dutchman who had worked at a prestigious consulting firm in the United States for several years later joined the top management team of a manufacturing company in the Netherlands. He compared the way the two companies were run: In the Dutch company, meetings were places where problems were discussed and attempts made to reach a common solution and consensus decisions. In the United States, on the other hand, meetings were an opportunity for the participants to show off how good they were, while decisions were made elsewhere. Feminine cultures tend to stress compromise and negotiation, while masculine cultures tend to think things should be resolved with a good fight—or the verbal equivalent.

One obvious advantage to learning about other cultures and what lies behind their customs and ways of doing things is to avoid misinterpretations and misunderstandings. Another, in this increasingly global world, is to better understand that adapting our training or management methods to other cultures requires a real knowledge of the different values and beliefs underlying those— and our own—cultures. But for our purposes, understanding other cultures' views on mistakes, success, and failure can help reshape biases we're often only dimly aware of. In chapter 2, I talked about the radically different ways Chinese and Americans viewed a student talking about his high performance. Through one (American) prism, it was showing off. Through another (Chinese) prism it was helping others improve. Sometimes such insights are like a door opening—I can choose, if I want, to change my old ways of thinking.

Take this poignant example: In 2008, a young German composer, Jan Moritz Onken, became conductor of the Kazakhstan Youth Orchestra, which was made up of students from the country's national conservatory. Brought up in the Soviet-style system, which taught them to obey orders and, above all, to avoid mistakes, they were very reluctant to take on the challenge of playing Igor Stravinsky's technically challenging *The Rite of Spring*. Some players wondered whether they should refuse to perform the piece rather than risk looking ridiculous. Those young musicians' prisms shifted when, after practicing a particularly difficult passage, Onken asked those who had made a mistake to raise their hands. Instead of criticizing them, he urged them to shout "Hurrah!" as a compliment to themselves. "Now we have something to work on!" Onken told them. They went on to perform the piece successfully to a packed hall.

When we're small children, we tend to think that how we live is how everyone lives. If you are a city dweller, then you might not know many homeowners. If you grow up in Southern California, then it can be surprising the first time you meet someone who resides in an apartment. When we discover these differences, we have to slightly rearrange our way of thinking—not everybody is like us. So it is when we investigate other cultures and their attitudes about mistakes; we reexamine our own way of measuring our successes and failures. The Japanese emphasis on effort, for example, can remind us that making mistakes while trying something new is to be commended, not disparaged, and that although it is difficult to always keep this in mind, we shouldn't revere results while diminishing the value of the process. If we effortlessly accomplish our goals, we haven't really learned anything—walking a smooth path through a park can be pleasant, but it rarely brings the same sense of accomplishment as breathlessly getting to the top of the peak. But all of life shouldn't be one test after another, either; we need to both conquer mountains and enjoy ambles in the park. Others, outside our own literal and figurative boundaries, can help us rethink our own assumptions and goals. It may take some effort, but it's worth it.

8.

I Want to Apologize

There's a *New Yorker* cartoon that shows a wife saying to her husband, "I don't want your apology—I want you to be sorry." Well, that pretty much sums up a large part of the apology problem: saying you're sorry doesn't really mean you are.

As we all should know well by now, mistakes happen. We need to learn from them. We also need to know how to apologize for them, which is something most of us are taught almost as soon as we can talk. "Say you're sorry," we instruct our two-year-old when she grabs someone else's pail in the sandbox. When they're toddlers, we know we can generally force our children to at least mutter, "I'm sorry." But often children argue that they shouldn't have to apologize because they didn't mean to hit Hannah with the swing. So we explain how doing something that hurts, even accidentally, requires an apology. As they get older, we don't want just rote apologies, but some sort of sign that children are genuinely regretful about breaking the lamp while playing living room football, or smacking each other with the remote control. How many times have I told my sons to apologize to each other, or to me, and I get a grudging "Sor-REE." It's clear they don't mean the apology and they don't even pretend to. "At least say, '*I'm* sorry,'" I shriek at them, particularly annoyed by the lack of the pronoun. It not only sounds ruder, but also seems a subconscious attempt to shed responsibility by avoiding the "I." So, even if we haven't read the literature, we all know from experience that some apologies work and some don't.

For such a seemingly simple interaction, apologies are surprisingly complex. I will look, of course, at apologies on the personal level—between friends and spouses and colleagues. But there is increasingly a debate over what role apologies should play in the public arena—in cases of lawsuits, medical malpractice, and corporate blunders or misdeeds. Lawyers often advise their clients, whether someone involved in a car accident or a multinational corporation, not to apologize. They know that saying "I'm sorry" could be interpreted as "I'm guilty." But we all know that a good apology, sincerely given, can defuse a volatile situation, perhaps avoid that lawsuit altogether, and save a company's reputation, a doctor's practice, or a politician's career. The study of apologies is an evolving field that, as Professor Jonathan Cohen of the Levin College of Law at the University of Florida told me, tries to find a fine balance between holding people accountable but "not build[ing] a distrusting adversarial relationship at the same time," said Cohen, an expert on the role of apologies in the legal field.

A proper apology has three elements: an acknowledgment of the fault or offense, regret for it, and responsibility for it—and, if possible, a way to fix the problem. Because we often don't separate these three aspects, we frequently get caught up in who is to blame and find it difficult to apologize when it shouldn't be. "We can acknowledge another's anger or dismay or regret [over] an offense even when we don't feel responsible for a wrong. . . . 'I want to apologize' is not an apology. It's no more an apology than 'I want to lose weight' is a loss of weight," consultant Holly Weeks writes in the *Harvard Management Update*. "Do the work. Deliver a clear, direct apology; don't hide behind vagueness, circumlocution or clichés."

I think we're all aware of the apology that violates Weeks's first tenet—acknowledgment of a fault or offense. It's the "I'm sorry if you were offended" or "I'm sorry I hurt your feelings." It somehow implies that the person wronged is at fault for being so sensitive. A classic example is Bishop Richard Williamson, who had his excommunication revoked by Pope Benedict in 2009. Williamson, who denies the existence of Nazi gas chambers and the scope of the Holocaust, said publicly, by way of apology, "I can truthfully say that I regret having made such remarks and that if I had known beforehand the full harm and hurt to which they would give rise, especially to the church, but also to survivors and relatives of victims of injustice under the Third Reich, I would not have made them." I don't think I need to explain what's wrong with that. Even on a less serious subject, apologies that dodge responsibility and accountability are infuriating. Drew Sharp, a *Detroit Free Press* columnist, expressed it succinctly when slamming Matt Millen, former chief executive for the Detroit Lions. Writing in 2009, as the Lions came off a 0–16 record, making it the worst team in NFL history, Sharp quoted Millen as saying, "I could give you excuses. I could give you reasons. To me that's just an excuse after the fact. You take the hit and move on." Millen blew it, Sharp says. "Simply saying you're responsible for the disaster doesn't make you accountable. If Millen truly seeks atonement, he must delve deeper into those additional 'reasons' of which he spoke." Millen is confusing excuses with explanations; nobody wants self-serving rationales, but an honest explanation is necessary.

Humor me as I look at one apology that hits very close to home. In a past chapter, I've mentioned Jayson Blair, who admitted fabricating and plagiarizing stories in *The New York Times* for more than a year. When his misdeeds came to light, the media world, of course, erupted. Speaking at a university forum in 2009, Blair, now a life coach, told his audience that "I've gotten to the point where I've forgiven myself for what I did." Well, that's nice for him, and Blair has more or less taken the blame for his transgressions, citing mental health issues and drug and alcohol abuse. But at the forum, when Blair was asked if he had apologized to the people he wrote lies about, Blair refused to answer. He said his conversations with his sources were private.

Just for the fun of it, contrast those so-called apologies with that of investment god Warren Buffett in his February 2009 statement to his shareholders. After laying out some positive news, he noted: "During 2008 I did some dumb things in investments. I made at least one major mistake of commission and several lesser ones that also hurt. Furthermore, I made some errors of omission, sucking my thumb when new facts came in that should have caused me to reexamine my thinking and promptly take action." Buffett went on to detail the mistakes he made, taking on the blame and explaining—not excusing—his decisions.

When apologizing, Weeks suggests, we should be thinking of communicating rather than expressing regret, because expression is one-sided—more like a monologue that aims to get something off your chest. Communicating should be a dialogue that works toward a resolution. It sounds simple, but just as we all have different ways of talking and different ways of interpreting conversations, apologies can mean one thing to one person and something else to another. Linguist Deborah Tannen, of Georgetown University, who has spent a lifetime looking at how people say what they say and at the meaning behind the words, delves into the different ways apologies are used. An apology can be part of a ritual. When we say "I'm sorry" at a funeral, we're not assuming blame for the death of the person, we're expressing sympathy for the loss a friend is feeling. Sometimes we (and yes, more often women) use "I'm sorry" as a way to grease the conversational wheels: "I'm sorry, I didn't hear what you were saying." When "I'm sorry" is accepting responsibility for something that went wrong, "it is often assumed to be the first step in a two-step ritual," she writes. "I say 'I'm sorry,' and take half the blame, then you take the other half." The example Tannen uses is a boss who tells his secretary that she missed inserting a phrase into a letter that she typed. She would apologize and he would usually follow up with something like, "Well, I wrote it so small it was easy to miss." When both parties share the blame, Tannen says, there's equal footing—it's a mutual face-saving device and no one is left in the one-down position. But ritual apologies, like other conversational rituals, work only when both parties share assumptions about their use, she points out.

Problems arise when someone feels that an apology or the appearance of an apology (and it doesn't always have to be the words "I'm sorry"—remorse can be conveyed in other ways) is a sign of weakness. And this often occurs between men and women. Studies show that women do apologize more often than men. To use just one example: I see this constantly when playing tennis. Women, unlike men, often apologize for hitting the ball out, missing it, and when a particularly strong player whacks an overhead so it bonks someone. This leads to not just one apology (which seems warranted) but numerous exclamations of regret. The court is virtually littered with as many sorries as tennis balls by the end. Tannen argues that such apologizing does not necessarily reflect a lack of self-confidence or a fear of appearing too competitive—although it can—but rather a focus on the other person. It's not necessarily "I'm sorry I hit the ball so hard" (because, after all, that won the point), but "I'm sorry you missed" or "I'm sorry the ball hit you." In the same way, "I'm sorry the dry cleaner didn't have your favorite shirt ready" doesn't mean I should have washed and pressed it myself, but rather "I know you are disappointed that you don't have the shirt you want." And while a good apology is important, we all also get annoyed by over-apologizers—those who can't seem to stop saying they're sorry.

On the other end of the spectrum from the over-apologizers are those (yes, more frequently men) who avoid apologizing at all costs, afraid it will imply weakness or won't resolve the problem anyhow, so what's the point? We all know the familiar cycle that grows out of this, especially in long-term relationships. One person makes a minor mistake—forgets to pick up milk—and so someone else has to run out to get it. A brief, if sincere, apology would remedy the situation, but the person who forgot thinks it's such a small slip it doesn't warrant an apology. Anger brews. And so on. The point is, while it's true that forgetting milk is not a federal case, an "I'm sorry" acknowledges the other's feeling of being slightly let down and slightly put out. Tannen told me that she has long thought about the contrasting ways men and women tend to view apologies, and one anecdote helped her see one potential source of difference. An adult daughter mentioned that she was curious about what had happened to her old boyfriend, Justin, but she didn't have his address or phone number. The father offered to get the information, and did so by first calling Justin's father and then Justin directly. When he passed on the information to his daughter, she exploded, embarrassed that her father had actually called the former beau. Her father didn't understand— he hadn't done anything wrong in his eyes. When his wife suggested calling his daughter and apologizing, he didn't want to because he felt he was in the right. And that may be true if you just look at his behavior, Tannen says—a father who thought he was helping his daughter. But if you look at the *effect* of the action, it was wrong. It upset his daughter, even if it was inadvertent. "If he defines *wrong* as a judgment of his behavior, the father understandably would be reluctant to apologize, because he feels his behavior was justified,"

Tannen writes. "But if he defines *wrong* as a judgment of the outcome, then he could acknowledge his daughter's distress without
feeling he was pleading guilty to a crime he did not commit."

We're often told to apologize immediately when we do something wrong, whether it is deliberate or not. However, a 2004 study
on the timing of apologies found that this is not necessarily good.
A victim has to be ready to receive an apology in order for it to be
effective. An apology offered too early during a conflict may "pressure someone who is not ready for de-escalation," the researchers
note. After all, we're supposed to forgive and forget, and if we're
still angry, that's awfully hard. They quote a colleague saying to
someone who was apologizing, "Don't apologize. I'm not done
being mad at you." Although long-delayed apologies are not necessarily effective, at least postponing an apology until the victim has a
chance to feel heard and understood is perhaps the best way to right
wrongs, the study found.

For those who really find it hard to apologize face-to-face—or
text-to-text—there are alternatives. There is the free online Apology Service, where people can post their apologies. The idea is to
help people deal with the many feelings of regret they encounter
every day. ApologyPros.com offers advice for different situations
you may find yourself in: How to Apologize to a Friend, or How to
Apologize for Cheating on Your Partner. In China, a small private
company called the Tianjin Apology and Gift Card Center sends
out one of its twenty employees to deliver an apology. They are
well-educated, well-dressed women in somber suits who, on behalf
of clients, will write letters, deliver gifts, and make explanations.
("I'm here to apologize on behalf of Jessica for sleeping with your

boyfriend" is a little hard to imagine, but maybe worth a shot.) Cohen imagines an American franchise of the Tianjin Apology and Gift Card Center. Would it be called McApology or McCulpa?

The last part of the apology triumvirate, accountability, is perhaps the area where most people fall short. Accountability does not necessarily—although it often should—mean some kind of restitution or changed behavior. But we expect that if someone is genuinely sorry and expresses regret, then as much as possible he will look back at what went wrong and try to avoid doing it again. If my son, to pull an example out of thin air, keeps breaking the glasses as he empties the dishwasher, saying "I'm sorry" and genuinely meaning it doesn't do much for me unless he changes his slapdash habits. Politicians, perhaps more than any others, seem to have become masters of apologies that aren't really apologies but rather appear to be well-honed PR exercises. Apologies are a tactic leaders now frequently use in an attempt to put behind them, at minimal cost, the errors of their ways. There is no such thing as a simple apology, Barbara Kellerman noted in a *Harvard Business Review* article: apologies are "prompted by fear, guilt and love—and by the calculation of personal or professional gain." Ronald Reagan became famous for many sayings while he was president; his line "Mistakes were made," referring to the Iran-contra scandal, is one of the classics. That is because it summed up so well the politician's ability to both acknowledge a blunder and somehow squirm out of responsibility. There is no active voice, no indication in the phrase of who made the mistakes. Carol Tavris and Elliot Aronson were so taken by the phrase that they used it as the title for their book; the subtitle—*But Not by Me*—makes explicit what is only implicit in Reagan's phrase.

Interestingly, although perhaps not surprisingly, that phrase actually has a long lineage with politicians. President Ulysses S. Grant, in a report to Congress, acknowledged the scandals engulfing his administration by writing that "mistakes have been made, as all can see and I admit it."

No one expects politicians to be perfect, although the intense media scrutiny of every small slipup—or perceived one—might lead us to believe otherwise. No doubt, it is partially this magnifying of any and all errors that makes it so difficult for those in the public eye to come clean. But politicians have been screwing up since the beginning of time; historian Barbara Tuchman brilliantly wrote about this in *The March of Folly*, outlining government disasters from the Trojan horse to the Vietnam War. And certainly, since the American colonists kicked the British out and formed their own government, there has been a long list of political blunders. A group of scholars once made up a list of the ten greatest presidential mistakes, and reading them, one wonders how this country ever survived. The list—which is *not* in chronological order—starts with James Buchanan's failure to oppose secession and ends with Bill Clinton and the Monica Lewinsky scandal. Smack in the middle, at number five, is Richard Nixon and Watergate.

There is a famous anecdote about Franklin Delano Roosevelt, who in 1932 gave a blistering speech in Pittsburgh denouncing his opponent, Herbert Hoover, and demanding a 25 percent cut in all federal expenditures. Four years after he won the presidency, he was due to return to Pittsburgh to give another speech while seeking reelection. His speechwriter came up to FDR and told him that they had a problem—during his last speech in Pittsburgh, he had promised to dramatically cut federal spending, but of course it hadn't happened. FDR was stumped for a moment and then said, "I know. Deny we were ever in Pittsburgh."

Denial and meaningless apologies, again, are nothing new (very little in politics is novel, after all). Congress in the nineteenth century was filled with insults, fistfights—and ritualized apologies. After all, in those days, members of Congress weren't just trying to avoid censure or a loss of voter support, but a duel. As Yale University historian Joanne Freeman states, "The formal apologies nearly always followed the same script. After harsh language or fisticuffs, the combatants would rise to their feet and apologize in open session." At the same time, "no one assumed such apologies were heartfelt, but even so," Freeman writes, "they meant something. By publicly apologizing to his colleagues, a congressman not only paid obeisance to the dignity and order of the House or Senate, but he also upheld the civility of Congressional proceedings as a whole."

But increasingly it's both the apparent lack of remorse and the complete unwillingness to shoulder responsibility—and really change behavior, not just promise to—that feeds the national cynicism about politicians. There is a seeming inability on the part of many politicians to stand up and say, "I was wrong. It was my fault. I'm sorry." Nothing offended commentators about President Clinton's "apology" in the Monica Lewinsky case more than its lack of regret. As columnist Mary McGrory wrote, echoing the feeling of many Americans: "Lying and adultery they could handle, but not being sorry, especially after you're caught and cornered, is unacceptable."

President George W. Bush was often criticized for this, even to the point of appearing physically uncomfortable if he came close to acknowledging an error. In 2004, when a reporter asked him what his biggest mistake was since September 11, 2001, he couldn't think of anything. Even cutting him some slack for being put on the spot at a press conference, one gets the feeling that given all the time in the world, he would still be hard-pressed to come up with one.

But all too often even when politicians ultimately do admit wrongdoing and apologize, the words seem empty. This is because an apology doesn't mean much without acknowledgment of a fault, regret for it, *and* responsibility. As author and lawyer Edward Lazarus notes, in the law, we can give a substantial break to defendants who accept responsibility by pleading guilty, even if they confess guilt after a jury has returned a guilty verdict. In politics, he says, we're sometimes willing to give politicians too much of a break for owning up to a mistake. "Public apologies and acceptances of responsibility can also serve as a strategy for escaping genuine accountability," he writes. "Most of the time, in public life, the real issue is not whether a politician is 'sorry' for what he or she has done, but rather whether the politician candidly discloses the full extent of the error made, how important the error was, what steps are being taken to correct the error and what consequences should flow from it. Expressions of regret and abstract claims of being held accountable are no substitute."

Take the case of FBI director Robert Mueller, who was in charge in 2007 when it was discovered that the FBI had repeatedly abused its power under the Patriot Act, in part by pretending, on about seven hundred occasions, that exigent circumstances existed—as required by law—to justify doing an end run around court supervision of information requests. In fact, no such exigent circumstances were present. Mueller, in testifying before Congress, reassuringly said, "I am accountable." But as Lazarus notes, so what? "His claim of accountability was worse than meaningless. It was a way of cloaking himself—Harry Truman style—with the aura of integrity and trustworthiness that goes with assuming personal responsibility. But the aura is far too often unaccompanied by any actual consequence for having already made some colossal blunder." How about resigning his position, or at least offering to resign? Otherwise, as Lazarus says, "his claim of accountability will actually amount, ironically, to a self-serving attempt to avoid accountability." Genuine accountability requires that serious mistakes have serious consequences.

When politicians' backs "are nailed to the wall, they may reluctantly acknowledge error, but not responsibility," Tavris and Aronson write. "We want to hear, we *long* to hear, 'I screwed up, I will do my best to ensure that it will not happen again.'" Of course, this isn't true with all politicians. They give a wonderful example of someone who, in 1944, was not yet an elected leader—Dwight D. Eisenhower—but was supreme commander of the Allied Forces in Europe. He had to make a crucial military decision: to invade Normandy. What we now know as the victory of D-Day could have gone terribly wrong. Eisenhower wrote out a short speech, which he planned to release if the invasion was unsuccessful: "Our landings in the Cherbourg-Havre area have failed to gain a satisfactory foothold and the troops have been withdrawn. My decision to attack at this time and place was based on the best information available. The troops, the Air [Force] and the Navy did all that bravery and devotion to duty could do. If any blame or fault attaches to the attempt, it is mine alone." After writing this note, Eisenhower made one small change—he crossed out "the troops have been withdrawn" and replaced it with "I have withdrawn the troops." It may be a small grammatical change, but by turning the passive into the active voice, Eisenhower signaled that he alone was taking on the mantle of accountability. Governors, presidents, mayors, are you listening?

When Tavris and Aronson published their book in 2007, they stated that the last American president to tell the country that he had made a terrible mistake—and show that he had learned from it— was John F. Kennedy back in 1961. Okay, granted, it was a doozy: he believed the claims and faulty intelligence of his top military advisors, who assured him that once America invaded Cuba at the Bay of Pigs, the people would rise up in relief and gratitude and overthrow Castro. (Hmm, this sounds eerily familiar to a current situation in another country and our inability to learn from mistakes.) The invasion was a disaster, but Kennedy actually took onboard the harsh lesson by reorganizing his intelligence system and no longer uncritically accepting the claims of his military advisors, a change that may have made all the difference in averting tragedy in the subsequent Cuban missile crises. Kennedy told newspaper publishers, "This administration intends to be candid about its errors. For as a wise man once said, 'An error does not become a mistake until you refuse to correct it.'" The final responsibility, Kennedy said, for the Bay of Pigs invasion was "mine and mine alone." Guess what? Kennedy's popularity soared.

Well, if Tavris and Aronson had written the book a few years later, they would have been able to point to another president willing to shoulder responsibility: Barack Obama. If you recall, his inauguration began with a slipup—Chief Justice John Roberts, while administering the oath of office, slightly mixed up the wording. In attempting to help him, Obama's response was worded improperly. The oath was given again privately shortly afterward, and although there was a small flurry of commentary in the days following, the incident was soon subsumed by bigger events. But in a letter to the editor, one reader found comfort in the mistakes: "As an editor who works on magazines, I usually find lapses in language annoying. But we all stumble from time to time. If these two titans can slip up while the whole planet watches, surely it makes our own small gaffes more bearable."

More relevant to our discussion here, when former Senator Tom Daschle was forced to withdraw as a nominee for Secretary of Health and Human Services because of a tax scandal, President Obama went on a series of television shows and bluntly announced about his choice of Daschle, "I screwed up." The casual wording as well as the active, not passive, voice was no accident. Obama's chief of staff, Rahm Emanuel, told *The New York Times* that "there were two words: not just 'mistake' but 'responsibility.' People like the fact that he said he made a mistake. They hadn't heard it from anybody in office for a long time."

Obama's frank admission of an error surprised most and delighted many, who saw it as a welcome change from how previous presidents had handled mistakes. "We drill into our children—with stories about young presidents, no less—that admitting mistakes is a fundamental hallmark of honesty. But it's not really something we've grown to expect of our leaders," said former Washington Post.com blogger Dan Froomkin in praising the president's approach.

But what about the last steps—accountability and changing behavior? That may prove a little more difficult in this, as in many cases. When White House press secretary Robert Gibbs was asked how such problems with potential nominees would be avoided in the future, he said, "The president doesn't need to write his staff a memo. We understand."

"How?" he was asked

"Clairvoyance," he responded, and left the podium.

Over the past few decades, research has shown that what we learned back in preschool also works in the corporate world: saying I'm sorry—and meaning it—makes the other person feel better. And therefore, she might be less likely to sue. Or take her business elsewhere. There are many examples of how things can rapidly escalate when the lesson of apologies is ignored. Look at the Eddie Bauer case in 1995. Alonzo Jackson, a black teenager, was stopped at an Eddie Bauer store in Fort Washington, Maryland. A security guard, Robert Sheehan, thought Alonzo was shoplifting a shirt and demanded a receipt. Jackson had actually bought the shirt the day before, but Sheehan didn't believe him—despite the fact that the store cashier confirmed Jackson's story. Sheehan proceeded to ask Jackson to take the shirt off and leave. Jackson's two friends, also high school students, were detained for about ten minutes. According to the lawsuit, when one of the friends protested, he was told, "Sit down or I'll lock you up." Jackson then returned to the store later that night with the receipt and retrieved the shirt. Guess what? Jackson and his friends then sued the clothing store for $85 million for consumer racism. Eddie Bauer's lawyers denied wrongdoing and blamed Sheehan, who they said was acting on his own and in violation of store policy. That may have been true, but does it sound familiar? "It's a bad apple—it's not us." Now, most of us may think that $85 million is extreme—so did the jury, which ultimately awarded $1 million: $850,000 to Jackson and $75,000 to each of his friends—but the point here is what role apologies played in escalating the situation. Although Eddie Bauer did apologize publicly, Jackson was looking for a more immediate and personal response. He said, "If they had apologized from the start or given some response, the lawsuit wouldn't have happened. It feels like they don't care."

Sydney Finkelstein, a management professor at the Tuck School of Business at Dartmouth, did a search of key words in the annual report to shareholders of more than one hundred Fortune 500 companies—many who had been performing poorly—over several years in the early 2000s. In only one annual report—and interestingly, this is from Intel's handling of the Pentium chip problem that I referred to in a previous chapter—did executives actually apologize and assume responsibility. The other companies blamed circumstances out of their control. "Apologies are not part of the makeup of CEOs," Finkelstein said. "They get to where they go by steamrolling other people. They're like a baseball player who strikes out—the focus is all on the next play, not the last one."

Of course, we don't have to go back a decade or more to find such examples. Chief executives of companies like Goldman Sachs, Lehman, and Bear Stearns all seemed to have a very difficult time finding words, let alone actions (remember the multimillion-dollar bonuses during the height of the latest recession?), to express their regret at their role in creating or adding to the nation's economic woes. Here's Lloyd Blankfein, chairman and chief executive officer of Goldman Sachs in June 2009: "While we regret that we participated in the market euphoria and failed to raise a responsible voice, we are proud of the way our firm managed the risk it assumed on behalf of our client before and during the financial crisis." It's a little hard to find the real remorse in there. Five months later, Blankfein sounded slightly more abject: "We participated in things that were clearly wrong and have reason to regret. We apologize." The real question, of course, is whether Blankfein and his fellow CEOs will implement the third part of a good apology: investigating what went wrong and changing behavior so that it's unlikely to occur again.

I could fill this whole chapter and book, in fact, with entire stories of companies that failed to give or poorly executed an apology. But let's look at one that worked well—the Tylenol poisoning incident back in 1982. It's a long time ago, but this case is still considered a rare and brilliant example of how a company should act—and apologize—in the midst of a crisis. I was a cub reporter at United Press International at the time, and I well remember the fear the case created. Seven people on Chicago's West Side died mysteriously after, it was determined, they had taken an Extra-Strength Tylenol laced with cyanide. The deaths included twelve-year-old Mary Kellerman and Adam Janus, a twenty-seven-year-old man—along with Adam's brother and wife, who, when gathering at Adam's house later that evening to mourn, took Tylenol from the same bottle. When Tylenol was discovered, after a few days, to be the connecting link in the deaths, word spread rapidly—police even drove through Chicago shouting warnings over loudspeakers—and nationwide panic ensued. As Johnson & Johnson, the manufacturers of Tylenol,

frantically tried to pinpoint where the poisonous Tylenol had origi-
nated and how much was out there, pundits predicted that Tylenol,
as a brand, was dead. "I don't think they can ever sell another product under that name," advertising genius Jerry Della Femina told
The New York Times in the days following the crisis.

But unlike other major companies that had been found to have
sold products dangerous to consumers, Johnson & Johnson, led
by chairman of the board James Burke, didn't try to shed responsibility, didn't try to cover up, didn't try to minimize the danger.
Burke and other executives went on television, telling people to
immediately return their bottles of Tylenol for a voucher. Production and advertising were halted. And Tylenol capsules already in
stores were recalled (at an estimated cost of some $100 million),
while company executives worked to resolve the crisis. In short,
say many who have studied this case, Burke extended the virtually perfect public apology. He promptly acknowledged the problem. He accepted responsibility. He expressed concern. And while
he couldn't undo the deaths, the company didn't stint in spending
what was needed—so he as much as possible repaired the problem.
Not only did he offer to exchange all Tylenol capsules already pur-
chased for Tylenol tablets, he promised new, secure packaging to
make certain that the problem would never be repeated. Marketing
experts had opined that the Tylenol brand would not survive—but
they were wrong. Within a year, Tylenol (in tamper-resistant packaging) had regained 90 percent of its market share. I take Tylenol
today and give it to my children without a second thought.

A more recent example of a company under fire for fatalities
caused by its product is Toyota. Unlike the response for Tylenol,

Toyota's handling of its crisis will more likely end up as a case study in the wrong way to do it. The trouble began in August 2009, when a Lexus (made by Toyota) spun out of control, killing all four members of the Saylor family. The car seemed to have no brakes, and a later investigation found that the wrong floor mats were installed, interfering with the gas pedal. Toyota recalled the floor mats on 4.2 million Toyotas and Lexuses, and Toyota CEO Akio Toyoda publicly apologized. But a few months later, the *Los Angeles Times*, in a series of reports, found that Toyota had actually been under investigation by the National Highway Traffic Safety Administration for numerous separate incidents of "unintended acceleration," resulting in nineteen fatalities since 2002. It also reported that hundreds of complaints about the issue had been filed with the federal government, which Toyota ignored. The car company continued to maintain, publicly and in letters sent out to car owners, that no defect existed. The NHTSA took the "highly unusual step of publicly rebuking Toyota," according to *Motor Trend* magazine, saying its press release was "inaccurate" and "misleading."

In December, a Toyota Avalon crashed into a lake in Texas after accelerating out of control, killing all four people in the car. Floor mats were ruled out as the cause of the accident, because they were in the trunk. Toyota recalled millions more of its cars, this time saying there seemed to be a "rare set of conditions" that caused the gas pedal to become harder to push down or sometimes stuck in a partially depressed position. It was unrelated to the floor mat problem, the company said. More questions arose about the cars' electronic throttle system. Finally, in January, Toyota halted sales and production of its best-selling models, and recalls eventually grew to about

8 million Toyota-made cars worldwide. The next month, Toyoda appeared before Congress to apologize, a gesture that was seen by many as too little too late.

I've covered in some depth medical errors and touched on the role of apologies in chapter 3, but I'll expand a little on them here because how the medical community handles this issue—and its relation to lawsuits—is in many ways trendsetting for other professions. For example, Sorry Works! is an advocacy and consulting group, started in 2005 by Doug Wojcieszak, that promotes the concept of what it calls "disclosure apology," primarily in the medical field. The idea, which is catching on, is that apologies, when appropriate, can reduce litigation. Wojcieszak was inspired to set up the organization following the death of his brother Jim in 1998. Jim, a fit thirty-nine-year-old, went into a Cincinnati hospital emergency room complaining of chest and arm pain—classic signs of a heart attack. After a few tests—but not for a possible heart attack—he was sent home. The next day Jim's parents, seeing he was worsening, brought him back to the ER, where he was checked in and given antibiotics for what doctors assumed was a bacterial infection. Jim's father had been at the hospital for a cardiac workup a few months previously, and Doug Wojcieszak said the hospital apparently mixed up the two files. Finally Jim was rushed to emergency open-heart surgery, and surgeons discovered that four major arteries were blocked. Jim died on the operating table.

"The surgeon, who had nothing to do with the initial diagnosis, was furious," Wojcieszak said. "He said, 'If you had got to me two days before, he would have lived.'" Jim's parents wanted to understand—and receive an apology for—the series of errors that led to their oldest son's death, but no one at the hospital would talk. Even the surgeon later said he was advised not to speak to the family. "In the summer of 2000 we received a settlement, but never an apology," Wojcieszak told me. "A lot of people think lawsuits are like winning the lottery, but it's awful. Imagine being deposed on the death of your firstborn." Money isn't irrelevant, he said, but "the big thing for families that are suffering is that this didn't happen in vain. We realize mistakes happen, but we want to know it will be fixed next time. As my mother said, that would have made all the difference."

Wojcieszak, who is in public relations, ended up doing work later for organizations trying to reform the tort system in the medical field, as well as for trial lawyers who were trying to expand the right to sue. Seeing the issue from both sides, "I realized that the way people were approaching this was all wrong," he said. He first started Sorry Works! as a PR vehicle, using his brother's story in an attempt to change the discussion. But a few years later, he created a separate consultancy group called The Sorry Works! Coalition. Among other things, it promotes a three-step formalized program that includes: initial disclosure, investigation, and resolution. That is, those responsible apologize—not necessarily admitting or assigning blame—and resolve the immediate needs of the clients. An effort is then made to learn the truth about what happened and whether a mistake was made. The results of the investigation are shared with the client and lawyer, if he has one, explaining what happened and how it can be prevented in the future. If no mistake was made, then this is also discussed with empathy. Sorry Works! calls its process "compassion with a backbone."

Compare Wojcieszak's case with that of Sebastian Ferrero, a three-year-old who went into a Florida hospital in 2007 for some routine diagnostic tests regarding his growth and, through a series of serious errors—including being administered a dose of an amino acid at more than ten times what was required—died forty-eight hours later. The hospital took full responsibility for Sebastian's death and quickly reached a settlement of $860,000 with the boy's parents. This was the public apology fifteen days later from Pediatrics Vice Chairman for Clinical Affairs Donald Novak: "Our investigation to date has identified a series of errors that collectively caused this tragic outcome, and the family has been made aware of our findings. Words cannot describe our profound regret for these events." The Ferreros went on to create the Sebastian Ferrero Foundation to partner with the institutions responsible for their boy's death and to work together to develop a nationally recognized program for patient safety, as well as advocate and help fund a state-of-the-art children's hospital in Gainesville.

Some real-life examples and academic research do show that people are apt to overestimate the cost of apologies and underestimate the benefits. In a British study of malpractice patients, 37 percent said they would never have gone to court in the first place had they been offered an explanation and an apology. A University of Missouri study showed that contrary to conventional wisdom, which says that a defendant should avoid any admission of guilt, full apologies are more, rather than less, likely to mean quick lawsuit settlement. At the University of Michigan Health System (UMHS), one of the first to experiment with full disclosure, existing claims and lawsuits dropped to 83 in August 2007 from 262 in

August 2001. In addition, the average time to process a claim fell from about twenty months to eight months, and average litigation costs were more than halved. Total insurance reserves dropped by more than two-thirds, which were then invested in areas such as patient safety and risk management. A study examining the UMHS disclosure system acknowledged that the dramatic decline was not simply due to its new process—that medical malpractice suits in general were decreasing during the same time for a variety of reasons. But nonetheless, "clearly transparency at UMHS has not been the catastrophe predicted—and it has yielded unquestionable benefits," the report states.

I don't want to oversimplify the disclosure system—it's not that doctors and patients simply sit in a room and talk, apologies are given, and everyone joins hands in a sing-along. Hospitals are often dealing with complex and tragic events that have more than one—or even two or three—interpretations. But just to give you a sense of how it works, I'll summarize the case of a woman identified as JW. She was a thirty-six-year-old schoolteacher, married and the mother of two boys, ages six and eight. In August 2003, JW had a breast exam at her annual physical at UMHS that revealed no problems. Several months later, she noticed a lump on her right breast. A doctor, covering for her usual physician, concluded that it was not a problem and told her to continue monthly self-exams and begin mammograms at age forty. A year later she returned to her regular doctors and reported no problems at all, but in July 2005, she discovered another lump. Tests showed cancer that had metastasized. She underwent chemotherapy, and ultimately had to have a complete mastectomy. JW sued UMHS, claiming that her doctor had failed on three occasions to diagnose breast cancer and seeking $2 million for lost wages since she could no longer work, college expenses for her sons, whom she feared she would not live long enough to see go to college, and other costs. UMHS investigated the situation and privately agreed that the situation was not clear-cut—JW should have followed up more closely herself, but the covering doctor's care was below expectations for UMHS faculty. Should they deny and defend—and probably win, since doctors and hospitals statistically win more than they lose at trial—or admit the problems and address what harm had occurred?

After much discussion, UMHS officials chose the latter. In August 2006, they met with JW and her lawyer and explored her concerns. She finished chemotherapy and radiation in September. The economics of JW's claim were reviewed. UMHS engaged a financial planner to calculate the cost of college funds for both boys, and the financial planner prepared proposals for the college funds. Counterproposals were offered. In December 2006, the doctor treating JW, her husband, their lawyer, and hospital representatives all met. It was an opportunity for JW and her husband to tell their story and for the doctors to share their thoughts and apologize, if appropriate.

The case was ultimately settled for $400,000 and an offer to videotape her story for educational purposes for other health care workers, which JW was pleased to do. In her video she said, "I was perfectly satisfied after that night. What that apology meant to me was they had listened and finally I had been heard. I can't even describe how euphoric I felt when I left that meeting." And JW's lawyer said this: "Instead of adversarial, it was conversational.

It was instead of trying to figure out what claims and defenses needed to be, I found myself trying to figure out some higher calling, what's the right thing to do here? What's the best thing to do here? My role changed from advocate to warrior to counselor is the best way that I can describe it."

In many states, apologies have even become codified into law for civil suits. Here's a little of the history: In the 1970s a Massachusetts state senator's daughter was killed while riding her bicycle, and the driver who hit her never apologized. The father couldn't believe that the driver never expressed contrition, and was told that the driver had dared not risk even saying "I'm sorry" because it could have been seen as an admission in the litigation surrounding the girl's death. When the state senator retired, he and his successor introduced and ultimately got passed a law that allowed a "safe harbor" for people to offer "benevolent gestures expressing sympathy or a general sense of benevolence." Of course, in some ways this opened up a can of worms: Could you say, "I'm sorry that you're hurt"? Or even more actively, "I'm sorry that I hurt you"? Would that indicate fault? Other states followed in the 1990s and 2000s, trying to answer some of these questions by making the laws more specific about what constituted expressions of sympathy versus fault. And now a majority of states have enacted such laws—some that address solely medical malpractice, others that apply to all civil cases. The wording varies, but all in some form ensure that an apology or expression of sympathy can't be regarded in court as an admission of liability by a defendant.

If I step back and look at this, it seems a bit ridiculous—and sad.

How did we get to this point, where lawmakers decide how we should apologize? Where we need to stifle, after a small fender-bender, the polite and customary "I'm sorry"? Jonathan Cohen, of the University of Florida, an expert on the law and apologies, traces some of this back to the changes in society. There's no question that lawsuits have long been among us—just read *Bleak House*, Charles Dickens's novel about a lawsuit that destroyed generations—but they were less likely when communities were more tightly woven, when lawyers were more a part of the local social web. But "as society has commodified, that has changed," Cohen said. "It's a question of how much people can trust each other." Of course some of the changes can be good, even if they lead to lawsuits. In the past, doctors used to be trusted much more, Cohen pointed out, but perhaps in certain cases—particularly if they were a long-established part of a town—they were blindly trusted. The trick is to hold people accountable, without escalating every conflict.

The role of dispute resolution and mediation, which has become increasingly popular over the past three decades, is an example of an effort that aims to get people to talk rather than yell. That doesn't necessarily mean that money isn't involved, but that as much as possible the conflict—whether it be a divorce or a business claim—is as harmonious as it can be. And teaching the parties how to apologize is often a part of that process. In fact, Cohen said, we can even look at the differences in the international arena in the response to genocide. After World War II we had the Nuremberg trials, a classic legal approach to trying those accused of murder. But more recently, we've seen the South African Truth and Reconciliation Committee, which aimed not just at bringing those guilty to justice, but also at creating a system where the accused would admit their wrongdoing—which was required as part of amnesty—and bring forth some sort of resolution with those they had wronged. Although far from perfect, it was an effort at a less hostile and hopefully more successful way to heal a shattered nation.

All too often this is a point that gets lost in the process—how important the apology is not only to the person wronged but to the one who is responsible. Cohen tells a story about when he was a small boy and enthusiastically signed his name—a skill he had just proudly learned—all over a bathroom wall in crayon. Although he had done it backward, by looking in a mirror, his mother soon figured out who the culprit was. Cohen was grounded, physically prohibited from leaving his yard except for going to school. But that grounding also gave him a moral foundation. He was punished not only for ruining the bathroom wall, but more important, for denying his act. His mother understood that he would make mistakes and do careless acts of mischief in the future, but it was important to his integrity to own up. And when people are told to deny responsibility for legal reasons—or because they're afraid they'll lose their job, or are simply worried they'll get in trouble—that poses a psychological and spiritual risk to the person who made the mistake. Of course, it's even better if the person we're confessing to absolves us, but the acknowledgment is often soul-cleansing in and of itself. I think we all know that sense of relief when we admit we did something wrong or made an error and stop trying to hide it. I still remember, although I couldn't have been more than six or seven, the time I stepped on a low concrete wall surrounding a neighbor's house. Although I had often played on it, this time, my shoe stuck. The concrete was newly laid and wet. I leaped off and ran home.

A while later, while I was playing in our front yard with friends, the neighbor came by and asked who had ruined his freshly paved wall. I, along with my friends, immediately denied it, but it felt like my shoe was glowing. The neighbor (admittedly a grumpy old guy) pointed to my shoe and said, "That looks like the imprint." I don't remember what else he said, but I ran inside the house and cowered there for hours. Sure, I was sorry I had accidentally ruined his wall, but what would happen when he found out I had lied? The denial lodged itself in my throat and I avoided his house for many months. I, of course, never told him the truth. That was more than four decades ago, yet the shame I felt and the fear that I would be found out—more than the act itself—remains a fresh memory.

You may recall Dr. David Hilfiker from chapter 4, who wrote a first-person article in *The New England Journal of Medicine* about facing his own mistakes as a doctor. He well knows the toll that the failure to do so takes. "The drastic consequences of our mistakes, the repeated opportunities to make them, the uncertainty about our culpability, and the professional denial that mistakes happen all work together to create an intolerable dilemma for the physician. We see the horror of our mistakes, yet we cannot deal with their enormous emotional impact. Perhaps the only way to face our guilt is through confession, restitution, and absolution. Yet within the structure of modern medicine there is no place for such spiritual healing."

Although some things have changed in the past quarter-century, allowing such "spiritual healing," too little has. A study regarding health care workers and how they cope after a medical error found that those who denied responsibility tended to develop coping habits that researchers called maladaptive—that is, by expecting perfection of themselves and others, some residents learned to "manage the vulnerability and discomfort of making mistakes through techniques such as denial, distancing and discounting." However, those who did hold themselves accountable—to themselves and others—had much healthier coping practices. In another study, one doctor said, "You would love to be just straightforward. 'Gosh, I wish I had checked that potassium yesterday. I was busy. I made a mistake, I should have checked that. I can't believe I wouldn't do that. I will learn from my mistake and I will do better next time, because this is how we learn as people." But, the doctor went on, there is always the overshadowing fear of a lawsuit that, sadly, prevents such honest exchanges. Doug Wojcieszak told me that when he talks at hospitals, "doctors first sit there with crossed arms and scowls on their faces—but after sixty minutes they're coming up and shaking our hands." The point is not only that Wojcieszak's family is still suffering, but that "the doctors involved are also still suffering. They're good people who had a bad day. Confession is good for the soul, it's good for the body."

Cohen couldn't agree more. He argues that when a lawyer or insurer tells you not to apologize for what you have done, for example, that "dismantles one of life's most basic moral lessons"— owning up to our mistakes. And only by doing this can we move on, turn the injury into a learning experience. Since a mistake or wrongdoing usually occurs in the context of a prior relationship—whether it be with colleagues, a parent, a child, a spouse, or a patient—it is very hard for that relationship to go forward unless the person who erred apologizes, Cohen observes. "Saying I'm sorry or asking forgiveness permits you to have a future relationship. In cases of what are perceived as public acts of betrayal, Cohen says, an apology is needed to "reestablish the moral universe."

If we can't apologize properly for our mistakes, or accept others' genuine apologies, then we haven't learned all we can from our mistakes. If we can't express contrition in a clear manner—acknowledgment of the transgression, regret and responsibility for it, and hopefully a way to fix it—then that may be because we have failed to come to terms with how we, or others, erred. An apology isn't separate from the mistake; rather, it's an integral part of the lesson to be learned. A genuine expression of remorse and offer of accountability aims not only to repair what went wrong in the past, but to help build greater understanding and trust in the future.

Conclusion

Reporters on a regular beat tend to be suscep-
tible to the issues they cover—a medical reporter often starts believing that she has the symptoms of the various diseases she writes
about, an environmental reporter, as I was for a time, starts viewing everything in relation to potential risks to health and nature. So
naturally, when I became immersed in writing this book, I started
thinking about virtually nothing but mistakes—how we make them,
how we respond to them, how we learn from them. Friends would
call to vent about something that went wrong—they stuck their
foot in their mouth when talking to the boss, they completely forgot
about a son's school concert—and I would launch into a historical,

sociological, psychological, and academic discourse about mistakes. I wouldn't even get to the part about why they shouldn't feel bad about their particular problem, because by then they would have long since abandoned the conversation. My point is not that my friends have suspiciously short attention spans, but that the way we handle mistakes affects every relationship we have.

When I started this book and was asked about the basic concept, I summarized it this way: "It explores the tension between the fact we're taught when young that we learn from mistakes, but the reality is that most of us hate and dread them." I sought to find out what creates that tension, and how we can return to and internalize the lesson from kindergarten—that mistakes help us because we learn from them. A few years—and a great deal of research—later, I've changed some of my assumptions, but that original thesis remains the same. There are no simple fixes, but there are ways all of us can shift our thinking about mistakes. Starting with our children, we can emphasize effort and deemphasize results. We can appreciate that we—and they—can't be perfect, nor is it a goal we should aim for. We should strive to do our best, but if the prize is ever elusive perfection, then the fear of failure will too often overshadow the willingness to experiment, take risks, and challenge ourselves. We should be careful of the contradictory message that it's all right to make mistakes but not where it counts, and of unintentionally absorbing assumptions about gender that reinforce stereotypes— that girls can't handle criticism or that boys don't want to talk about their mishaps. We can create a community of like-minded friends who support us in our efforts not to succumb to the idea that all that matters is good grades and awards. Yes, our children need to succeed, but we have to know—and repeat it to ourselves over and over and over—that they also need to fail.

The type of children we raise will be the employees and employers of tomorrow, and they will carry what they learn about mistakes when young right into the workplace. Will they be adults who point fingers, or will they be more interested in solving problems than placing blame? As we've seen, there is usually not one incompetent person at the root of most mistakes. While this may make it more difficult to affix culpability, it does make it easier to eventually uncover the factors that underlie errors and resolve them in the long term. Research in the area of human error has taught us the importance of figuring out and uncovering the multitude of latent errors that led up to the blatant one.

It has also taught us how necessary it is to avoid hindsight bias— that is, as much as possible, walking through the steps and missteps leading up to a mistake, not judging it in retrospect while standing at the finish line. And especially in light of our recent economic turmoil, it is clear how important it is not to assume that there are those—through perceived talent or brains or experience—who are somehow above mistakes. That some people—or we ourselves— are immune to needing to be questioned or challenged.

One overarching theme is the value of clear communication. But like so many clichés, this term has lost real meaning—if we just conversed more, things would be better. In fact, research has shown us that there are tools we can use to help us share information more successfully. Remember the checklists in surgery? Just casually telling people to be more aware of what they are doing and to talk more wouldn't change anything. Those who developed the checklists had to study how other such systems were developed, conduct pilot studies, and constantly revise. Something as seemingly minor as knowing each other's names, studies found, fosters closer teamwork. We don't have to reinvent the wheel and figure it all out ourselves; there is a lot of helpful information out there to create better communication within our families, in the workplace, and with our friends, if we are only willing to access it.

What other kinds of information do we need? In developing systems to avoid errors, observation and feedback are crucial. We all make too many assumptions about how we and others act based on what we want to be true, not necessarily on what is true. As we read, many pilots and doctors believe that fatigue and stress don't cause them to make mistakes. That's simply not correct. In all walks of life, we need to identify underlying attitudes that can be harmful and then work hard to change them. We also need to learn from other cultures that our ways of looking at mistakes and errors aren't the only ways.

Finally, I think we have all been in situations where we knew that if we sincerely said we were sorry and acknowledged our accountability, it would defuse a situation—but we don't and it escalates. And the opposite is true as well—I know the anger and helplessness I feel when someone has done me wrong but brushes it off, refuses to admit it, or somehow turns it around to be my fault. The original mistake becomes completely clouded in the ensuing rage and resentment. I think most of us want others to be able to make mistakes without it being considered a sin, but we also want them to own up and take responsibility for their actions. We want them to offer sincere apologies, not just lip service. But as much as we want others to react that way, we need to want that for *ourselves*—to be a person who can recognize which mistakes are serious and which aren't, to be able to genuinely apologize (but not over-apologize) when needed, to take on board whatever lessons need to be learned and then to move on. We also need to be the kind of people who are willing to acknowledge the imperfection in others, to sincerely *accept* an apology and then let go.

It is not easy. Yet despite what many of us think, we can choose, to some extent, to become that kind of person. Yes, some are born with a more easygoing or accepting temperament, where slip-ups seem to roll off their back, while others with more intense or uptight personalities may agonize about every little blooper. But just because we're hardwired one way doesn't mean we can't, through a willingness to listen and understand, shift our perceptions. Even though the process may seem painstakingly slow, we can change our attitudes little by little. *C'est la vie* may never be my life motto, but just by learning what I have while researching this book, I can say that I am more accepting of my own and others' mistakes (yes, even my husband's and children's). I am more willing to look at what really happened when things go wrong and try to learn rather than go on autopilot, expending useless energy flagellating myself or pointing fingers at others.

The truth also is, sometimes a faux pas is just a faux pas and there is no great lesson or wonderful epiphany at the end. It might just be a blunder that messes up your workday or causes your spouse to get mad at you or ruins that great cashmere sweater you got on sale (hypothetically speaking, of course). We all make our share of those, and that's okay also. But if we can all forgive ours and others' errors more often, if we can acknowledge that perfection is a myth and that human beings screw up on a regular basis—and we can either simply feel bad about it and find someone to accuse or learn from it—then we are on the right track. Make no mistake about it.

ACKNOWLEDGMENTS

I always read acknowledgments wondering how so many people can be involved in producing a book. Well, now I know.

My thanks first of all to the two people who have shown great faith in this project from its infancy: my agent, Miriam Altshuler, who shepherded it with great skill and humor from a vague idea to a full-blown book, and my editor at Riverhead, Megan Lynch, who has consistently been thoughtful, generous, and inspiring.

I also want to thank Jim Impoco, who initiated a whole new phase in my life when he asked me to write the "ShortCuts" column, and Mickey Meese, my first wonderful editor of that column. Phyllis Messenger, who took over and edited the mistakes column that set this whole book in motion, has been the best editor a reporter could have.

My heartfelt appreciation to my friend Nancy Miller, who pointed me in the right direction from the very beginning and was always there with valuable advice. To Andraya Dolbee, a good and true friend and most faithful reader of my column. To Nina Easton, who always believed I could do this. To Leah Murphy, who celebrates my victories as if they were her own. To my neighbor Peter Kinsman: I am forever in his debt for using his computer skills to rescue a lost chapter. And to all those who have supported me and been there during my many mistakes throughout the years: Mollie Sokolov, Mary-Kay Demetriou, Christine Knights, Faye Fiore, Christin Putnam, and Nancy Winkelstein. A special mention, of course, to my fabulous sisters and their families: Orlee Raymond and her husband, Danny, and children, Talia, Yaniv, and Maya; and Ronit Austgen and her husband, Tim, and children, Hannah, Jake, and Zach.

I want to thank all those who took the time to speak with me and go over my research to keep it as error-free as possible. In particular, Carol Dweck, Robert Helmreich, Peter Pronovost, James Bagian, and Jim Stigler were exceptionally generous with their time. All mistakes (as there inevitably will be) are mine alone.

Although I don't say it often enough, I am so grateful to have parents who have always encouraged me. And to have two wonderful sons, Ben and Gabriel, who are growing into fine human beings despite their imperfect mother. And even as a writer, words fail me when it comes to my appreciation and love for my husband, Mark, who is always there for me. I only wish my grandmother could have been alive to see this book published. As she did with the many poems I wrote as a child, she would no doubt have handed copies out to all her friends (and a few strangers as well).

NOTES

Introduction

Page 3 *Social psychologists Carol Tavris and Elliot Aronson:* Tavris, C., and Aronson, E. (2007) *Mistakes Were Made (But Not by Me)*. New York: Houghton Mifflin Harcourt, p. 230.

Page 5 *A student of hers, "David":* Bryans, P. (1999) What Do Professional Men and Women Learn from Making Mistakes at Work? *Research in Post-Compulsory Education*, p. 185.

Chapter 1. (Mis)Understanding and (Re)Defining Mistakes

Page 10 *The dictionary separates out error:* Bryans, p. 189.

Page 10 *how mistakes can foster innovation:* Prather, C. (March 2008) Use Mistakes to Foster Innovation, *Research Technology Management*, p. 14.

Page 11 *Reason defines an error:* Reason, J. (1990) *Human Error.* New York: Cambridge University Press, p. 9.

Page 11 *To explain the difference:* Ibid., p. 55.

Page 12 *Reason's book* Human Error: Ibid., p. 1.

Page 14 *For instance, in January:* Ibid., p. 5.

Page 14 *"active failures are like mosquitoes":* Reason, J. (March 18, 2000) Human Error: Models and Management, *British Medical Journal,* 320, pp. 768–770.

Page 15 *As Reason points out:* Reason, *Human Error,* pp. 192, 253.

Page 17 *Once we put mistakes under the microscope:* Pearn, M., and Honey, P. From Error Terror to Wonder Blunder, *People Management,* March 1997, pp. 42–43.

Page 18 *We've always been told:* Dekker, S. (2006) *The Field Guide to Understanding Human Error.* Burlington, VT: Ashgate, p. 13.

Page 19 *As historian Barbara Tuchman:* Tuchman, B. (1981) *Practicing History.* New York: Alfred A. Knopf, p. 75.

Page 20 *As the chairman of the investigation:* Dekker, p. 23; Hidden, A. (1989) *Investigation into the Clapham Junction Railway Accident.* London: Department of Transport.

Pages 21–22 *It was back in the early 1990s:* Ullsperger, M. (Minding) Mistakes, *Scientific American Mind,* August/September 2008, pp. 52–54.

Page 22 *But in addition to recognizing:* Author interview with Markus Ullsperger.

Page 23 *In 1998, two Japanese neuroscientists:* Ullsperger, p. 55.

Page 24 *But according to Jonah Lehrer's book:* Lehrer, J. (2009) *How We Decide.* New York: Houghton Mifflin Harcourt, pp. 46–48.

Page 24 *What's interesting is that people:* Ullsperger, p. 57.

Page 25 *Lehrer points out:* Lehrer, p. 51.

Page 25 *One of the very important aspects:* Author interview with Markus Ullsperger.

Page 26 *Ullsperger noted that if we:* Author interview with Markus Ullsperger.

Page 27 *It may seem as if we've wandered:* Author interview with Stephen Taylor.

Page 28 *Perfectionists often get caught:* Author interview with Jeff Szymanski.

Page 28 *Rabbi Irving Greenberg, a Jewish scholar:* Greenberg, I. (1988) *The Jewish Way.* Northvale, NJ: Jason Aronson, pp. 209–210.

Page 29 *Those who have perfectionist tendencies:* Author interview with Jeff Szymanski.

Page 30 *"Excellence involves enjoying":* Marano, H. E. Pitfalls of Perfectionism, *Psychology Today,* March 1, 2008.

Page 31 *One of Frost's studies shows:* Frost, R. O., and Marten, P. A. (1990) Perfectionism and Evaluative Threat, *Cognitive Therapy and Research,* 14, no. 6, pp. 559–572.

NOTES

Page 32 *Multidimensional Perfectionism Scale:* Reprinted with generous permission from Professor Randy Frost.

Page 36 *Frost asked university students:* Frost, R. O., Turcotte, T. A., Heimberg, R. G., Mattia, J. I., Holt, C. S., and Hope, D. A. (1995) Reactions to Mistakes Among Subjects High and Low in Perfectionistic Concern over Mistakes, *Cognitive Therapy and Research*, 19, no. 2, pp.195–205.

Page 37 *It's good to remember:* Saints Misbehavin' by Thomas Craughwell, *Wall Street Journal*, October 27, 2006.

Page 38 *In some ways, do these shows:* Author interview with Mark Andrejevic.

Page 40 *So what have we learned:* Reason, *Human Error*, p. 148.

CHAPTER 2. IT STARTS EARLY

Page 41 *I first heard about:* Bronson, P. How Not to Talk to Your Kids, *New York*, February 19, 2007.

Page 41 *When we applaud children:* Author interview with Carol Dweck.

Page 47 *Children as young as three or four years old:* Blackwell, L.S., Trzesniewski, K. H., Dweck, C.S. (January/February 2007) Implicit Theories of Intelligence Predict Achievement Across an Adolescent Transition: A Longitudinal Study and an Intervention, *Child Development*, 78, no. 1, pp. 246–263.

Page 49 *First of all, there's simply how we're hardwired:* Klein, T., Neumann, J., Reuter, M., Hennig, J., von Cramon, D. Y., and Ullsperger, M. Genetically Determined Differences in Learning from Errors, *Science*, 318, no. 5856, pp. 1642–1645.

Page 50 *For example, some studies have shown:* Folmer, A. S., Cole, D. A., Sigal, A. B., Benbow, L. D., Satterwhite, L. F., Swygert, K. E., and Ciesla, J. A. (February 2008) Age-Related Changes in Children's Understanding Effort and Ability: Implications for Attribution Theory and Motivation, *Journal of Experimental Child Psychology*, 99, no. 2, pp. 114–134; Nicholls, J. G. (1978) The Development of the Concepts of Effort and Ability, Perception of Academic Attainment and the Understanding That Difficult Tasks Require More Ability, *Child Development*, 49, pp. 800–814.

Page 51 *Second, one person can have both:* Quihuis, G.., Bempechat, J., Jimenez, N. V., and Boulay, B. A. (Summer 2002) Implicit Theories of Intelligence Across Academic Domains: A Study of Meaning Making in Adolescents of Mexican Descent, *New Directions for Child and Adolescent Development*, no. 96, pp. 87–100.

Page 54 *In his best-selling book:* Gladwell, M. (2008) *Outliers.* New York: Little, Brown, p. 268.

Page 54 *The concept that the best naturally rise:* Author interview with K. Anders Ericsson.

Page 55 *So how does that all fit together?* Seligman, M. E. P. (2007) *The Optimistic Child.* New York: Houghton Mifflin, pp. 31–35.

Page 57 *"While we do not want our children":* Brooks, R., and Goldstein, S. (2003) *Nurturing Resilience in Our Children.* Chicago: Contemporary Books, pp. 161–163.

Page 58 *Wendy Mogel, a psychologist:* Mogel, W. (2001) *The Blessing of a Skinned Knee.* New York: Penguin Compass, p. 77.

Page 58 *The first and most benign:* Mogel, pp. 201–202.

Page 59 *For parents, it's often hard:* Coloroso, B. (2005) *Kids Are Worth It!* New York: CollinsLifestyle, pp. 10–41, 148.

Page 61 *"How we respond to their many mistakes":* Coloroso, B. (2007) *Just Because It's Not Wrong Doesn't Make It Right.* Toronto: Penguin Canada, p. 168.

Page 61 *One of the difficulties, of course:* Seligman, pp. 65–66.

Pages 62 *The same, of course, is true with teachers:* Bray, W. Learning from Mistakes During Class Discussion of Mathematics: The Role of Teachers' Beliefs and Knowledge. Paper presented at the Association of Mathematics Teacher Educators Annual Meeting, Orlando, Florida, February 6, 2009.

Page 67 *The psychologist John Nicholls argues:* Nicholls, J. G. (1989) *The Competitive Ethos and Democratic Education.* Cambridge, MA: Harvard University Press.

Page 67 *Gail Heyman, a professor of psychology:* Heyman, G., Fu, G., and Lee, K. (2008) Reasoning About the Disclosure of Success and Failure to Friends Among Children in the United States and China, *Developmental Psychology*, 44, no. 4, pp. 908–918.

Page 69 *Such insight may help explain:* Author interview with Hazel Markus.

Page 71 *It can seem overwhelming to think:* Author interview with Daniel Pink.

CHAPTER 3. "FAIL OFTEN, FAST, AND CHEAP"

Page 74 *Remember poor David:* Gladwell, M. The Talent Myth, *New Yorker*, July 22, 2002.

Page 76 *As we know, there are many different:* Argyris, C. (1992) *On Organizational Learning.* Cambridge, MA: Blackwell.

Page 77 *Sometimes, however, it may seem:* Argyris, C. Good Communication That Blocks Learning, *Harvard Business Review*, July/August 1994, pp. 77–85.

NOTES

Page 78 *Years of empirical research:* Ibid.; author interview with Chris Argyris.

Page 78 *This is not surprising:* Tavris and Aronson, p. 2.

Page 79 *But "mindless self-justification":* Ibid., p. 9.

Page 79 *Most companies—like most people:* Schoemaker, P. J. H., and Gunther, R. E. The Wisdom of Deliberate Mistakes, *Harvard Business Review*, June 2006, pp. 109–115.

Page 81 *"Unfortunately, the people who most need":* Author interview with Paul Schoemaker.

Page 82 *Speaking of the* Times: Rose, M., and Cohen, L. Amid Turmoil, Top Editors Resign at *New York Times, Wall Street Journal*, June 6, 2003.

Page 83 *A recurring theme, in work:* Prather.

Page 83 *Researchers from Stanford University:* Fast, N. J., and Tiedens, L. Z. (2010) Blame Contagion: The Automatic Transmission of Self-Serving Attributions, *Journal of Experimental Social Psychology*, 46, pp. 97–106.

Page 85 *Such experiments underline:* Bennis, W., and Nanus, B. (1997) *Leaders: Strategies for Taking Charge.* New York: HarperCollins, p. 70.

Page 85 *Some companies have gone even further:* Prather.

Page 86 *But wacky awards won't go far:* Heslin, P. A., Latham, G. P., and VandeWalle, D. (2005) The Effect of Implicit Person Theory on Performance Appraisals, *Journal of Applied Psychology*, 90, no. 5, pp. 842–856.

Page 87 *"airline pilots, nuclear power plant operators":* Heslin, P. A., and VandeWalle, D. (June 2008) Managers' Implicit Assumptions About Personnel, *Current Directions in Psychological Science*, 17, pp. 219–223.

Page 88 *"How a company deals with mistakes":* Gates, B. Failure Is Part of the Game and Should Be Used, *Seattle Post-Intelligencer*, April 26, 1995.

Page 88 *In order for companies:* Schoemaker and Gunther, The Wisdom of Deliberate Mistakes.

Page 90 *realizing which tasks are routine . . . "One of the most helpful things":* Argyris, C. Empowerment: The Emperor's New Clothes, *Harvard Business Review*, May/June 1998, pp. 98–105.

Page 90 *Creating an environment:* Agyris, Good Communication That Blocks Learning.

Page 90 *There are ways to resolve:* O'Toole, J., and Bennis, W. A Culture of Candor, *Harvard Business Review*, June 2009.

Page 91 *Researchers have determined:* Garvin, D. A., Edmondson, A.C., and Francesca, G. Is Yours a Learning Organization? *Harvard Business Review*, March 2008.

Page 91 *One way to make employees:* Prather.

Page 91 *Changing a work culture:* Heslin and VandeWalle.

Page 92 *While most people will do anything:* Gully, S. M., Payne, S. C., Koles, K. L. K., and Whiteman, J. A. K. (February 2002) The Impact of Error Training and Individual Differences on Training Outcomes: An Attribute-Treatment Interaction Perspective, *Journal of Applied Psychology*, 87, no. 1, pp. 143–155; author interview with Stanley Gully.

Page 94 *First let me go back:* Argyris, On Organizational Learning, p. 85.

Page 95 *The star system, where individual brilliance:* Gladwell, The Talent Myth.

Page 96 *Carol Dweck argues that this adulation:* Author interview with Carol Dweck.

Page 96 *Executives confidently went on:* Author interview with Peter Heslin.

Page 96 *Merrill Lynch, Countrywide Financial:* Anderson, J. Chiefs' Pay Under Fire at Capitol, *New York Times*, March 8, 2008; Wingfield, B. Puzzling Pay Packages, Forbes.com, March 7, 2008.

Page 97 *O'Neal is an example:* Cassidy, J. Subprime Suspect, *New Yorker*, March 31, 2008.

Page 97 *And we seem to have learned nothing:* Sterngold, J. How Much Did Lehman CEO Dick Fuld Really Make? *Bloomberg Businessweek*, April 29, 2010.

Page 98 *Michael Jenson, a professor emeritus:* Author interview with Michael Jenson.

Page 98 *The fact that their performance:* Gladwell, The Talent Myth.

Page 98 *Or, as the caption:* Mankoff, B. *New Yorker*, March 2, 2009.

Page 98 *one of the most dangerous myths:* Author interview with Warren Bennis.

Page 99 *"Success is a lousy teacher":* Gates, B. (1995) *The Road Ahead*. New York: Viking Penguin.

Page 99 *"There is no chance that pretty much":* Carney, J. John Thain Admits He Didn't Understand Merrill's Risks, *Business Insider*, October 7, 2009.

Page 99 *Yet at the end of 2009:* Tse, T. M. Fresh Round of Wall Street Bonuses Rekindles Scrutiny, *Washington Post*, January 12, 2010.

Page 100 *But as for other lessons?:* Author interview with Joe Nocera.

Page 101 *"The same patterns emerge":* Author interview with Carmen Reinhart.

Page 101 *But why don't we see what has consistently failed?* www.century-of-flight.net.

Page 101 *"Finance is like sex":* Author interview with Joe Nocera.

Page 102 *a great example:* Andrews, E. L. My Personal Credit Crisis, *New York Times*, May 17, 2009.

Page 104 *"Done right, an apology":* Weeks, H. (May 19, 2003) The Art of the Apology, *Harvard Management Update*.

Page 104 *Take the Intel Pentium chip tale:* Emergy, V. (February/March 1996) The Pentium Chip Story: A Learning Experience, www.emery.com; Miller, G. S., and

Narayanan, V. G. Accounting for the Intel Pentium Chip Flaw, *Harvard Business Review*, June 26, 2001.

Page 106 *None of this is going to be quick or easy:* Learning from Others' Mistakes, *In Sight*, July 2005. http://www.collision-insight.com/news/archives/200507-feature .htm.

CHAPTER 4. IT'S NOT BRAIN SURGERY . . . BUT WHAT IF IT IS?

Page 108 *The mistake in Rebecca's hospital:* Kohn, L.T., Corrigan, J. M., and Donaldson, M. S., eds. (2000) *To Err Is Human: Building a Safer Health System.* Washington, DC: Institute of Medicine, National Academy Press.

Page 109 *A poll by the Kaiser Family Foundation: Kaiser/Harvard Health News,* 4, no. 6 (November/December 1999) .

Page 109 *staggering statistic:* Kohn, Corrigan, and Donaldson, p. 26.

Page 109 *One of the report's authors:* Weiss, R. Medical Errors Blamed for Many Deaths, *Washington Post,* November 30, 1999.

Page 109 *Let's return to definitions:* Kohn, Corrigan, and Donaldson, p. 4.

Page 109 *The authors divided types of errors:* Ibid., p. 36.

Page 110 *The initial step, of course:* Ibid., p. 3.

Page 110 *"the pilot has a certain enlightened":* Author interview with James Bagian.

Page 111 *"the majority of medical errors":* Kohn, Corrigan, and Donaldson, p. 4.

Page 111 *the "person approach" and the "systems approach":* Reason, Human Error: Models and Management.

Page 111 *"Blaming individuals is emotionally more satisfying":* Ibid.

Page 111 *"the complete absences of such a reporting culture":* Ibid.

Page 112 *"When an adverse event occurs":* Ibid.

Page 112 *"their accumulation actually makes":* Kohn, Corrigan, and Donaldson, p. 56.

Page 112 *Let me put a human face:* Allen, S. With Work, Dana-Farber Learns from '94 Mistakes, *Boston Globe,* November 30, 2004; Agency for Healthcare Research and Quality. (2004) Organizational Change in the Face of High Public Errors: The Dana-Farber Cancer Institute Experience, www.webmm.ahrq.gov; Chemo Overdoses Overview, U.S. Department of Veterans Affairs Getting at Patient Safety (GAPs) Center. www.gapscenter.va.gov/stories/BetsyDesc.asp.

Page 113 *Teacher Maureen Bateman:* Maureen Bateman, A Cancer Patient and Chronicler, *New York Times,* June 1, 1997.

Page 113 *In 1995, a Florida man:* Doctor Who Cut Off Wrong Leg Is Defended by Colleagues, *New York Times,* September 17, 1995.

Page 113 *The same year, a seven-year-old boy:* Thompson, D., and Lemonick, M. D. Doctors' Deadly Mistakes, *Time,* December 13, 1999.

Page 114 *Those deaths created:* Reason, *Human Error,* p. 213.

Page 114 *"The natural human tendency":* Ibid.

Pages 114–15 *If accidents are viewed as unique:* Author interview with David Woods.

Page 115 *It "truly changed the conversation":* Leape, L. L., and Berwick, D. M. (May 18, 2005) Five Years After *To Err Is Human, Journal of the American Medical Association (JAMA),* 93, no. 19, pp. 2384–2390.

Page 115 *Fewer patients die from:* Ibid.

Page 116 *But far less has changed:* Consumers Union. To Err Is Human—To Delay Is Deadly, SafePatientProject.org, May 2009, p. 5.

Page 116 *Confusion caused by similar drug names:* Medication Errors Injure 1.5 Million People and Cost Billions of Dollars Annually, National Academies news release, July 20, 2006.

Page 116 *Perhaps the best-known example:* Dennis Quaid Acts on Medical Errors, *Wall Street Journal* health blog, March 21, 2008.

Page 116 *"The more complex any system is":* Leape and Berwick, p. 2387.

Page 116 *"The 'hidden curriculum'":* Berlinger, N. (2008) Medical Error, in *From Birth to Death and Bench to Clinic: The Hastings Center Bioethics Briefing Book for Journalists, Policymakers, and Campaigns,* ed. Mary Crowley. Garrison, NY: The Hastings Center, pp. 97–100.

Pages 118–119 *Each year what are known as central lines:* Pronovost, P., Needham, D., Berenholtz, S., Sinopoli, D., Chu, H., Cosgrove, S., Sexton, B., Hyzy, R., Welsh, R., Roth, G., Bander, J., Kepros, J., and Goeschel, C. (December 28, 2006) An Intervention to Decrease Catheter-Related Bloodstream Infections in the ICU, *New England Journal of Medicine,* 355, no. 26, pp. 2725–2732; author interview with Peter Pronovost and e-mail from Peter Pronovost to author.

Page 119 *intensive care units barely existed:* Gawande, A. The Checklist, *New Yorker,* December 10, 2007.

Pages 119–120 *medicine has now entered the phase:* Ibid.

Page 120 *Here is Pronovost's checklist:* Ibid.

Page 120 *Pronovost asked his nurses:* Author interview with Peter Pronovost.

Page 121 *When Pronovost and his colleagues:* Gawande, The Checklist.

Page 121 *Then, in 2003, the Michigan:* Pronovost et al.

Page 121 *The typical ICU:* Gawande, The Checklist.

Page 121 *"There's an expectation of perfection":* Author interview with Peter Pronovost.

Page 123 *When he was asked in 2007:* Gawande, A. (2009) *The Checklist Manifesto.* New York: Metropolitan Books/Henry Holt, p. 88.

Page 123 *Gawande describes how:* Ibid., p. 112.

Page 123 *Gawande went back to the drawing board:* Ibid., p. 123.

Page 124 *He developed one for safe surgery:* Ibid., pp. 141–146.

Page 124 *In October 2008, the results came in:* Ibid., pp. 153–154.

Page 124 *In a survey of 250 surgeons:* Ibid., p. 157.

Page 124 *One of the requirements:* Ibid., p. 107.

Page 125 *WHO Checklist for Surgery:* http://whqlibdoc.who.int/publications/2009/9789241598590_eng_Checklist.pdf.

Page 127 *Even at such an enlightened hospital:* Author interview with resident.

Page 127 *Before the Johns Hopkins resident:* Hilfiker, D. (January 12, 1984) Facing Our Mistakes, *New England Journal of Medicine*, 310, pp 118–122.

Page 128 *Hilfiker told me:* Author interview with David Hilfiker.

Page 129 *Changing a deeply embedded culture:* Institute for Healthcare Improvement. Pursuing Perfection: Report from McLeod Regional Medical Center on Leadership Patient Rounds. http://www.ihi.org/IHI/Topics/LeadingSystemImprovement/Leadership/ImprovementStories/PursuingPerfectionReportfromMcLeodRegional-MedicalCenteronLeadershipPatientRounds.htm.

Page 129 *Another way to encourage:* The Patient Safety and Quality Improvement Act of 2005, Agency for Healthcare Research and Quality, www.ahrq.gov/qual/psocat.htm.

Page 130 *As I was writing this book:* Author interview with James Bagian; Changing the Safety Culture at VA, *U.S. Medicine*, August 2002.

Page 132 *In 2000, the Department of Veterans Affairs*: Author interview with James Bagian.

Page 133 *Linda Connell, program director:* Author interview with Linda Connell.

Page 134 *The concept of Just Culture:* Author interview with David Marx.

Page 134 *In an effort to address this tension:* Page, A. H. (October 2007) Making Just Culture a Reality: One Organization's Approach, AHRQ WebM&M serial, webmm.ahrq.gov/perspective.aspx?perspectiveID=50.

Page 134 *Let's take the case of a hospital-wide requirement:* Ibid.

NOTES

Page 135 *In 2010, the American Nurses Association:* American Nurses Association, Position Statement, January 28, 2010.

Page 136 *Things have changed:* Author interview with Avrum Bluming.

Page 137 *Even though the pendulum:* Gallagher, T. H., Garbutt, J. M., Waterman, A. D., Flum, D. R., Larson, E. B., Waterman, B. M., Dunagan, W. C., Fraser, V. J., and Levinson, W. (August 14–18, 2006) Choosing Your Words Carefully: How Physicians Would Disclose Harmful Medical Errors to Patients, *Archives of Internal Medicine*, 166, pp. 1585–1593.

Page 138 *But it is not just the patient:* Waterman, A. D., Garbutt, J., Hazel, E., Dunagan, W. C., Levinson, W., Fraser, V. J., and Gallagher, T. H. (August 2007) The Emotional Impact of Medical Errors on Practicing Physicians in the United States and Canada, *The Joint Commission Journal on Quality and Patient Safety*, 33, no. 8, pp. 467–475.

Page 139 *"Because doctors do not discuss":* Hilifiker, Facing Our Mistakes.

CHAPTER 5. LESSONS FROM THE COCKPIT

Page 144 *He became involved in pilot safety:* Author interview with Robert Helmreich.

Page 144 *It turns out that what Helmreich:* UT Professor Studies Parallels Between Cockpit Crews, Medical Teams, *ONCampus* (The University of Texas at Austin), 26, no. 12 (March 30, 1999).

Page 145 *"Plane crashes rarely happen":* Gladwell, *Outliers*, p. 183.

Page 145 *Historically, the statistic bandied about:* Helmreich, R. (March 18, 2000) On Error Management: Lessons from Aviation, *British Medical Journal*, 320, pp. 781–785.

Page 145 *However, many aviation experts:* Author interview with Robert Sumwalt.

Page 146 *Such surveys help shed light:* Helmreich, On Error Management.

Page 147 *The three main programs:* Helmreich, R. L., Merritt, A. C., Wilhelm, J. A. (1999) The Evolution of Crew Resource Management Training in Commercial Aviation, *International Journal of Aviation Psychology*, 9, no. 1, pp. 19–32.

Page 148 *A classic and tragic example:* Fischer, U., and Orasanu, J. (August 2000) Error-Challenging Strategies: Their Role in Preventing and Correcting Errors, in *Proceedings of the International Ergonomics Association 14th Triennial Congress and Human Factors and Ergonomics Society 44th Annual Meeting in San Diego, California.*

Page 149 *Two years after that:* Captain Al Haynes, speech at NASA Ames Research Center, Dryden Flight Research Facility, Edwards, California, May 24, 1991.

Page 150 *The three-member crew:* Helmreich, R. Managing Human Error in Aviation, *Scientific American,* May 1997, pp. 62–67.

Page 150 *Research shows that highly effective:* Sexton, J. B., Thomas, E. J., and Helmreich, R. (March 18, 2000) Error, Stress and Teamwork in Medicine and Aviation: Cross Sectional Surveys, *British Medical Journal,* 320, pp. 745–749.

Page 151 *And in case we need any more evidence:* Frank, T., and Levin, A. Hudson River Hero Is ex–Air Force Fighter Pilot, *USA Today,* January 16, 2009.

Page 151 *Observing how pilots work:* Helmreich, On Error Management; Office of the Secretary General, International Civil Aviation Organization. (2002) Line Operations Safety Audit (LOSA) manual.

Page 152 *Another way the aviation industry:* Author interview with Linda Connell.

Page 154 *What has been so effective:* Author interview with Linda Connell; Wald, M. Panel Backs Letting Airlines Confess Errors Unpunished, *New York Times,* September 11, 2008; Otto, D. (July 2004) Aviation Safety Reporting in the 90th FS, *Flying Safety Magazine* (United States Air Force), 60, p. 22.

Page 154 *Selective incidents are published: Callback,* no. 337 (January 2008), www.asrs.arc.gov/publications/callback.

Page 155 *Critics say that with ASRS:* Author interviews with Robert Helmreich and Linda Connell.

Page 156 *Such systems are, of course, not a panacea:* Wellman, J. (Fall 2007) Lessons Learned About Lessons Learned, *Organization Development Journal,* 25, no. 3, pp. 65–72.

Page 156 *So has this worked?:* Information from the National Transportation Safety Board, Table 6, Accidents, Fatalities and Rates 1975–2008 for U.S. Carriers Operating Under 14 CFR 121 Scheduled Service (Airlines).

Page 157 *In addition, observation and data:* Helmreich, R., et al. The Evolution of Crew Resource Management Training in Commercial Aviation; Pizzi, L. T., Goldfarb, N., and Nash, D. B. (July 2001) Crew Resource Management and Its Application in Medicine, chap. 44 in *Making Health Care Safer: A Critical Analysis of Patient Safety Practices,* Shojania, K. G., Duncan, B. W., McDonald, K. M., and Wachter, R. M., eds. AHRQ Publication No. 01-E058.

Page 157 *"We have to believe":* Author interview with Robert Sumwalt.

NOTES

CHAPTER 6. BLAMING YOU, BLAMING ME

Page 161 *In the 1970s and 1980s, some of this:* Gilligan, C. (1993) *In a Different Voice.* Cambridge, MA: Harvard University Press.

Page 161 *Gilligan's writings have had:* Sadker, M. and D. (1995) *Failing at Fairness: How Our Schools Cheat Girls.* New York: Touchstone/Simon & Schuster, p. 228.

Page 162 *And more recently, using:* Weil, E. Testosterone, *New York Times Magazine,* March 2, 2008.

Page 162 *"Scientists themselves no longer pit":* Eliot, L. (2009) *Pink Brain, Blue Brain.* New York: Houghton Mifflin Harcourt, p. 7.

Page 163 *over one hundred samples of 28,920 college students:* Twenge, J. (2006) *Generation Me.* New York: Free Press/Simon & Schuster, p. 193.

Page 163 *For those who work:* Dey, J. G., and Hill, C. (2007) *Behind the Pay Gap.* Washington, DC: American Association of American Women Educational Foundation, p. 2.

Page 163 *"Although people may be more accepting":* Author interview with Amanda Diekman.

Pages 164 *one of the few studies directly looking:* Bryans, P., and Mavin, S. (2007) The Emotional Impact of Making Mistakes at Work: Gender Schemas and Emotion Norms, chap. 7 in *Gendering Emotions in Organizations,* Lewis, P., and Simpson, R., eds. London: Palgrave MacMillan.

Page 164–166 *"women tend to internalize" and following quotations from study:* Bryans and Mavin, pp. 135–140.

Page 166 *One study asked undergraduates:* Beyer, S., and Langenfeld, K. (2003) Gender Differences in the Recall of Performance Feedback. Paper presented at the annual meeting of the American Psychological Association, Atlanta, May 2003.

Page 167 *What about how women are viewed by others?:* Carli, L. L. (1990) Gender, Language, and Influence, *Journal of Personality and Social Psychology,* 59, no. 5, pp. 941–951.

Page 168 *A 2004 study found that women:* Thomas-Hunt, M. C., and Phillips, K. W. (December 2004) When What You Know Is Not Enough: Expertise and Gender Dynamics in Task Groups, *Personality and Social Psychology Bulletin,* 30, no. 12, pp. 1585–1598.

Page 170 *It depends on how central:* Author interview with Carol Tavris.

Page 171 *A 2000 study, for example:* Eliot, pp. 66–67.

NOTES

Page 171 *"resist the temptation to see the work":* Tavris, C. (1992) *The Mismeasure of Woman.* New York: Touchstone/Simon & Schuster, p. 333.

Page 172 *"The male-female differences":* Eliot, pp. 6–7.

Page 172 *Some of the interesting studies:* Ibid., p. 84.

Page 173 *For example, Eliot notes:* Ibid., p. 74.

Page 173 *"Unlike a generation ago":* Ibid., p. 14.

Page 173 *She emphasizes the amazing plasticity:* Ibid., p. 18.

Page 174 *The real metaphor for men and women:* Ibid., p. 13.

Page 174 *The way boys and girls:* Sadker, p. 96.

Page 175 *In case we think that's all:* Girls Just Want to Have Sums, *The Simpsons,* season 17, episode 19, originally aired April 30, 2006.

Page 176 *What would happen to your language:* Tavris, *The Mismeasure of Woman,* p. 298.

Page 177 *"The low status [people]":* Carli, p. 949.

Page 177 *While society is changing:* Simmons, R. (2009) *The Curse of the Good Girl.* New York: The Penguin Press, p. 78.

Page 179 *In 2002, there were eleven:* National Association for Single Sex Public Education, www.singlesexschools.org.

Page 179 *There are those who promote:* Weil, Testosterone; Eliot, L., and Bailey, S. M. Gender Segregation in Schools Isn't the Answer, *USA Today,* August 28, 2008.

Page 179 *Then there are those:* Author interview with Rosemary Salomone.

Page 180 *Three Reactions to Constructive Criticism:* Simmons, used with permission of the Girls' Leadership Institute; inspired by Stone, D., Patton, B., Heen, S., and Fisher, R. (2000) *Difficult Conversations: How to Discuss What Matters Most.* New York: Penguin.

Page 182 *Simply understanding that someone:* Exline, J. J., Baumeister, R. F., Zell, A. I., Kraft, A. J., and Witvliet, C. V. O. (2008) Not So Innocent: Does Seeing One's Own Capability for Wrongdoing Predict Forgiveness? *Journal of Personality and Social Psychology,* 94, no. 3, pp. 495–515.

Page 184 *Although Exline's study:* Author interview with Julie Exline.

Page 184 *And here's something concrete:* Johnson, C. Y. Tech's Feminine Side, *Boston Globe,* February 18, 2008; Mintz, J. Computing Reasons for the Gender Gap, *Connecticut Post* online, September 28, 2007.

Page 185 *Beckwith says that while there is a relationship:* Author interview with Laura Beckwith.

267

NOTES

CHAPTER 7. YOU SAY MISTAKE, I SAY LESSON

Page 189 *Geert Hofstede, an influential Dutch psychologist:* Hofstede, G., and Hofstede, G. J. (2005) *Cultures and Organizations: Software of the Mind* (2nd ed.). New York: McGraw-Hill, pp. 11–12.

Page 191 *One of the main differences:* Author interview with Hazel Markus.

Page 191 *This approach to mistakes:* Lewis, C. C. (1995) *Educating Hearts and Mind: Reflections on Japanese Preschool and Elementary Education.* Cambridge, England: Cambridge University Press, pp. 168–169.

Page 192 *James Stigler, a UCLA psychology professor:* Stigler, J. W., and Stevenson, H. W. (1991) How Asian Teachers Polish Each Lesson to Perfection, *American Educator*, 15, no. 1, pp. 12–20, 43–47.

Page 192 *So in Japanese culture:* Author interview with James Stigler.

Page 194 *Steven Heine, a psychology professor:* Heine, S. J. (2005) Constructing Good Selves in Japan and North America, chap. 5 in *Culture and Social Behavior: The Ontario Symposium*, vol. 10, Sorrentino, R. M., Cohen, D., Olson, J. M., and Zanna, M. P., eds. Mahwah, NJ: Lawrence Erlbaum.

Page 194 *In one study that Heine conducted:* Heine, S. J., Kitayama, S., Lehman, D. R., Takata, T., Ide, E., Leung, C., and Matsumoto, H. (2001) Divergent Consequences of Success and Failure in Japan and North America: An Investigation of Self-Improving Motivations and Malleable Selves, *Journal of Personality and Social Psychology*, 81, no. 4, pp. 599–615.

Page 196 *In one survey, Americans:* Heine, Constructing Good Selves in Japan and North America, p. 106.

Page 196 *Chris Arnold, a former San Francisco:* Whiting, R. (1990) *You Gotta Have Wa.* New York: Vintage, p. 52.

Page 196 *In the charming book:* Ibid., pp. 52–58.

Page 196 *The emphasis on making the effort:* Heine, Constructing Good Selves in Japan and North America, p. 106.

Page 197 *These traits are also highly prized:* Interview conducted by Marco Werman, *The World*, Public Radio International, January 21, 2010.

Page 197 *I would agree with Heine:* Author interview with Steven Heine.

Page 197 *"We are not a nation of effort":* Dweck, C. S. (2006) *Mindset: The New Psychology of Success.* New York: Ballantine, p. 41.

Page 199 *"Dissonance reduction operates":* Tavris and Aronson, p. 30.

Page 199 *But since the Japanese emphasis:* Heine, S. J., Lehman, D. R., Markus, H. R., and Kitayma, S. (1999) Is There a Universal Need for Positive Self-Regard? *Psychological Review*, 106, no. 4, pp. 766–794.

Page 199 *This is not to say that people from Japan:* Heine, Constructing Good Selves in Japan and North America, p. 96.

Page 199 *They must perform their role:* Heine, Is There a Universal Need for Positive Self-Regard? p. 773.

Page 200 *I asked James Stigler a question:* Author interview with James Stigler.

Page 200 *"was designed to avoid unpleasant confrontations":* Whiting, p. 16.

Page 201 *If we screw up publicly:* Author interview with Steven Heine.

Page 201 *compared American and Italian teachers' use:* Santagata, R. (2004) "Are You Joking or Are You Sleeping?" Cultural Beliefs and Practices in Italian and U.S. Teachers' Mistake-Handling Strategies, *Linguistics and Education*, 15, pp. 141–164.

Page 201 *When Italian and American students were separately:* Santagata, pp. 157–159.

Page 202 *"I don't think the Italian way":* Author interview with Rossella Santagata.

Page 203 *Geert Hofstede, the Dutch psychologist:* www.geert-hofstede.com; www.geerthofstede.nl.

Page 205 *First the power-distance dimension:* Hofstede and Hofstede, p. 42.

Page 205 *In comparing seventy-four countries:* Ibid., p. 43.

Page 206 *Hofstede found that if a country:* Ibid., p. 50.

Page 206 *I was told an anecdote:* Author interview with P. Christopher Earley.

Page 206 *Individualism versus collectivism:* Hofstede and Hofstede, p. 76.

Page 207 *Now, it probably won't surprise you:* Ibid., pp. 78–79.

Page 208 *Eighteen hundred pilots:* Merritt, A. C., and Helmreich, R. L. (1996) Human Factors on the Flight Deck: The Influence of National Culture, *Journal of Cross-Cultural Psychology*, 27, no. 5, pp. 5–24.

Page 209 *Helmreich indicated high power distance:* Gladwell, *Outliers*, p. 207.

Page 209 *The point, as with gender comparisons:* Merritt and Helmreich, Human Factors on the Flight Deck, p. 20.

Page 210 *"This is my last leg":* Merritt, A., and Helmreich, R. L. CRM: I Hate It, What Is It? (Error, Stress and Culture). Paper presented at the Orient Airlines Association Air Safety Seminar, Jakarta, Indonesia, April 13–15, 1996.

Page 211 *A Dutchman who had worked:* Hofstede and Hofstede, p. 143.

Page 212 *In 2008, a young German composer:* Stern, D. L. Creating a Melody from Fear of Failure, *New York Times*, June 4, 2008.

Chapter 8. I Want to Apologize

Page 215 *There's a* New Yorker *cartoon:* Smaller, B. *New Yorker*, December 15, 2008.

Page 216 *The study of apologies:* Author interview with Jonathan Cohen.

Page 217 *A proper apology:* Weeks, H. (April 2003) The Art of Apology, *Harvard Management Update.*

Page 217 *"I can truthfully say that I regret":* Donadio, R. Bishop Offers Apology for Holocaust Remarks, *New York Times*, February 27, 2009.

Page 218 *"I could give you excuses":* Sharp, D. Millen Hides Behind Camera, *Detroit Free Press*, January 4, 2009.

Page 218 *"I've gotten to the point":* Bratu, B., and Steele, C. The *Chronicle's* Weekend with Jayson Blair, *Commonwealth Chronicle*, November 10, 2009.

Page 219 *"During 2008 I did some dumb things":* Warren Buffett, February 2009 statement to Shareholders of Berkshire Hathaway Inc., www.berkshirehathaway.com/letters/2008ltr.pdf.

Page 219 *When apologizing, Weeks suggests:* Weeks, The Art of Apology.

Page 219 *Linguist Deborah Tannen:* Tannen, D. (1994) *Talking from 9 to 5.* New York: Quill/HarperCollins, p. 46.

Page 221 *Tannen told me that she has long thought:* Author interview with Deborah Tannen.

Page 221 *"If he defines wrong":* Tannen, D. (2001) *I Only Say This Because I Love You.* New York: Ballantine, pp. 102–103.

Page 222 *We're often told to apologize:* Frantz, C. M., and Bennigson, C. (2005) Better Late Than Early: The Influence of Timing on Apology Effectiveness, *Journal of Experimental Social Psychology*, 41, pp. 201–207.

Page 222 *In China, a small private company:* Cohen, J. R. (2002) Legislating Apology: The Pros and Cons, *University of Cincinnati Law Review*, 70, pp. 819–895.

Page 223 *There is no such thing:* Kellerman, B. When Should a Leader Apologize—and When Not? *Harvard Business Review*, April 2006.

Page 224 *President Ulysses S. Grant, in a report:* Safire, W. (2008) *Safire's Political Dictionary.* New York: Oxford University Press, p. 432.

Page 224 *But politicians have been screwing up:* Tuchman, B. W. (1984) *The March of Folly: From Troy to Vietnam.* New York: Alfred A. Knopf.

Page 224 *A group of scholars once made up:* Dunbar, E. Scholars Rate 10 Worst Presidential Errors. Associated Press, February 18, 2006.

Page 224 *There is a famous anecdote:* Smith, R. N. (November 15, 2006) Roosevelt and Reagan: Eternal Optimists. Speech given at Grand Valley State University (Hauenstein Center for Presidential Studies), Grand Rapids, Michigan.

Page 225 *Denial and meaningless apologies:* Freeman, J. B. Joe Wilson's War, *New York Times*, September 19, 2009.

Page 225 *"Lying and adultery":* McGrory, M. A Sorry Confession, *Washington Post*, August 20, 1998.

Page 226 *In 2004, when a reporter:* Text of President Bush's Press Conference, *New York Times*, April 13, 2004.

Page 226 *As author and lawyer Edward Lazarus notes:* Lazarus, E. (March 29, 2007) Why Full Disclosure Is Far More Valuable Than an Apology in Areas Ranging from DOJ Scandals to Iraq War Votes, FindLaw, Legal News and Commentary, http://writ.news.findlaw.com/lazarus/20070329.html.

Page 227 *When politicians' backs "are nailed":* Tavris and Aronson, pp. 3, 218.

Page 227 *They give a wonderful example:* Carol Tavris and Elliot Aronson. (2008) *Mistakes Were Made (But Not by Me)*. New York: Mariner Books, p. 236.

Page 228 *When Tavris and Aronson published:* Ibid., p. 218.

Page 229 *his inauguration began with a slipup:* Kelley, T. Letter to the editor, *New York Times*, January 25, 2009.

Page 229 *when former Senator Tom Daschle:* Nagourney, A. The Pros and Cons of Admitting a Presidential Error, *New York Times*, February 4, 2009.

Page 229 *"We drill into our children":* Froomkin, D. When Mistakes Are Made, Washingtonpost.com, February 4, 2009.

Page 230 *When White House press secretary Robert Gibbs:* Nagourney.

Page 230 *Look at the Eddie Bauer case:* Loviglio, J. Eddie Bauer Will Pay $1 Million in "Consumer Racism" Case, *Oregonian*, October 10, 1997.

Page 231 *Sydney Finkelstein, a management professor:* Martin, A. and Maynard, M. For Bankers, Saying "Sorry" Has Its Perils, *New York Times*, January 12, 2010.

Page 231 *Chief executives of companies like Goldman Sachs:* Goldman Regrets "Market Euphoria" That Led to Crisis, *New York Times*, June 16, 2009.

Page 232 *Seven people on Chicago's West Side:* Fletcher, D. A Brief History of the Tylenol Poisonings, *Time*, February 10, 2009; Kaplan, T. The Tylenol Crisis: How Effective Public Relations Saved Johnson & Johnson, www.aerobiologicalengineering.com/wxk116/TylenolMurders/crisis.html.

Page 233 *A more recent example of a company:* MacKenzie, A., and Evans, S. The Toyota

Recall Crisis, *Motor Trend*, January 2010; Kitamura, M. Toyota President Toyoda Apologizes for Recall Crisis, Bloomberg.com, February 5, 2010; Tabuchi, H., and Maynard, M. President of Toyota Apologizes, *New York Times*, October 2, 2009.

Page 235 *For example, Sorry works!:* Author interview with Doug Wojcieszak.

Page 236 *Among other things, it promotes:* Wojcieszak, D., Saxton, J. W., and Finkelstein, M. M. (2008) *Sorry Works! Disclosure, Apology, and Relationships Prevent Medical Malpractice Claims.* Bloomington, IN: AuthorHouse.

Page 237 *Compare Wojcieszak's case:* Dooley, K. (Fall 2008) How One Boy Changed the College of Medicine, *Florida Physician.*

Page 237 *In a British study of malpractice patients:* Kellerman.

Page 237 *A University of Missouri study:* Ibid.

Page 237 *At the University of Michigan Health System:* Boothman, R. C., Blackwell, A. C., Campbell, D. A., Jr., Commiskey, E., and Anderson, S. A. (January 2009) Better Approach to Medical Malpractice Claims? The University of Michigan Experience, *Journal of Health & Life Sciences Law*, 2, no. 2, pp. 125–159.

Page 240 *In many states, apologies have even:* Cohen, p. 827.

Page 241 *But "as society has commodified":* Author interview with Jonathan Cohen.

Page 242 *Cohen tells a story:* Cohen, J. R. (2004–2005) The Immorality of Denial, *Tulane Law Review*, 79, pp. 903–953; see p. 909.

Page 243 *"The drastic consequences of our mistakes":* Hilfiker.

Page 243 *A study regarding health care workers:* White, A. A., Waterman, A. D., McCotter, P., Boyle, D. J., and Gallagher, T. H. (May 2008) Supporting Health Care Workers After Medical Error: Considerations for Health Care Leaders, *Journal of Clinical Outcomes Management*, 15, no. 5, pp. 240–246.

Page 244 *In another study, one doctor said:* Gallagher, T. H., Waterman, A. D., Ebers, A. G., Fraser, V. J., and Levinson, W. (February 26, 2003) Patients' and Physicians' Attitudes Regarding the Disclosures of Medical Error, *Journal of the American Medical Association (JAMA)*, 289, no. 8.

Page 244 *"doctors first sit there":* Author interview with Doug Wojcieszak.

Page 244 *Cohen couldn't agree more:* Author interview with Jonathan Cohen.

BIBLIOGRAPHY

Allen, Scott. "With Work, Dana-Farber Learns from '94 Mistakes." *The Boston Globe*, November 30, 2004.

Anderson, Jenny. "Chiefs' Pay Under Fire at Capitol." *The New York Times*, March 6, 2008.

Andrews, Edmund L. "My Personal Credit Crisis." *The New York Times*, May 17, 2009.

Argyris, Chris. *On Organizational Learning*. Cambridge, MA: Blackwell Publishers, 1992.

———. "Good Communication That Blocks Learning." *Harvard Business Review* (July/ August 1994): 77–85.

———. "Empowerment: The Emperor's New Clothes." *Harvard Business Review* (May/ June 1998): 98–105.

Bennis, Warren, and Burt Nanus. *Leaders: Strategies for Taking Charge*. New York: HarperCollins, 1997.

Bennis, Warren, Daniel Goleman, and James O'Toole. *Transparency: How Leaders Create a Culture of Candor.* San Francisco: Jossey-Bass, 2008.

Berlinger, Nancy. "Medical Error." In *From Birth to Death and Bench to Clinic: The Hastings Center Bioethics Briefing Book for Journalists, Policymakers, and Campaigns.* Edited by Mary Crowley. Garrison, NY: The Hastings Center.

Beyer, Sylvia, and Langenfeld, Kelly. "Gender Differences in the Recall of Performance Feedback." Paper presented at the annual meeting of the American Psychological Association, Atlanta, Georgia, May 2003.

Blackwell, Lisa S., Kali H. Trzesniewski, and Carol S. Dweck. "Implicit Theories of Intelligence Predict Achievement Across an Adolescent Transition: A Longitudinal Study and an Intervention." *Child Development* 78, no. 1 (January/February 2007): 246–263.

Boothman, Richard C., et al. "A Better Approach to Medical Malpractice Claims? The University of Michigan Experience." *Journal of Health & Life Sciences Law* 2, no. 2 (January 2009): 125–159.

Bratu, Becky, and Cameron Steele. "The Chronicle's Weekend with Jayson Blair." *Commonwealth Chronicle*, November 10, 2009.

Bray, Wendy. "Learning from Mistakes During Class Discussion of Mathematics: The Role of Teachers' Beliefs and Knowledge." Paper presented at the Association of Mathematics Teacher Educators Annual Meeting, Orlando, Florida, February 6, 2009.

Bronson, Po. "How Not to Talk to Your Kids: The Inverse Power of Praise." *New York*, February 11, 2007.

Brooks, Robert, and Sam Goldstein. *Nurturing Resilience in Our Children.* Chicago: Contemporary Books, 2003.

Bryans, Patricia. "What Do Professional Men and Women Learn from Making Mistakes at Work?" *Research in Post-Compulsory Education* 4, no. 2 (1999): 183–194.

———, and Sharon Mavin. "The Emotional Impact of Making Mistakes at Work: Gender Schemas and Emotion Norms." Chapter 7 in *Gendering Emotions in Organizations.* London: Palgrave MacMillan, 2007.

Buffett, Warren. February 2009 statement to shareholders of Berkshire Hathaway Inc. www.berkshirehathaway.com/letters/2008ltr.pdf.

Callback (Aviation Safety Reporting System), no. 337 (January 2008). www.asrs.arc.gov/publications/callback.

Carli, Linda L. "Gender, Language, and Influence." *Journal of Personality and Social Psychology* 59, no. 5 (1999): 941–951.

BIBLIOGRAPHY

Carney, John. "John Thain Admits He Didn't Understand Merrill's Risks." *Business Insider*, October 7, 2009.

Cassidy, John. "Subprime Suspect." *The New Yorker*, March 31, 2008.

"Changing the Safety Culture at VA." *U.S. Medicine*, August 2002.

"Chemo Overdoses Overview." U.S. Department of Veterans Affairs Getting at Patient Safety (GAPs) Center, www.gapscenter.va.gov/stories/BetsyDesc.asp.

Cohen, Jonathan R. "Legislating Apology: The Pros and Cons." *University of Cincinnati Law Review* 70 (2002): 819–895.

———. "The Immorality of Denial. *Tulane Law Review* 79 (2004–2005): 90–953.

Coloroso, Barbara. *Kids Are Worth It*. New York: CollinsLifestyle/HarperCollins, 2002.

———. *Just Because It's Not Wrong Doesn't Make It Right: From Toddlers to Teens, Teaching Kids to Think and Act Ethically*. Toronto: Penguin Canada, 2005.

Craughwell, Thomas. "Saints Misbehavin'." *The Wall Street Journal*, October 27, 2006.

Dekker, Sidney. *The Field Guide to Understanding Human Error*. Burlington, VT: Ashgate, 2006.

"Dennis Quaid Acts on Medical Errors." The *Wall Street Journal* health blog, March 21, 2008.

Dey, Judy G., and Catherine Hill. *Behind the Pay Gap*. Washington, DC: American Association of University Women Educational Foundation, 2007.

"Doctor Who Cut Off Wrong Leg Is Defended by Colleagues." *The New York Times*, September 17, 1995.

Dooley, Karen. "How One Boy Changed the College of Medicine." *Florida Physician* (Fall 2008).

Donadio, Rachel. "Bishop Offers Apology for Holocaust Remarks." *The New York Times*, February 27, 2009.

Dunbar, Elizabeth. "Scholars Rate 10 Worst Presidential Errors." *Associated Press*, February 18, 2006.

Dweck, Carol S. *Mindset: The New Psychology of Success*. New York: Ballantine Books, 2008.

Eagley, Alice H., and Linda L. Carli. *Through the Labyrinth: The Truth About How Women Become Leaders*. Boston: Harvard Business School Press, 2007.

Eliot, Lise. "Gender Segregation in Schools Isn't the Answer." *USA Today*, August 28, 2008.

———. *Pink Brain, Blue Brain*. New York: Houghton Mifflin Harcourt, 2009.

Emery, Vince. "The Pentium Chip Story: A Learning Experience." February/March 1996. www.emery.com.

Exline, Julie J., et al. "Not So Innocent: Does Seeing One's Own Capability for Wrong-doing Predict Forgiveness?" *Journal of Personality and Social Psychology* 94, no. 3 (2008): 495–515.

Fast, Nathanael J., and Larissa Z. Tiedens. "Blame Contagion: The Automatic Trans-mission of Self-Serving Attributions." *Journal of Experimental Social Psychology* 46 (2010): 97–106.

Fischer, Ute, and Judith Orasanu. "Error-Challenging Strategies: Their Role in Pre-venting and Correcting Errors." In *Proceedings of the International Ergonomics Asso-ciation 14th Triennial Congress and Human Factors and Ergonomics Society 44th Annual Meeting in San Diego, California.* August 2000.

Fletcher, Dan. "A Brief History of the Tylenol Poisonings." *Time*, February 10, 2009.

Folmer, Amy S., et al. "Age-Related Changes in Children's Understanding Effort and Ability: Implications for Attribution Theory and Motivation." *Journal of Experimen-tal Child Psychology* 99, no. 2 (February 2008): 114–134.

Frank, Thomas, and Alan Levin. "Hudson River Hero Is ex-Air Force Fighter Pilot." *USA Today*, January 16, 2009.

Frantz, Cynthia M., and Courtney Bennigson. "Better Late Than Early: The Influence of Timing on Apology Effectiveness." *Journal of Experimental Social Psychology* 41 (2005): 201–207.

Freeman, Joanne B. "Joe Wilson's War." *The New York Times*, September 19, 2009.

Froomkin, Dan. "When Mistakes Are Made." White House Watch blog, Washington-post.com, February 4, 2009.

Frost, Randy O., and Patricia A. Marten. "Perfectionism and Evaluative Threat." *Cogni-tive Therapy and Research* 14, no. 6 (1990): 559–572.

——., et al. "Reactions to Mistakes Among Subjects High and Low in Perfectionistic Concern over Mistakes." *Cognitive Therapy and Research* 19, no. 2 (1995): 195–205.

Gallagher, Thomas H., et al. "Patients' and Physicians' Attitudes Regarding the Dis-closures of Medical Error." *Journal of the American Medical Association* 289, no. 8 (February 26, 2003): 1001–1007.

——. "Choosing Your Words Carefully: How Physicians Would Disclose Harmful Medical Errors to Patients." *Archives of Internal Medicine* 166 (August 14–18, 2006): 1585–1593.

Garvin, David A., Amy C. Edmondson, and Francesca Gino. "Is Yours a Learning Organization?" *Harvard Business Review* (March 2008).

Gates, Bill. "Failure Is Part of the Game and Should Be Used." *Seattle Post-Intelligencer*, April 26, 1995.

———. *The Road Ahead*. New York: Penguin Group, 1995.

Gawande, Atul. "The Checklist." *The New Yorker*, December 10, 2007.

———. *The Checklist Manifesto: How To Get Things Right*. New York: Metropolitan Books, 2009.

Gilligan, Carol. *In a Different Voice: Psychological Theory and Women's Development*. 32nd edition. Cambridge, MA: Harvard University Press, 1993.

"Girls Just Want to Have Sums." *The Simpsons*, season 17, episode 19, originally aired April 30, 2006.

Gladwell, Malcolm. "The Talent Myth." *The New Yorker*, July 22, 2002.

———. Outliers: The Story of Success. New York: Little, Brown, 2008.

"Goldman Regrets 'Market Euphoria' That Led to Crisis." *The New York Times*, June 16, 2009.

Greenberg, Irving. *The Jewish Way: Living the Holidays*. Northvale, NJ: Jason Aronson, 1988.

Gully, Stanley M., et al. "The Impact of Error Training and Individual Differences on Training Outcomes: An Attribute-Treatment Interaction Perspective." *Journal of Applied Psychology* 87, no. 1 (February 2002): 143–155.

Hallinan, Joseph, T. *Why We Make Mistakes*. New York: Broadway Books, 2009.

Hallowell, Edward M. *The Childhood Roots of Adult Happiness*. New York: Ballantine, 2002.

Haynes, Al. Speech given at NASA Ames Research Center, Dryden Flight Research Facility, Edwards, California, May 24, 1991.

Heine, Steven J. "Constructing Good Selves in Japan and North America." Chapter 5 in *Culture and Social Behavior: The Ontario Symposium*, vol. 10. Mahwah, NJ: Lawrence Erlbaum, 2005.

———, et al. "Is There a Universal Need for Positive Self-Regard?" *Psychological Review* 106, no. 4 (1999): 766–794.

———, et al. "Divergent Consequences of Success and Failure in Japan and North America: An Investigation of Self-Improving Motivations and Malleable Selves." *Journal of Personality and Social Psychology* 81, no. 4 (2001): 599–615.

Helmreich, Robert L. "Managing Human Error in Aviation." *Scientific American* (May 1997): 62–67.

——. "On Error Management: Lessons from Aviation." *British Medical Journal* 320 (March 18, 2000): 781–785.

——, Ashleigh C. Merritt, and John A. Wilhelm. "The Evolution of Crew Resource Management Training in Commercial Aviation." *International Journal of Aviation Psychology* 9, no. 1 (1999): 19–32.

"Helmreich's Maneuvers: UT Professor Studies Parallels Between Cockpit Crews, Medical Teams." *ONCampus* (The University of Texas at Austin) 26, no. 12 (March 30, 1999).

Heslin, Peter A., Gary P. Latham, and Don VandeWalle. "The Effect of Implicit Person Theory on Performance Appraisals." *Journal of Applied Psychology* 90, no. 5 (2005): 842–856.

Heslin, Peter A., and Don VandeWalle. "Managers' Implicit Assumptions About Personnel." *Current Directions in Psychological Science* 17 (June 2008): 219–223.

Heyman, Gail, Genyue Fu, and Kang Lee. "Reasoning About the Disclosure of Success and Failure to Friends Among Children in the United States and China." *Developmental Psychology* 44, no. 4 (2008): 908–918.

Hilfiker, David. "Facing Our Mistakes." *New England Journal of Medicine* 310 (January 12, 1984): 118–122.

Hofstede, Geert, and Gert J. Hofstede. *Cultures and Organizations: Software of the Mind.* Second edition. New York: McGraw Hill, 2005.

Institute for Healthcare Improvement. "Pursuing Perfection: Report from McLeod Regional Medical Center on Leadership Patient Rounds." http://www.ihi.org/IHI/Topics/LeadingSystemImprovement/Leadership/ImprovementStories/Pursuing-PerfectionReport from McLeodRegionalMedicalCenteronLeadershipPatientRounds.htm.

Investigation into the Clapham Junction Railway Accident. London: Department of Transport, 1989.

Johnson, Carolyn Y. "Tech's Feminine Side." *The Boston Globe*, February 18, 2008.

Kaplan, Tamara. The Tylenol Crisis: How Effective Public Relations Saved Johnson & Johnson. Pennsylvania State University. www.aerobiologicalengineering.com/wxkll6/TylenolMurders/crisis.html.

Kellerman, Barbara. "When Should a Leader Apologize—and When Not?" *Harvard Business Review*, April 2006.

Kitamura, Makiko. "Toyota President Toyoda Apologizes for Recall Crisis." Bloomberg.com, February 5, 2010.

Klein, Tilmann A., et al. "Genetically Determined Differences in Learning from Errors." *Science* 318, no. 5856 (December 7, 2007): 1642–1645.

Kohn, Linda T., et al, eds. *To Err Is Human: Building a Safer Health System*. Washington, DC: National Academy Press, 2000.

Layton, Charles. "State of the American Newspaper: What Do Readers Really Want?" *American Journalism Review* (March 1999).

Lazarus, Edward. "Why Full Disclosure Is Far More Valuable Than an Apology in Areas Ranging from DOJ Scandals to Iraq War Votes." FindLaw, Legal News and Commentary (March 29, 2007). http://writ.news.findlaw.com/lazarus/20070329.html. March 29, 2007.

Leape, Lucien L., and Donald M. Berwick. "Five Years After To Err is Human." *Journal of the American Medical Association* 93, no. 19 (May 18, 2005): 2384–2390.

"Learning from Others' Mistakes." *In Sight* (July 2005). http://www.collision-insight.com/news/archives/200507-feature.htm.

LeBaron, Michelle. *Bridging Cultural Conflict: A New Approach for a Changing World*. New York: John Wiley & Sons, 2003.

Lehrer, Jonah. *How We Decide*. New York: Houghton Mifflin Harcourt, 2009.

Lewis, Catherine C. *Educating Hearts and Minds: Reflections on Japanese Preschool and Elementary Education*. New York: Cambridge University Press, 1995.

Lewis, Patricia, and Ruth Simpson, eds. *Gendering Emotions in Organization*. Hampshire, UK: Palgrave MacMillan, 2007.

Line Operations Safety Audit, first edition. International Civil Aviation Organization, 2002.

Loviglio, Joann. "Eddie Bauer Will Pay $1 Million in 'Consumer Racism' Case." *The Associated Press*, October 10, 1997.

MacKenzie, Angus, and Scott Evans. "The Toyota Recall Crisis." *Motor Trend* (January 2010).

Marano, Haro E. "Pitfalls of Perfectionism." *Psychology Today* (March 1, 2008).

Martin, Andrew, and Michelene Maynar. "For Bankers, Saying 'Sorry' Has Its Perils." *The New York Times*, January 12, 2010.

Marx, David. *Whack a Mole: The Price We Pay For Expecting Perfection*. Plano, TX: By Your Side Studios, 2009.

"Maureen Bateman, A Cancer Patient and Chronicler, 55." *The New York Times*, June 1, 1997.

McGrory, Mary. "A Sorry Confession." *Washington Post*, August 20, 1998.

BIBLIOGRAPHY

"Medication Errors Injure 1.5 Million People and Cost Billions of Dollars Annually." News release from the National Academies, July 20, 2006.

Merritt, Ashleigh, and Robert L. Helmreich. "CRM: I Hate It, What Is It? (Error, Stress and Culture)." Paper presented at the Orient Airlines Association Air Safety Seminar, Jakarta, Indonesia, April 13–15, 1996.

———. "Human Factors on the Flight Deck: The Influence of National Culture." *Journal of Cross-Cultural Psychology* 27, no. 5 (1996): 5–24.

Miller, Geoffrey S., and V. G. Narayanan. "Accounting for the Intel Pentium Chip Flaw." *Harvard Business Review*, June 26, 2001.

Mintz, Jessica. "Computing Reasons for the Gender Gap." *Connecticut Post*, September 28, 2007.

Mogel, Wendy. *The Blessing of a Skinned Knee*. New York: Penguin Compass, 2001.

Multidimensional Perfectionism Scale. First appeared in Frost Randy O., et al. "The Dimensions of Perfectionism." *Cognitive Therapy & Research* 14 (1990): 449–468.

Nagourney, Adam. "The Pros and Cons of Admitting a Presidential Error." *The New York Times*, February 4, 2009.

National Association for Single Sex Public Education. www.singlesexschools.org.

Nicholls, John, G. *The Competitive Ethos and Democratic Education*. Cambridge, Mass.: Harvard University Press, 1989.

———. "The Development of the Concepts of Effort and Ability, Perception of Academic Attainment and the Understanding That Difficult Tasks Require More Ability." *Child Development* 49 (1978): 800–814.

Nuland, Sherwin B. *The Soul of Medicine: Tales from the Bedside*. New York: Kaplan Publishing, 2009.

"Organizational Change in the Face of High Public Errors: The Dana-Farber Cancer Institute Experience." Agency for Healthcare Research and Quality (2004). www.webmm.ahrq.gov.

Otto, Dave. "Aviation Safety Reporting in the 90th FS." *Flying Safety Magazine* (United States Air Force) 60 (July 2004): 22.

O'Toole, James, and Warren Bennis. "A Culture of Candor." *Harvard Business Review* (June 2009).

Page, Alison H. "Making Just Culture a Reality: One Organization's Approach." Agency for Healthcare Research and Quality, Web M&M serial (October 2007). http://webmm.ahrq.gov/perspective.aspx?perspectiveID=50.

BIBLIOGRAPHY

Page, Ann, ed. *Keeping Patients Safe: Transforming the Work Environment of Nurses.* Washington, DC: The National Academies Press, 2004.

Pearn, Michael, and Peter Honey. "From Error Terror to Wonder Blunder." *People Management* (March 1992): 42–43.

Pizzi, Laura, Neil I. Goldfarb, and David B. Nash. "Crew Resource Management and Its Application in Medicine." Chapter 44 in *Making Health Care Safer: A Critical Analysis of Patient Safety Practices.* AHRQ Publication No. 01-E058, July 2001.

Prather, Charles. "Use Mistakes to Foster Innovation." *Research Technology Management* 51, no. 2 (March–April 2008): 14.

Pronovost, Peter, et al. "An Intervention to Decrease Catheter-Related Bloodstream Infections in the ICU." *New England Journal of Medicine* 355, no. 26 (December 28, 2006): 2725–2732.

Quihuis, Gisell, et al. "Implicit Theories of Intelligence Across Academic Domains: A Study of Meaning Making in Adolescents of Mexican Descent." *New Directions for Child and Adolescent Development* no. 96 (Summer 2002): 87–100.

Reason, James. *Human Error.* New York: Cambridge University Press, 1990.

———. "Human Error: Models and Management." *British Medical Journal* 320 (March 18, 2000): 768–770.

Reinhart, Carmen M., and Kenneth S. Rogoff. *This Time Is Different: Eight Centuries of Financial Folly.* Princeton, NJ: Princeton University Press, 2009.

Rose, Matthew, and Laura P. Cohen. "Amid Turmoil, Top Editors Resign at New York Times." *Wall Street Journal,* June 6, 2003.

Sadker, Myra and David. *Failing at Fairness: How Our Schools Cheat Girls.* New York: Touchstone/Simon & Schuster, 1994.

Safire, William. *Safire's Political Dictionary.* New York: Oxford University Press, 2008.

Salmone, Rosemary C. *Same, Different, Equal: Rethinking Single-Sex Schooling.* New Haven: Yale University Press, 2003.

Santagata, Rosella. "'Are You Joking or Are You Sleeping?' Cultural Beliefs and Practices in Italian and U.S. Teachers' Mistake-Handling Strategies." *Linguistics and Education* 15 (2004): 141–164.

Schoemaker, Paul J. H., and Robert E. Gunther. "The Wisdom of Deliberate Mistakes." *Harvard Business Review* (June 2006): 109–115.

Seligman, Martin E. P. *The Optimistic Child.* New York: Houghton Mifflin, 2007.

Sexton, J. Bryan, Eric J. Thomas, and Robert L. Helmreich. "Error, Stress and Team-work in Medicine and Aviation: Cross Sectional Surveys." *British Medical Journal* 320 (March 18, 2000): 745–749.

Sharp, Drew. "Millen Hides Behind Camera." *Detroit Free Press.* January 4, 2009.

Simmons, Rachel. *The Curse of the Good Girl: Raising Authentic Girls with Courage and Confidence.* New York: The Penguin Press, 2009.

Smith, Richard Norton. "Roosevelt and Reagan: Eternal Optimists." Speech given at Grand Valley State University sponsored by the Hauenstein Center for Presidential Studies, Grand Rapids, Michigan, November 15, 2006.

Stern, David L. "Creating a Melody from Fear of Failure." *The New York Times,* June 4, 2008.

Sterngold, James. "How Much Did Lehman CEO Dick Fuld Really Make?" *Bloomberg Business Week,* April 29, 2010.

Stigler, James W., and Harold W. Stevenson. "How Asian Teachers Polish Each Lesson to Perfection." *American Educator* (1991).

Tabuchi, Hiroko, and Micheline Maynard. "President of Toyota Apologizes." *The New York Times,* October 2, 2009.

Tannen, Deborah. *I Only Say This Because I Love You.* New York: Ballantine Books, 2001.

———. *Talking from 9 to 5: Men and Women at Work.* New York: Quill/HarperCollins, 2001.

Tavris, Carol. *The Mismeasure of Woman.* New York: Touchstone/Simon & Schuster, 1992.

———, and Elliot Aronson. *Mistakes Were Made (But Not by Me).* New York: Harcourt, 2007. Reprint: Mariner Books, 2008.

Text of President Bush's Press Conference. *The New York Times.* April 13, 2004.

The History of Flight. www.century-of-flight.net.

The Patient Safety and Quality Improvement Act of 2005. Agency for Healthcare Research and Quality. www.ahrq.gov/qual/psocat.htm.

Thomas-Hunt, Melissa C., and Katherine W. Phillips. "When What You Know Is Not Enough: Expertise and Gender Dynamics in Task Groups." *Personality and Social Psychology Bulletin* 30, no. 12 (December 2004): 1585–1598.

Thompson, Dick, and Michael D. Lemonick. "Doctors' Deadly Mistakes." *Time,* December 13, 1999.

"To Err Is Human—To Delay Is Deadly." Safe Patient Project, Consumers Union (May 2009). http://www.safepatientproject.org/pdf/safepatientproject.org-to_delay_is_deadly-2009_05.pdf.

Tobin, Joseph J., David Y. Wu, and Dana H. Davidson. *Preschool in Three Cultures: Japan, China and the United States.* New Haven: Yale University Press, 1989.

Trapp, Roger. *My Biggest Mistake.* Oxford, UK: Butterworth-Heinemann and *The Independent on Sunday,* 1993.

Triandis, Harry, C. *Fooling Ourselves: Self-Deception in Politics, Religion and Terrorism.* Westport, CT: Praeger Publishers, 2009.

Tse, Tomoch M. "Fresh Round of Wall Street Bonuses Rekindles Scrutiny." *Washington Post,* January 12, 2010.

Tuchman, Barbara W. *Practicing History: Selected Essays.* New York: Ballantine Books, 1982.

———. W. *The March of Folly: From Troy to Vietnam.* New York: Alfred A. Knopf, 1984.

Twenge, Jean M. *Generation Me: Why Today's Young Americans Are More Confident, Assertive, Entitled—and More Miserable Than Ever Before.* New York: Free Press/ Simon & Schuster, 2006.

Ullsperger, Marcus. "(Minding) Mistakes." *Scientific American Mind* (August/September 2008): 52–59.

Wald, Matthew. "Panel Backs Letting Airlines Confess Errors Unpunished." *The New York Times,* September 10, 2008.

Waterman, Amy D., et al. "The Emotional Impact of Medical Errors on Practicing Physicians in the United States and Canada." *The Joint Commission Journal on Quality and Patient Safety* 33, no. 8 (August 2007): 467–475.

Weeks, Holly. "The Art of the Apology," *Harvard Management Update,* May 19, 2003.

———. *Failure to Communicate: How Conversations Go Wrong and What You Can Do to Right Them.* Boston: Harvard Business Press, 2008.

Weiss, Rick. "Medical Errors Blamed for Many Deaths." *Washington Post,* November 30, 1999.

Weil, Elizabeth. "Teaching to the Testosterone." *The New York Times Magazine,* March 2, 2008.

Wellman, Jerry. "Lessons Learned About Lessons Learned." *Organization Development Journal* 25, no. 3 (Fall 2007): 65–72.

White, Andrew A., et al. "Supporting Health Care Workers After Medical Error: Considerations for Health Care Leaders." *Journal of Clinical Outcomes Management* 15, no. 5 (May 2008): 240–246.

Whiting, Robert. *You Gotta Have Wa.* New York: Vintage Books, 1990.

Wingfield, Brian. "Puzzling Pay Packages." Forbes, March 7, 2008.

BIBLIOGRAPHY

Wojcieszak, Doug, James W. Saxton, and Maggie M. Finkelstein. *Sorry Works! Disclosure, Apology and Relationships Prevent Medical Malpractice Claims.* Bloomington, IN: Authorhouse, 2008.

World Health Organization's Surgical Safety List. http://whqlibdoc.who.int/publications/2009/9789241598590_eng_Checklist.pdf.

INDEX

INDEX